The Development Frontier

The Development Frontier

Essays in Applied Economics

Peter Bauer

Harvard University Press

Cambridge, Massachusetts

1991

This book is printed on acid-free paper, and its binding materials have been chosen for strength and durability.

Library of Congress Cataloging-in-Publication Data
Bauer, Péter Tamás
  The development frontier : essays in applied economics / P. T. Bauer.
      p.   cm.
  Includes bibliographical references and index.
  ISBN 0-674-20033-0
  1. Developing countries—Economic policy—Case studies.
2. Economic development—Case studies.   I. Title.
HC59.7.B359   1991
338.9'09172'4—dc20   90-5124
                    CIP

Contents

Preface   vii

1. Traders and the Development Frontier   1
2. Economic Progress and Occupational Distribution: Numbers, Roles, and Categories   6
3. Population, Welfare, and Development: Gloom Dispelled   20
4. Foreign Aid: Central Component of World Development?   38
5. The Third World Debt Crisis: Can't Pay or Won't Pay?   56
6. Marketing Reform: An Inventory of Intervention   64
7. Cooperative Societies in Less Developed Countries   87
8. Commodity Stabilization: Disguised Restrictionism   92
9. Wage Regulation in Less Developed Countries: On Not Helping the Poor   99
10. Price Control in Less Developed Countries: Unexpected Consequences   112
11. Industrialization and Development: Nigeria   122
12. Policy and Progress: The Hong Kong Story   141
13. Import Capacity and Economic Development: India   147
14. Price Response: Cocoa and Palm Oil in Nigeria   152
15. Competition and Prices: Groundnut Buying in Nigeria   158

16. Economic History as Theory: An Unrealistic
    Prospectus   166
17. Development Economics: A Retrospective View   187

    Notes   207
    Index   231

Preface

These essays describe and analyze major features of the emergence of less developed countries from subsistence to exchange economies, and from their subsequent advance. They focus on significant topics and issues that are neglected or treated inadequately or inappropriately in the literature on economic development. The book does not cover the full range of topics found in most textbooks on development economics; rather, it serves both as a supplement and as a corrective to them. The essays are also written to be accessible to the general reader, who will find that in their analysis and implications they differ substantially from those usually encountered in public and political discussion.

In applying economic reasoning in the setting of less developed countries, the economist needs to use a variety of information, including primary sources and the findings of cognate disciplines such as anthropology, demography, and history; to become familiar with the social and political situation and its antecedents; to examine the interaction of the usual economic variables with social and political forces; and while using conventional sources and sources of statistical information to be sensitive to the limitations of information condensed into statistics. I have tried to be mindful of these requirements throughout.

Essays 1, 3, 4, 5, 7, and 8 have been written specifically for this volume, although here and there they draw on ideas and material published earlier. Essays 16 and 17 are reprinted with only minor changes. Each of the remaining essays is a recognizable version of a previous publication which has undergone substantial revision.

I have worked very closely with Professor Basil Yamey on all the essays in this volume. I wish also to thank him for permission to make use of previously published studies of which he was coauthor.

As on previous occasions, I have relied greatly on the help of Léonie Glen-Thorogood, which has ranged well beyond what is usually understood as editorial assistance. Her quick understanding, thoughtful drafting, and sense of language and form have been of the greatest value in marshaling the argument.

Essay 1 incorporates suggestions by Richard A. Ware, Essay 3 suggestions by Professor Partha Dasgupta, and Essay 4 suggestions by Professors Milton Friedman, Deepak Lal, and Dr. W. Allen Wallis. I wish also to thank Michael Aronson of Harvard University Press for his interest, encouragement, and help at various stages of the preparation of this book.

Thanks are also due to the Earhart Foundation, in Ann Arbor, Michigan, and to the Institute of Educational Affairs, in Washington, D.C., for financial assistance for work on the book.

I am grateful to the publishers of *Economica* (Essays 15 and 16), *Economic History Review* (Essay 11), *Economic Journal* (Essays 2, 13, and 14), *Journal of Development Studies* (Essay 10), *Journal of Political Economy* (Essay 6), and *The Spectator* (Essay 12) for permission to publish revised versions of essays that first appeared there; to Philip D. Bradley for permission to publish a revised version of "Regulated Wages in Underdeveloped Countries," in *The Public Stake in Union Power*, edited by Philip D. Bradley (Charlottesville, 1961) (Essay 9); and to Oxford University Press for permission to publish a revised version of "Remembrance of Studies Past: Retracing First Steps," in *Pioneers in Development*, edited by Gerard M. Meier and Dudley Seers (New York, 1984; © the International Bank for Reconstruction and Development / The World Bank) (Essay 17).

The Development Frontier

1
Traders and the Development Frontier

When economists discuss wholesaling and retailing in advanced Western economies they focus on such subjects as the organization of these activities, the nature and extent of competition, concentration, economies of scale, vertical integration, and restrictive practices. The emphasis is on the efficiency in the provision of distributive services, in broad terms, the link between production and consumption. It is unusual to examine the possibility of any relationship between the activities of traders and the growth of the economy, except to the extent that efficiency in the provision of their services releases resources for other purposes. In short, the emphasis is on the allocation of given resources. In this respect, trading activity is treated very much like any other branch of economic activity.

This orientation is justified. It focuses on the main issues of interest to both economists and policymakers. But this orientation, though appropriate now, would be misleading if it were applied to the same economies as they were two or more centuries ago. Yet in that earlier period those economies were in many ways far more advanced than those of most less developed countries (LDCs) today. In particular, they were already very largely exchange economies in which subsistence or near-subsistence production was relatively unimportant. It has been recognized by some historians that the economic repercussions of trading activities in, say, seventeenth- and eighteenth-century England went well beyond those of efficiency in the use of resources in the trading activities themselves. For example, the two authors of a recent book on shopkeeping in eighteenth-century England conclude:

> If the major purpose of all these activities by shopkeepers was to drum up business, by so doing they eased the flow of goods

and at the same time helped to stimulate as well as satisfy an increasingly widespread demand, a demand that encouraged expansion in industry and overseas trade. It was not an unimportant contributor to the overall economic development of the country—industry, overseas trading and inland distribution moved in tandem, each fructifying the other.[1]

Professor Jacob Price has observed that in seventeenth- and eighteenth-century Britain the activities of merchants "left behind" much more than "specific markets for specific products." Their activities helped to create commercial institutions and practices and to raise the level of human capital, which proved to be "of great utility to the entire economy in the ensuing era of rapid industrialization and attendant export growth."[2] Richard Grassby wrote that it was "merchant capital which created markets, financed manufactures, floated the American colonial economies and launched banking and insurance."[3]

And in the words of Adam Smith, a contemporary observer, "the habits besides of order, economy and attention to which mercantile business naturally forms a merchant render him much fitter to execute, with profit and success in any project of improvement."[4]

These observations about trading activity in seventeenth- and eighteenth-century Britain on the eve of what is still known as the Industrial Revolution apply at least as cogently to development in much of the Third World. Nevertheless, the pertinent considerations are still ignored in the formulation of official policies in many LDCs, and for that matter are also neglected in many influential academic publications.

Economic development brings with it improved living standards and the widening of choice. It begins with the replacement of subsistence activities by production for sale. Producers will move out of subsistence production only if they see the advantages of doing so and if it is made possible for them to do so. They need the incentive, the opportunity, and the resources. This is where the traders come in. Traders make consumption goods available to the producers. The availability of some of these goods, which used to be known as incentive goods (a term that has largely dropped out of the contemporary development literature), widens the horizons of producers by showing the possibilities of a more varied and richer pattern of consumption. It helps to overcome what has sometimes been called the wantlessness of backward peoples.

Simultaneously, traders both large and small create new opportunities. With their knowledge of the requirements of local regional and export markets traders provide outlets for farm products. They buy the traditional products and at the same time acquaint farmers with new products and the methods of growing them. Further, they make available to them the necessary inputs, such as seeds, fertilizers, and implements. Thus the traders encourage new wants, convey new opportunities, and help farmers to take advantage of them. The activities of traders set in motion and maintain the process by which participation in the exchange economy replaces subsistence production.[5]

It is therefore misleading to look upon the network of traders in an LDC as serving only as a pipeline for conveying from producer to consumer a given volume and composition of output. Although none of the traders is trying to transform the economy, their perception and pursuit of opportunities for profit encourage that process.

In many LDCs, large numbers of people in rural areas respond to the incentives and opportunities conveyed to them through traders. That response often involves capital formation. The investment includes the establishment, extension, and improvement of agricultural holdings, taking such forms as the clearing of bush or jungle, the terracing of soil, fencing, drainage, and the planting of crops, often tree crops, which begin to yield returns only after several years. Related categories of investment include consideration of storage facilities and the acquisition of simple farming and transport equipment.

These types of capital formation are often undertaken by farmers with very low incomes. In order to secure improved living standards in the future, they work harder and give up some of their leisure. A large volume of effective capital investment has been undertaken in LDCs by people who are very poor by Western standards.

There is a very large volume of direct investment in agriculture by small-scale producers in the Third World, investment encouraged and made possible by the activities of traders. This category of capital formation is generally ignored in the development literature.[6] This neglect results in a misleading picture of economic activity in LDCs in that it suggests that small farmers there are unable or unwilling to save. Moreover, this disregard of their capital formation has had practical consequences. It means that the repercussions of official policies are not fully recognized. For example, a government wishing to encourage capital formation is likely to frame its taxation rather differently if it recognizes the importance of direct investment in agriculture than if it believes that farmers do not save and invest.

Traders, including small-scale traders, also build up capital in the form of buildings, transport equipment, and stocks of goods. They also often provide credit to their farmer customers, which facilitates both production for the market and capital formation on the farms.

Many traders in LDCs also own and farm land. Thus they can be classified as farmers as well as traders. The pioneers of manufacturing and processing activities have often come from their ranks. In LDCs traders have been among the first to operate repair shops and transport enterprises, to establish plants for the processing of farm produce (cotton ginneries, for example, and nut-crushing plants), and to set up manufacturing establishments. When such businesses prosper, they can develop into substantial enterprises. Such developments are not surprising. Trading activity, as Adam Smith observed in the passage already quoted, serves as preparation for other economic activities that call for the same attitudes and attributes as does trading itself. All this applies to farmer traders as well—that is, to farmers, often small farmers, who also undertake some trading.

Such movement from trading to other economic activities, including manufacturing, is familiar in the economic history of the advanced economies as well as in the recent history of the contemporary LDCs. In the early history of textile manufacture in Europe, the merchant entrepreneurs occupied a key position as organizers of production, supplying materials to outworkers, providing finance, and marketing the products. In eighteenth-century Britain merchants involved themselves in many financial and industrial enterprises, either directly or as major investors. Such giant enterprises as Royal Dutch Shell and Unilever had their origins in very small trading enterprises established a century or so ago.

In British West Africa in the 1950s, every single successful local industrialist had started his business life as a trader. Much the same is true of Southeast Asia. Indeed, the history of these two regions provides examples of the transformation of large economies in which the role of traders has been critical along the lines analyzed here.

The process of transformation can also operate in reverse, and this can be observed on the contemporary scene. The maltreatment of traders and the suppression of trading activity in the 1960s and 1970s in many LDCs, especially in Africa and to some extent also in South Asia, have been contributory factors to economic stagnation, retrogression, and even collapse, including reversion to subsistence production with all its hazards.

The Sahel, Ethiopia, Tanzania, Uganda, and Zaire have provided examples of such negative, even destructive effects.

The central theme of this essay has been the role of trade in helping to propel and maintain the development of an exchange economy from a subsistence base. This emphasis on the expansion and advance of an economy, and on the dynamic effects of trade, has been deliberate because these effects have been so largely ignored, both in the development literature and in development policy. However, trading activity in LDCs is highly important also in securing the effective deployment of available resources, often in uncongenial conditions. This aspect of trading activity will be examined in the next two essays.

2
Economic Progress and Occupational Distribution: Numbers, Roles and Categories

This essay examines the validity and significance of the widely accepted generalization that economic progress is associated with certain distinct, necessary, and predictable changes in occupational distribution, in particular with a relative increase in the numbers engaged in tertiary activities.[1] The method used here is largely analytical; but since a strong empirical basis is claimed for the generalization being examined, it is necessary to make frequent descriptive reference to the composition of economic activity in economies at different stages of development. Most of the description is concentrated in the first section, which describes and analyzes the volume and significance of trading activity in Nigeria and the Gold Coast (Ghana).[2]

The occupational statistics of backward economies purport to show that the great bulk of the population is occupied in agriculture. This claim is often made in official statements on economic activity in these territories. Lord Hailey's authoritative *An African Survey* affords an example:

> In the Northern Province of Nigeria, at the census of 1931, about 84% of occupied males whose returns permitted them to be classified were shown as engaged in agriculture and fishing, about 9% in manufacture, and under 3% in commerce and finance . . . For Southern Nigeria less detailed information is available. The returns, which are less reliable than those for Northern Nigeria, would suggest that the proportion of males engaged in agriculture is about 82% and that concerned with handicrafts about 4.7%.[3]

Trade and transport are not mentioned. No attempt is made to reconcile this with another statement (on the same page) that almost 30 percent of the population of Nigeria lived in towns of over 5,000 inhabitants. In the same vein, the official *Annual Report on Nigeria* stated year after year that the great majority of the population was occupied in agriculture: trade was not among the other occupations listed.

In contrast to these statements and statistics, a remarkable multitude of traders, especially of small-scale sellers of both local produce and imported merchandise, is a most conspicuous feature of West Africa. This is so apparent that it has not escaped attention. It is freely said by responsible administrators that in the southern parts of Nigeria and the Gold Coast everybody over ten years of age is engaged in trade, and this is hardly an exaggeration.

It is not possible to give specific quantitative information about the volume of trade or the numbers engaged in it. Certain sporadic but conservative data relating, for example, to numbers of market stallholders and hawkers' licenses indicate that there are many traders in the principal markets. But the figures give an imperfect idea of the great numbers of people engaged either part-time or full-time in selling small quantities of goods or conveying them to numerous and often distant points of sale. In the aggregate there is an enormous amount of activity, the quantitative significance of which is obvious to the observer.

The seriously misleading impression created by official statistics derives from the use of classification by distinct occupational categories. Such classification is not appropriate for economies in which most people are far from being specialized in particular occupations. The economic activity of a large proportion of the population of West Africa is better described as doing a number of different things rather than as pursuing a definite occupation. In many households officially described as agricultural, the head of the household trades part of the time, even during the normally short farming season, and more actively outside the season; and other members of the family trade intermittently throughout the year.

Imperfect specialization of economic activity is not confined to the agricultural community. Many African doctors, lawyers, and chiefs have extensive trading interests. Government employees and servants of the European population trade part-time, either importing merchandise or dealing in merchandise and foodstuffs bought locally. The fluidity of activity extends to personal relations in circumstances in which they bear closely on economic life. A prominent African trader in Lagos whose children are being educated at expensive universities and schools in England includes his wife among his principal retailer customers.

Even where the conceptual and statistical difficulties arising from imperfect occupational specialization are fully appreciated, it is difficult to collect the required information on subsidiary activities of individuals, particularly on part-time trade. Africans frequently do not regard trade as an occupation, especially when carried on by dependents, and would not refer to it as such when questioned because they regard it as part of existence and not as a distinct occupation. In many cases it may not be possible to draw the line between the social and commercial activities of, say, a group of women traders in the market. There is, however, no doubt that the commercial element is generally substantial.

Once the level of economic activity has risen from that of a subsistence economy to that of an emerging exchange economy—a process that is encouraged and promoted by the activities of traders—the task of distribution may require a substantial volume of resources. Much depends upon physical and climatic conditions. But the circumstances of West Africa are certainly not exceptional in requiring much distributive activity. The large number of dispersed farmers and holdings, poor natural communications and long distances, and the difficulties of prolonged storage in the open, together postulate a substantial volume of resources in distribution and transport for raising and maintaining the economy above the subsistence level at an early stage in economic development. In this type of economy the indispensable tasks of assembly, bulking, transport, breaking of bulk, and dispersal require a large proportion of available resources. Moreover, in an economy that has recently emerged from the subsistence level, some transactions are still likely to be on a barter basis. Barter tends to use more resources, especially labor, than does a fully developed money economy for transacting a given volume of trade.

Entry into small-scale trade is easy, as no technical or administrative skill is required at this level, and virtually no capital (since short-term credit is commonplace). Trade is attractive even for very low rewards in view of the absence of more profitable opportunities.[4]

The type of resources to be found in trade and transport depends, given the state of technique, upon the relative terms at which different productive resources are available. In an economy such as that of West Africa, where capital is scarce and expensive and unskilled labor abundant and cheap, the large volume of resources in distribution and transport consists very largely of labor. As compared with more advanced economies, there is a mass emphasis on labor rather than on capital. This tendency, which may proceed very far and reveal unsuspected possibilities, permeates West African trading arrangements, as a few examples will show.

In West Africa there is an extensive trade in empty containers such as kerosene, cigarette, and soup tins; flour, salt, sugar, and cement bags; and beer bottles. Some types of container are turned into household articles or other commodities. Small oil lamps are made from cigarette and soup tins; salt bags are made into shirts or tunics. But more usually the containers are used again for storage and movement of goods. Those who seek out, purchase, carry, and distribute secondhand containers maintain the stock of capital. They prevent the destruction of the containers, usually improve their condition, distribute them to where they can best be used, and so extend their usefulness, the intensity of their use, and their effective life. The activities of the traders represent a substitution of labor for capital. Most of the entrepreneurs in the container trade are women or children. The substitution is economic as long as six or eight hours of their time are less valuable (in view of the lack of other opportunities) than the small profit to be made from the sale of a few empty containers. So far from being wasteful, the system is highly economic in substituting abundant for scarce resources. Within the limits of available technical skill nothing is wasted in West Africa.

For various reasons, of which the low level of capital is one, the individual agriculturalist produces on a very small scale.

Moreover, the same lack of capital is reflected in the absence of suitable storage facilities and of cash reserves. As a result, each producer has to dispose of small quantities of produce at frequent intervals as it becomes available during and immediately after the harvesting season. This postulates a large number of intermediaries, who, because of the high cost of capital, employ methods of transport using relatively little capital and much labor. Donkey and bicycle transport are examples, while in some cases there is still head loading and human porterage, especially in the short-distance movement of local crops. Subject to frequent breakdowns as a result of poor roads and low technical skill, the available transport equipment is used continuously with the assistance of large quantities of labor.

The same phenomenon of the more intensive use of capital—that is, its more rapid turnover—can be observed in the breaking of bulk into the minute quantities in which imported merchandise is bought by the ultimate consumer. The purchase of a box of matches is often still a wholesale transaction; the buyer frequently breaks bulk and resells the contents to the final consumer in small bundles of ten to fifteen matches. Similarly, at the petty retail stage sugar is sold in lots of three cubes, trade perfume by the drop, salt by the cigarette tin, and cheap biscuits by the small heap of three or six. The small purchases are the result of low incomes and low capital, and the activities of the numerous petty retailers represent a substitution of labor for capital.

The small number of telephones and the low rate of literacy render it necessary for importing firms and larger distributors to use the services of numerous intermediaries to keep contact with smaller traders and to distribute their goods to them at an economic rate of turnover. The intermediaries reduce the size of stocks that need to be held. This saving is of particular importance, since the low level of fixed capital tends to enhance the economy's requirements of working capital.

The narrowness of markets and the backwardness of communications are reflected in interregional price differences, which provide profitable opportunities for successful arbitrage (particularly in locally produced goods) from region to region. These opportunities attract traders and intermediaries and also make it profitable for nontrading travelers to take part in trade, which they frequently do on a casual basis.

In West Africa, then, as in other emerging economies, the indispensable task of commodity distribution is costly in terms of available resources; of the available resources, capital is scarce and unskilled labor abundant; the multiplicity of traders is the result of the mass use of unskilled labor instead of capital in the performance of the task of distribution. There is an extensive demand for the services of intermediaries, and there is a large section of the population available to perform these services at a low supply price in terms of daily earnings.

In many Third World countries the numbers engaged in trade, and in the informal sector in general, are somewhat increased by the fact that wages in larger-scale employment are above the market-clearing level. Employment in the so-called organized sector is restricted, thereby increasing the supply of labor available in the informal sector.[5]

There are severe limitations and qualifications to the view that a high proportion of labor in tertiary production is both a consequence of and a pointer to a high standard of living. As is well known, this generally held view derives from the statistical investigations and analysis of Colin Clark and A. G. B. Fisher. Thus according to Clark:

> Studying economic progress in relation to the economic structure of different countries, we find a very firmly established generalization that a high average level of real income per head is always associated with a high proportion of the working population engaged in tertiary industries . . . Low real income per head is always associated with a low proportion of the working population engaged in tertiary production and a high percentage in primary production, culminating in China, where 75–80% of the population are primary producers. High average real income per head compels a large proportion of producers to engage in tertiary production.[6]

Professor Fisher writes:

> We may say that in every progressive economy there has been a steady shift of employment and investment from the essen-

tial "primary" activities, without whose products life in even its most primitive forms would be impossible, to secondary activities of all kinds, and to a still greater extent into tertiary production . . . The shifts of employment towards secondary and tertiary production revealed by the census are the inescapable reflection of economic progress.[7]

These general propositions are based partly on analytical reasoning and partly on statistical evidence. Both types of verification are defective.

The analytical reasoning supporting the generalization is based on the view that tertiary production is less essential than primary or secondary production; that its products are in the nature of luxuries. The argument is that the income elasticity of demand for tertiary products is higher than that for the products of primary and secondary activities; and that therefore the demand for tertiary products increases relatively more rapidly with economic progress. It is also suggested that technical progress is relatively slower in tertiary production. For these reasons it is argued that the proportion of employment in tertiary production must rise with economic progress.

The analytical basis of the generalization is open to criticism on several independent grounds. First, a substantial proportion of tertiary products are not luxuries with a relatively high income elasticity of demand; conversely, some products of primary and secondary production, possibly on a large scale in their aggregate, are such luxuries. Much of the output of tertiary production consists of intermediate rather than consumption goods; and there is no reason why the income elasticity of demand for such goods should be high. Second, there may be large-scale substitution of capital for labor in tertiary production in the course of economic progress. Third, the concept of the income elasticity of demand applied to a whole economy raises problems of aggregation, especially when relative factor prices and the distribution of incomes change.

For reasons already mentioned, the distributive task in the early stages of economic development is likely to be expensive in terms of all resources. A considerable volume of trading and transport is necessary to develop and sustain an exchange economy at an early stage of its development; it is an essential prerequisite for the development of specialization and therefore for the raising of productivity in primary production. Thus the proportion of resources engaged in tertiary production, notably in trade and transport, is likely to be high. It is possible that this proportion may fall at certain stages because the distributive task becomes easier and less costly in terms of resources as the economy develops. The task may become lighter with the growth of internal security, the development and improvement of communications, and the growth and stabilization of markets, all of which contribute toward more regular and continuous commercial contacts, more intensive use of available resources in distribution, and an increase in the size of trading units. These improvements are likely to have differential effects on productivity in various types of economic activity.

In richer economies, there is no a priori reason why, as incomes increase, a greater proportion of the luxuries consumed should be services, that is, products of tertiary activities. The durable consumer goods of Western economics provide numerous examples of heavy expenditure on the products of secondary activities with higher incomes. Expensive motor cars, jewelry, works of art, mass-produced but high-grade textiles, and handmade bespoke clothes and shoes are products of secondary activities.[8]

The proportion of all resources in tertiary production is not an index of economic progress. Moreover, even if it were, it would not follow that the proportion of employment in tertiary production must rise with economic progress. This would happen only if additionally labor and other productive resources were employed in tertiary production in fixed proportions. And this would occur only if substitution were not possible in the whole range of tertiary production, or if the relative terms upon which labor and other factors of production could be obtained remained unchanged throughout the whole course of economic progress. In fact, substitution between productive resources is obviously possible in tertiary production; and the terms on which labor and capital are available are then bound to change.

The emphasis on the use of labor rather than capital in tertiary production in an underdeveloped economy has been discussed above. The trade in used containers exemplifies how a tertiary activity expands with a lavish use of labor to economize in the products of secondary production. Conversely, in more advanced industrialized economies capital frequently replaces labor in tertiary activities, and secondary production tends to expand to economize on labor-intensive tertiary activities. There are familiar examples on a large scale in domestic service, laundry and repair services, and restaurant and retailing services, where capital equipment is now used instead of labor. The mass substitution of capital for labor in tertiary activity in North America is as striking as the reverse substitution in West Africa.[9] Altogether, the possibility of substitution between resources undermines the validity of the proposition connecting society's real income and the proportion of population occupied in tertiary production.

Changes in relative factor prices and differential rates of technical progress in different branches of production also affect the relative prices at which different luxuries (that is, goods or services with relatively high income elasticities of demand, whether they are the products of primary, secondary, or tertiary activities) are available to consumers. Such changes need not necessarily favor the luxuries that are the products of tertiary activities. If it were true, as is sometimes assumed, that productivity increases faster in secondary than in tertiary production, there would be a tendency for consumers to substitute luxuries that are produced by secondary production for those produced by tertiary production. There is, however, no reason why technical progress should always be more rapid in primary and secondary production than in tertiary production.

In any society it is unlikely that all members spend the same proportion of their incomes on tertiary products. People's incomes, tastes, and circumstances all differ. The share of the total national expenditure on tertiary products is obviously an average for the population as a whole. There is no ground for assuming a unique relationship between changes in this average and changes in national income. Indeed, this average may well fall if the bulk of any increase in the national income accrues to people whose relative expenditure on tertiary products is below the average. In these circumstances the average can be pulled down, even though each person's income elasticity of demand for tertiary products exceeds unity (which, of course, is by no means necessary). Moreover, a general increase in productivity is likely to reduce the supply of cheap labor formerly available for employment in certain types of tertiary activity, notably domestic service and petty trade, and thus reduce the volume of labor in those activities.

Tertiary production, then, is an aggregation of many dissimilar activities, including domestic service, government service, transport, retail and wholesale distribution, entertainment, and education. Some tertiary services are in the nature of inputs—that is, they are intermediate goods; other tertiary services are in the nature of consumption goods—that is, they are final goods. There is no reason why the demand for every one of these should follow a common trend. The only feature common to all tertiary production is that the output is nonmaterial. This characteristic does not produce a logical category of significance in the analysis either of demand or of economic progress. On the supply side, moreover, the proportion of the labor force in tertiary production depends upon a number of different forces, the individual and total effects of which are in no way unambiguously determined by secular changes in the national income.

Empirical verification of the relation between occupational distribution and economic progress is based on statistics that generally show both a higher proportion of the occupied population in tertiary industries in advanced countries than in underdeveloped countries and an increasing proportion in time series for particular countries. These types of comparison are vitiated principally on two counts. First, occupational statistics cannot convey ambiguities arising from imperfect occupational specialization. Second, the comparability of these statistics is affected by shifts of labor between unpaid and paid activities.

Clear-cut occupational classifications are inappropriate in underdeveloped countries where specialization is imperfect. What matters in this context is not the accuracy or adequacy of the statistics but their significance as a picture of economic activities. As noted earlier, statistics focus on only one of the activities performed by the head of the household only part of the time. They disregard his other activities, as well as those performed by the other members of his household. Over a considerable period of development many activities, especially trading, porterage, and domestic service, would not be regarded as separate occupations either by official enumerators or by the subjects themselves, particularly where activities are carried on by part-time workers or dependents. As specialization becomes more definite and pronounced and these activities come to be carried out by specialists, the performers and their performance are more easily identified and recognized and their extent looms larger, possibly much larger, in occupational statistics, even though the total volume of these activities may be unchanged or even reduced.

The classification of economic activities into three categories, while superficially convenient and clear, conceals large arbitrary elements that greatly reduce its usefulness. The activities of the agricultural producer selling his crops can be regarded partly as primary and partly as tertiary; this is particularly evident when he sells to the final consumer. Yet until they are taken over by an intermediary, his activities will be regarded as primary. When the intermediary is a member of the family, the activity may continue to be classed as primary. Its tertiary character is likely to be recognized only when the intermediary is an independent middleman. Since the emergence of an intermediary is likely to reduce the total effort in marketing a given volume of produce, tertiary activity may appear to be increasing at a time when it is actually decreasing.

These difficulties of classification do not disappear in more advanced economies. On a smaller scale, similar difficulties appear in the classification of the activities of different departments of large-scale enterprises. Again, the activities of the cobbler and the milliner are likely to be classified as tertiary when these are carried out in shops dealing with the public. Under factory conditions the activities would be treated as secondary production.

The substitution of unpaid labor, with or without capital, for paid labor (or vice versa) is the second reason why little reliance can be placed on occupational statistics in comparative studies. Such substitution takes place with economic progress. An obvious example in an advanced economy is the substitution of the activities of the household for those of the paid domestic servant; conversely, the household may frequently purchase the services of restaurants and repair agencies. Economic progress provides no general indication of the direction in which the shift between paid and unpaid labor will take place. Retail trade provides examples. In a poor economy, the poverty of consumers prevents them from buying in advance of requirements and from storing their purchases. The tasks of holding stocks and of breaking bulk into the small quantities required for almost daily consumption devolve upon the paid intermediary. In these instances, the activities of middlemen arise in response to the needs of poor consumers, who gain access to commodities otherwise outside their reach. By contrast, in advanced economies today housewives may store substantial quantities of consumer goods, especially of food, and may actually break bulk themselves. The tertiary activity remains, but the unpaid labor of consumers and their own capital are being substituted for the services of the intermediary.

The analysis of economic change and occupational movements in a particular economy requires a search for the causes of the existing distribution of employment (including unpaid employment) and for the forces making for change or obstructing it. When the relevant facts of a particular economy are ascertained, they can usefully be analyzed and interpreted, inter alia, in terms of relative factor prices, relative product prices, terms of trade, distribution of income, characteristics of demand for different products, opportunities for substitution between capital and different sorts of labor, demand for money income in terms of leisure or the fruits of unpaid efforts, and institutional rigidities. The fact that a particular economic activity is primary, secondary, or tertiary, in the customary senses of those terms, is not relevant for the necessary process of analysis. An activity becomes no more amenable to analysis by being labeled primary, secondary, or tertiary. In the present context, the only common feature of tertiary activities, namely that they produce services, is of no analytical interest to the economist. Moreover, while aggregation may be necessary and useful in some branches of economics, aggregation of economic activities and their division into three broad categories is misplaced in that branch of economics that is concerned with the structure of an economy.

Some of the main themes developed in Professor Fisher's writings are, of course, valid—in particular the necessity and desirability of occupational shifts in a changing economy and the importance of institutional impediments to such shifts in both more advanced and less advanced economies. But the validity of these themes does not depend upon a tripartite classification of production; and the concept of tertiary production is not necessary or useful "for driving home the fundamental truth that there is no invariable natural 'balance' between types of production, and that the relations between them require never-ending readjustment to changing circumstances."[10] The necessity and desirability of occupational shifts are independent of any correlation (or lack of correlation) between tertiary production and economic progress. If anything, the tripartite classification of economic activity, by appearing to neglect changes *within* each of the three categories, would seem to hinder rather than to help in the recognition of the causes, concomitants, and consequences of economic change and growth. The formulation of some "inescapable"[11] relationship between labor in tertiary production and economic progress is apt to lead, however unintentionally, to those very ideas of some desirable or necessary balance between categories of production of which Fisher properly disapproves; moreover, the formulation is likely to bring about confusion between effects and their causes.

Misgivings about the usefulness of the classification of economic activities into primary, secondary, and tertiary are reinforced by Fisher's references to at least three (and possibly four) quite different criteria or approaches for identifying tertiary production, and by his observation that no "exclusive choice" in favor of any of these is necessary.[12] When, furthermore, the classification of the cultivation of strawberries and mushrooms as tertiary is supported on the grounds that those who "defend the interests of primary producers" do not have such products in mind, one may doubt whether the concept has any "identifiable hard core of meaning," let alone usefulness for economic analysis.[13]

Professor Fisher's reluctance to define his concept is not helpful. But although it appears that he does not want to commit himself to a rigorous definition, he nevertheless seems to incline to the view that production should be regarded as tertiary if the product has a high income elasticity of demand (presumably greater than unity). Hence, for example, the claim that the concept of tertiary production is useful as a guide for "recognising the 'growing points' of a progressive economy."[14] However, the income elasticity of demand for a product is not the same in all countries; and it does not remain the same in any one country. A definition of tertiary production in terms of high income elasticity of demand for its products would require the statistician or economist to treat the same activity as tertiary in some countries and as nontertiary in others, as tertiary in one period and as nontertiary in others, which would invalidate the classification for purposes of intertemporal and international comparison.

3
Population, Welfare, and Development: Gloom Dispelled

Since the Second World War it has been widely argued that population growth is a major, perhaps decisive, obstacle to the economic progress and social betterment of the underdeveloped world, the majority of mankind. Thus Robert S. McNamara, former president of the World Bank, wrote:

> To put it simply: the greatest single obstacle to the economic and social advancement of the majority of peoples in the underdeveloped world is rampant population growth . . .
>
> The threat of unmanageable population pressures is very much like the threat of nuclear war . . . Both threats can and will have catastrophic consequences unless they are dealt with rapidly and rationally . . .
>
> Governments must divert an inordinately high proportion of their limited national savings away from productive effort simply in order to maintain the current low level of existence for the expanding population . . . Capital that ought to have been invested was not available. It had been dissipated by the ever-rising tide of children.[1]

Mr. McNamara's words of 1973 were repeated practically verbatim in March 1990 by the Duke of Edinburgh. According to *The Times*,

> The Duke of Edinburgh warned yesterday that the consequences of unimpeded population growth would be more devastating to the world than a nuclear holocaust.
>
> In a speech prepared for the United Nations' Population Fund, he said it was high time that political leaders began to "face the facts" and make efforts to solve the crisis. "The fuse of the population bomb has already been ignited," he said.[2]

The Pearson Commission, whose members included Nobel laureates, sounded the same note: "No other phenomenon casts a darker shadow over the prospects of international development [of LDCs] than the staggering growth of population."[3]

These apprehensions rest primarily on three assumptions. The first is that national income per head (as conventionally calculated) measures economic well-being. The second is that economic performance and progress depend critically on land and capital per head. The third is that people in the Third World are ignorant of birth control or careless about family size: they procreate regardless of consequences. A subsidiary or supporting assumption is that population trends in the Third World can be forecast with accuracy for decades ahead.

Conflicting views on mankind are discernible behind these assumptions and, indeed, behind debates on population. One view envisages people as deliberate decision-making persons in matters of family size. The other view treats people as being under the sway of uncontrollable sexual urges, their numbers limited only by forces outside themselves, either Malthusian checks of nature or the power of superior authority. However, proponents of both views agree that LDC governments, urged by the West, should encourage or, if necessary, force people to have smaller families.

The central issue in population policy is whether the number of children people have should be decided by the parents or by agents of the state.

Suppose for the moment that an increase in population reduced income per head, a contingency examined later in the essay. Such a reduction need not mean that the well-being either of families or of the wider community has been reduced.

As conventionally measured, national income per head is usually regarded as a satisfactory index of economic welfare, even of welfare as such. This index registers the flow of goods and services yielding benefit and satisfactions that can conventionally be evaluated by the measuring rod of money. Familiar problems arise in defining and measuring national income in this sense. These include the problem of demarcation between inputs and outputs in both production and consumption (such as the treatment of the costs of travel to work or to the shops); the problem of standardizing for age distributions when the index is used for intertemporal and international comparisons; and the choice of exchange rates in international comparisons. These are not simply minor technical difficulties, but relate to major limitations in the use of the concept of national income per head.

In the economics of population, national income per head founders completely as a measure of welfare. It takes no account of the satisfaction people derive from having children or from living longer. The birth of a child immediately reduces income per head for the family and also for the country as a whole. The death of the same child has the opposite effect. Yet for most people, the first event is a blessing, and the second a tragedy. Ironically, the birth of a child is registered as a reduction in national income per head, while the birth of a farm animal shows up as an improvement.

The wish of the great majority of mankind to have children has extended across centuries, cultures, and classes. This is evident from the survival of the human race: most people have been ready to bear the cost of raising two or more children to the age of puberty. Widely held ideas and common attitudes reflect and recognize the benefits parents expect from having children. The biblical injunction is to "be fruitful and multiply." Less well known in the West is the traditional greeting addressed to brides in India, "May you be the mother of eight sons."

The uniformly unfavorable connotation of the term *barren* reflects the same sentiment.[4] The practice of adoption and the demand for artificial insemination in some countries also indicate the desire for children. All this refutes the notion that children are simply a cost or a burden.

These general considerations and their applicability to contemporary LDCs can be easily illustrated. Professor John Caldwell, a leading Australian demographer, has quoted from a study of the Fulani in northern Nigeria.

The prospect of a secure and relatively carefree old age under the care of their sons will often restrain young women from deserting or divorcing their husbands. Both men and women in many respects show a remarkable disposition to forego present convenience (or pleasure) in the interests of future benefits. Such attitudes are universally reported by field researchers, even among the businessmen of Ghana's capital Accra.[5]

Another example is from the Indian subcontinent.

A Punjabi water carrier, mistaking an anthropologist for a family planner who had visited him many years earlier, is reported to have said: "You were trying to convince me . . . that I shouldn't have any more sons. Now, you see, I have six sons and two daughters and I sit at home in leisure. They are grown up and they bring me money. One even works outside the village as a labourer. You told me I was a poor man and couldn't support a large family. Now you see, because of my large family, I am a rich man."[6]

Some have argued that high birth rates in LDCs, especially among the poorest, result in lives so wretched as not to be worth living: that over a person's life, suffering or disutility may exceed utility. If this were so, fewer such lives would increase the sum total of happiness. This view implies that external observers are qualified to assess the joys and sorrows of others. It implies that life and survival are of no value to the people involved. This outlook, which raises far-reaching ethical issues, is unlikely to be morally acceptable to most people, least of all as basis for forcible action to restrict people's reproductive behavior, especially when it is remembered how widely it was espoused about the poor in the West only about two generations ago. Nor is this opinion consistent with simple observation, which suggests that even very poor people prefer to live rather than not to live, as is shown by their striving to remain among the living by, for instance, seeking medical help to prolong their lives.[7]

Thus these considerations make clear that the much-deplored population explosion of recent decades is seen more appropriately as a blessing rather than as a disaster because it reflects a fall in mortality which is an improvement in people's welfare.

In welfare economics, situations are assessed in terms of the satisfaction of people's revealed preferences. In the terms of the discussion above, people reveal their preferences when they have children and when they take decisions to remain alive. However, economists also take account of certain considerations other than people's revealed preferences. In the present context, three of these may be pertinent: ignorance, external effects, and income distribution.

Much of the advocacy of state-sponsored birth control is predicated on the implicit assumption that people in high-fertility LDCs do not know about contraceptives and that, in any case, they do not take into account the long-term consequences of their actions. People in the Third World do know about birth control, and many practice it. In most Third World societies, fertility is well below fecundity; that is, the number of actual births is well below the biologically possible number. Traditional methods of birth control were widely practiced in societies much more backward than contemporary LDCs with high fertility.

Moreover, for many decades now, cheap Western-style consumer goods such as hardware, cosmetics, soft drinks, watches, and cameras have been conspicuous trade goods in Southeast and South Asia, the Middle East, West Africa, and Latin America. More recently, transistor radios and pocket calculators have become common in LDCs. It follows that had there been a large demand for modern contraceptives, these would have been equally conspicuous as trade goods. In fact, condoms, intra-uterine devices, and the contraceptive pill so far have spread only slowly in much of the Third World, even when heavily subsidized. Indeed, those contraceptives are often absent where sophisticated articles of feminine hygiene are on sale. All this suggests that the demand for modern contraceptives has been small, either because people do not want to restrict their families or because they prefer other ways of doing so.[8]

The inference is that in the Third World, the children who are born are generally wanted by their parents. This statement is subject to the qualification that one of the parents may not want a child but has to bow to the wishes of the other parent. This situation may apply particularly to women in Catholic or Muslim societies. How far external observers can or should attempt to enforce changes in mores in such societies raises issues that cannot be pursued here; in any case the argument of this essay is not affected by the presence of such conditions.

Children are certainly avoidable. And people in LDCs generally are not ignorant of the long-term consequences of their actions. Indeed, young women in LDCs often say that they want more children and grandchildren to provide for them in their old age.[9] The readiness to take the long view is evident also in other decisions such as the planting of slow-maturing trees or embarking on long-distance migration.

The next issue is that of externalities. The first question under this rubric is whether parents bear the full cost of having and raising their children. If they did not bear these costs fully, they would have more children than they would otherwise. According to the usual assumption of welfare economics, the satisfaction of the parents from the additional children would be less than the weight of the burden falling on others. It is often assumed that parents in LDCs do not bear the full costs of having children, in particular the costs of health care and education, and that a substantial part of those costs is in fact borne by taxpayers.[10] The particular costs are unlikely to be heavy in LDCs. They are likely to be lower relative to the national income than in the West. For instance, schools are often simple, inexpensive structures. For social and institutional reasons, basic health services are extensively performed by medical auxiliaries and nurses rather than by fully qualified doctors. In any event, if the externalities in question were considered to be so large as to call for remedial action, this should take the form of changes in the volume and direction of the relevant public expenditures, as well as in their financing. Imposed reductions in family size constitute a far less satisfactory or effective alternative.

The extended family provides a further example of the same negative externality. Parents may have more children if they know that part of the cost is borne by other members of their extended family. However, as just noted, the burden falling on others is likely to be small. Moreover, the extended family is embodied in the mores of much of the less developed world. And any effect of the operation in this context of the extended family will diminish or disappear if the extended family system

gives way with modernization, a matter examined in the concluding section of this essay.

Rapid population growth might produce adverse externality
effects in other ways also. Congestion in cities is sometimes
instanced.

The rapid growth of cities in LDCs is not generally the result
of high population growth. Rather, it derives from the pull of
large cities, especially the capitals. This attraction results from
the limitations to many people of rural life and from the higher
incomes and other benefits available or expected in the cities.
The income differences are increased when rural earnings are
depressed as a result of policies benefiting the urban population.
That the growth of large cities is the result of these influences is
evidenced by large conurbations in sparsely populated LDCs
such as Brazil and Zaire, and generally by the more rapid
increase in the urban populations of LDCs than in the countries
as a whole. In any case, undesirable crowding in large cities is
not a function of their size or growth, much less of the growth of
the national population: it is the inevitable consequence of the
pricing of housing and transport, unrelated to the scarcity of
these resources.

Similar considerations apply to other supposed adverse
external effects of population growth on the environment,
including deforestation, soil erosion, and depletion of fish
stocks. The rate of use of such assets can be controlled by pricing
and the assignment of property rights.

Altogether, it is highly unlikely that population growth sets up
net adverse externalities of such magnitude as to result in loss of
welfare in the community as a whole, let alone such a loss as to
warrant the apprehensions noted in the first section, or official
pressure on people to have fewer children. Where serious
adverse externalities are present, much less drastic interven-
tions will produce the desired results much less painfully as well
as more rapidly and effectively. This will be developed later in
this essay.

Moreover, population growth can have favorable external
effects. It can facilitate the more effective division of labor and
thereby increase real incomes. In fact, in much of Southeast
Asia, Africa, and Latin America, sparseness of population
inhibits economic advance. It retards the development of trans-

port facilities and communications, and thus inhibits the movement of people and goods and the spread of new ideas and methods. These obstacles to enterprise and economic advance are particularly difficult to overcome.

At the later stage of development, there are also significant positive externalities arising from greater scope for the division of labor in economic activity in science, technology and research generally.

The positive externalities in the early stages of development amid a sparse population are plain.

Beyond that stage, opinion about the relative importance of positive and negative (favorable and unfavorable) externalities of population growth must be speculative.

The practically exclusive preoccupation with adverse externalities is unwarranted. And even if it could be shown that they are significant and outweigh the positive externalities, this would call for policies quite different from pressure on parents to have fewer children, as will be argued later.

Finally, the implications of population growth for income distribution need consideration.

The rapid population growth in the less developed world in recent years is often said to have increased differences in recorded per capita income between advanced countries and LDCs. Somewhat similar changes are said to have taken place within individual countries between richer and poorer groups. These outcomes are often deplored as a worsening of income distribution. Those who deplore the so-called worsening of income distribution are outside observers, often Westerners. They are certainly not the parents or the children. Population growth is the result of the conduct of the parents and the survival of their children. As has been explained above, conventionally measured income does not include the satisfaction of having children and of living longer. There is a great improvement in the welfare of those who have not died and of those whose children live longer. But the outside observers would presumably remain critical of what is called a worsening of income distribution even if it were established that the welfare of the poor, or indeed their conventionally measured income, had increased over the period under discussion.

*   *   *

Having seen that population growth is unlikely to reduce welfare, we can now consider whether even conventionally measured income per head is likely to be reduced by population growth.

It seems prima facie commonsensical that prosperity depends on natural resources—land, mineral resources, and capital—and that population growth reduces the per capita supply of these critical determinants and therefore per capita income. Indeed, if nothing else changed, an increase in population must reduce income per head: and this must be true in the very short run.[11] However, this elementary analysis reveals nothing about developments over a longer period. This is so because over a longer period other influences affecting productivity are significant, and some of these can be elicited or reinforced by an increase in population. These influences include the spread of knowledge, division of labor, changes in attitudes and habits, redeployment of resources, and technical change. Economic analysis, in short, cannot demonstrate that an increase in population must entail reduction in income per head over a longer period.

There is ample evidence that rapid population growth has certainly not inhibited economic progress either in the West or in the contemporary Third World. The population of the Western world has more than quadrupled since the middle of the eighteenth century. Real income per head is estimated to have increased fivefold at least. Much of the increase in incomes took place when population increased as fast as in most of the contemporary less developed world, or even faster.

Similarly, population growth in the Third World has often gone hand in hand with rapid material advance. In the 1890s, Malaya was a sparsely populated area of hamlets and fishing villages. By the 1930s it had become a country with large cities, extensive commerce, and extensive plantation and mining operations. The total population rose through natural increase and immigration from about one and a half million to about six million, and the number of Malays from about one million to about two and a half million. The much larger population had much higher material standards and lived longer than the small numbers of the 1890s. Since the Second World War a number of

LDCs have combined rapid population increase with rapid, even spectacular economic growth for decades on end—witness Taiwan, Hong Kong, Malaysia, Kenya, the Ivory Coast, Mexico, Colombia, and Brazil, to name but a few.

Conventional views on the effects of population growth assume that endowments of land and other natural resources are critical for economic performance. As we have seen, this assumption is refuted by experience in both the distant and more recent past. And there is much additional evidence that works in the same direction. Amid abundant land, the American Indians before Columbus were backward at a time when most of Europe, with far less land, was already advanced. Europe in the sixteenth and seventeenth centuries included prosperous Holland, much of it reclaimed from the sea; and Venice, a wealthy world power built on a few mud flats. At present, many millions of poor people in the Third World live amid ample cultivable land. Indeed, in much of Southeast Asia, Central Africa, and the interior of Latin America, land is a free good. Conversely, land is now very expensive in both Hong Kong and Singapore, probably the most densely populated countries in the world with originally very poor land. For example, Hong Kong in the 1840s consisted largely of eroded hillsides, and much of Singapore in the nineteenth century was empty marsh land. Both these countries are now highly industrialized and prosperous communities. The experience of other countries both in the East and in the West points in the same direction. Obvious examples include Japan and Taiwan, West Germany, and Switzerland. All these instances underline the obvious: the importance of people's economic qualities and the policies of governments.

It is pertinent also that productivity of the soil in both prosperous and poor countries owes very little to the "original and indestructible powers of the soil," that is, to land as a factor in totally inelastic supply. The productivity of land is the result largely of human activity: labor, investment, science, and technology. Moreover, the factor price of land, including return on investment, is a small part of the national income in most countries; and this proportion has tended to fall rather than rise in those Western countries for which reasonably reliable statistics are available. This would not be so if land were acutely scarce relative to other productive resources.[12]

The wide differences in economic performance and prosperity between individuals and groups in the same country with access to the same natural resources also make clear that the availability of natural resources cannot be critical to economic achievement. Such differences have been, and still are, conspicuous the world over. Salient examples of group differences in the same country are those among Chinese, Indians, and Malays in Malaysia; Chinese and others elsewhere in Southeast Asia; Parsees, Jains, Marwaris, and others in India; Greeks and Turks in Cyprus; Asians and Africans in East and Central Africa; Ibo and others in Nigeria; and Chinese, Lebanese, and West Indians in the Caribbean. The experience of Huguenots, Jews, and Nonconformists in the West also makes clear that natural resources are not critical for economic achievement. For long periods, these prosperous groups were not allowed to own land or had their access to it severely restricted.

Mineral resources have often yielded substantial windfalls to those who discovered or developed them or expropriated their proprietors. Latin American gold and silver in the sixteenth century and the riches of contemporary oil-producing states are often cited as examples of prosperity conferred by natural resources. But the precious metals of the Americas did not promote economic progress in pre-Columbian America, nor did their capture ensure substantial development in Spain. The oil reserves of the Middle East and elsewhere were worthless until discovered and developed by the West, and it must be conjectural whether they will lead to sustained economic advance.

It is often argued that population growth reduces capital formation, and thus the growth of per capita incomes. This is so because resources have to be diverted to the maintenance of more children. However, the work of leading scholars suggests that capital formation is not a major factor in long-term development. As we have already noted, other factors have been far more important.

Population growth as such can induce changes in economic behavior favorable to capital formation. The parents of enlarged families may well work harder and save more in order to provide for the future of their families. It is evident that poor people in LDCs are not precluded from saving and investment by virtue of their poverty. They can save and invest by sacrificing leisure for work and by transferring their labor and land to more productive use, perhaps by replacing subsistence production by cash crops. Poor and illiterate traders have often accumulated capital by working harder and opening up local markets.

Population growth is often thought to bring about certain special problems; the risk of famine, exhaustion of mineral resources, and large-scale unemployment are often specified in this context.

There is no danger that malnutrition or starvation through shortage of land will arise from population growth. Contemporary famines and food shortages occur mostly in sparsely populated subsistence economies such as Ethiopia, the Sahel, Tanzania, Uganda, and Zaire. In these countries land is abundant and, in places, even a free good. Recurrent food shortages or famines in these and other LDCs reflect features of subsistence and near-subsistence economies such as nomadic style of life, shifting cultivation, and inadequate communications and storage facilities. These conditions are exacerbated by lack of public security, official restrictions on the activities of traders, the movement of food, and imports of both consumer goods and farm supplies. Unproductive forms of land tenure such as tribal systems of land rights can also bring about shortages. Finally, the very poor may suffer acute hardship if adverse external shocks abruptly reduce their disposable income. All these actual or potential adverse conditions have nothing to do with population growth or pressure. No famines are reported in such densely populated regions of the less developed world as Taiwan, Hong Kong, Singapore, western Malaysia, and the cash-crop-producing areas of West Africa. Indeed, where a greater density of population in sparsely populated countries brings about improved transport facilities and greater public security, it promotes emergence from subsistence production.

With the exception of fossil fuels, mineral deposits and concentrations of minerals are not exhaustible resources. The discovery and extraction of mineral deposits or less readily recoverable minerals depend on price, cost, technology, and government policy. When minerals are used they do not disappear. They can be largely recovered by processes governed by the same factors as determine their discovery and extraction. Fossil fuel is the one exception because it disappears with use. But population growth or pressure is no threat to the continued supply of energy. Substantial and lasting increases in the real cost of fossil fuel would encourage both the use of other sources of energy and also various energy-saving methods. Moreover, fossil fuels are not used extensively as sources of energy in Asia and Africa, so that population increases there would not be a major factor in raising the cost of fossil fuel.

There is no reason why population growth should lead to unemployment. A large population means more consumers as well as more producers: if it is true that with every mouth God sends a pair of hands, it is equally true that with every pair of hands, God sends a mouth. The large increase in population in the West over the last two centuries has not brought about persistent mass unemployment. Substantial unemployment emerged in the twentieth century, when population growth was already much slower than it had been in the nineteenth. And when in the 1930s and 1940s an early decline in population was widely envisaged, this was generally thought to portend more unemployment because a decline in population would reduce the mobility and adaptability of the labor force and would also diminish the incentive to invest.

Contemporary experience in the less developed world confirms that rapid increase in population does not result in unemployment, and also that the issue cannot be discussed simply on the basis of numbers and physical resources. Until recently, population grew very rapidly in densely populated Hong Kong and Singapore without resulting in unemployment. There is far less land per head in Singapore than in neighboring Malaysia; yet many people move from Malaysia to Singapore, both as short-term or long-term migrants and as permanent settlers in search of employment and higher wages. They are an appreciable portion of the labor force of Singapore and are significant also in relation to the labor force of Malaysia.

The idea that population growth results in unemployment implies that labor cannot be substituted for land or capital in particular activities, and also that resources cannot be moved from less labor-intensive to more labor-intensive activities. In other words, it implies that the elasticity of substitution between labor and other resources is zero in both production and consumption. That this is not so is shown by the development of more intensive forms of agriculture in many LDCs, including the development of double and treble cropping. Substitution in consumption is evidenced by the frequent changes in patterns of consumption. The argument that population growth causes large-scale and persistent unemployment in LDCs involves further unrealistic and inadmissible assumptions such as a closed economy and unchanging technology.

Certain characteristics of the labor markets in some LDCs could lead to unemployment. These have nothing to do with population growth or pressure. An important instance is the operation of a formal or informal minimum wage above the market-clearing level for the type of labor involved. This need not in itself cause unemployment but merely a reduction in the numbers employed in those activities. However, the attraction of being employed at those wages, together with the need to be available for employment when required, can result in the formation of pools of unemployed or intermittently employed labor around centers of relatively highly paid employment in the formal sector.

Dramatic long-term population forecasts are often put forward with much confidence. Such confidence is unwarranted. It is useful to recall the population forecasts of the 1930s and 1940s when a substantial decline of population, primarily in the West but to some extent world wide, was widely predicted. Confidence in these forecasts was based on improvements in demographic techniques, notably the development and use of the concepts of gross and net reproduction rates. Even the extinction of the species was seriously envisaged in the writings of prominent academics under such headings as "The End of the Human Experiment" and "The Suicide of the Human Race."

Within less than one human generation, the population

problem has come to mean the exact opposite of what it was formerly held to be. The earlier scare of a decline has come to be replaced by the scare of an increase, primarily in LDCs. The scare has remained but the sign has been reversed from minus to plus.[13] It would be interesting to speculate what would have happened if in the 1930s public policy measures then widely advocated had been adopted and had succeeded in increasing the world population.

Once again, the predictions put forward so confidently are accompanied by far-reaching proposals for dealing with the supposed problem. Yet for many reasons only the roughest forecasts of population trends in the Third World are warranted. The basis for confident predictions for the Third World, or even for individual LDCs, is far more tenuous than it was for the forecasts of long-term population trends in the West in the 1930s and 1940s that proved so unsuccessful.

To begin with, vital statistics are seriously deficient in many LDCs. In much of the Third World there is no registration of births and deaths, and even where there is, it is often incomplete. Estimates of the population of African countries differ by as much as a third or more, and for large countries such as Nigeria, this means tens of millions of people. Estimates of the population of the People's Republic of China, the most populous country in the world, also differ substantially. Such deficiencies in the statistics put into perspective such widely canvassed and officially endorsed practices as forecasting to the nearest million the population of the world for the year 2000 or beyond.

In the coming decades, major political, cultural, and economic changes are bound to occur in much of the Third World. These changes are unpredictable, and so are people's responses. For instance, contrary to expectations, the economic improvement in recent decades in some Third World countries has resulted in higher not lower fertility. Similarly, decline in mortality in many LDCs has not been accompanied by the corresponding decline in fertility that had been widely expected in the belief that people had many children to replace those who died young. Moreover, in some of these countries urban and rural fertility rates are about the same while in others there are wide differences. The relationship of fertility to social class and occupation is also much more varied in the Third World than in the West.

There is one demographic relationship of considerable generality that bears upon population trends in LDCs. Professor Caldwell has found that systematic restriction of family size in the Third World is practiced primarily by women who have adopted Western attitudes toward childbearing and child-rearing, as a result of exposure to Western education, media, and contacts. Their attitude to fertility control does not depend on income, status, or urbanization, but on Westernization.[14] In the context, Westernization means the readiness of parents to forgo additions to family income from the work of young children and also to incur increased expenditure on education, reflecting greater concern with the material welfare of their children.

Caldwell's conclusion is more plausible and more solidly based than the widely held view that high incomes lead to reduced fertility. It is true that in the West, and in the Westernized parts of the Third World, higher incomes and lower fertility are often, though by no means always, associated. But it is not the case that higher incomes as such lead to smaller families. Both the higher incomes and the smaller families reflect greater ambition for material welfare for oneself and one's family. Both, in other words, reflect a change in motivation. By contrast, when parental incomes are increased as a result of subsidies or windfalls, without a change in attitudes the parents are likely to have more children, not fewer. This last point is pertinent to the proposals of many Western observers who, without recognizing the contradiction, urge both population control and also more aid to poor people with large families.

Some broad, unambitious predictions of Third World population prospects may be in order. Although the speed and extent of Westernization are uncertain, the process is likely to make some headway. The result would be some decline in fertility. But the large proportion of young people and the prevailing reproductive rates will ensure significant increases in population in the principal regions of the Third World over the next few decades. Population growth in the Third World as a whole is unlikely to fall much below 2 percent, and may for some years continue around 2.5 percent, the rough estimate of growth rates in the early and mid-1980s. It is therefore likely to remain considerably higher than in the West, Japan, and Australasia.

If this difference in population growth continues, the population of the West, Japan, and Australasia will, over the years, shrink considerably relative to that of Asia, Africa, and Latin America. Such an outcome will have wide political and cultural consequences. But these consequences cannot be explored in an essay that addresses the relation between population growth and economic attainment and well-being, and not the ethnic, racial, or national composition of mankind.

We have seen that it is most unlikely that Third World population growth could be such as to jeopardize the well-being of families and societies. But if this well-being were for any reason to be seriously impaired by population growth, reproductive behavior would change without official pressure. There is, therefore, no cause for trying to force people to have fewer children than they would like. And when such pressure emanates from outside the local culture it is especially objectionable. It is also likely to provoke resistance to modernization generally.

The central issue in population policy, then, is whether the number of children people may have should be decided by individuals and families or by politicians and national and international civil servants.

Advocates of officially-sponsored population policies often argue that they do not propose compulsion but intend only to extend the options of people by assisting the spread of knowledge about contraceptive methods. As we have seen, people in LDCs usually know about both traditional and more modern methods of birth control. Moreover, in many Third World countries, especially in Asia and Africa, official information, advice, and persuasion in practice often shade into coercion. In most of these societies people are more subject to authority than in the West. And especially in recent years, the incomes and prospects of many individuals have come to depend heavily on official favors. In India, for example, promotion in the civil service, allocation of driver and vehicle licences, and access to subsidized credit, official housing, and other facilities have all been linked at times to restriction of family size. Forcible mass sterilization, which took place in India in the 1970s, and the extensive coercion in the People's Republic of China are only extreme cases in a spectrum of measures extending from publicity to compulsion.

Policies and measures pressing people to have fewer children can provoke acute anxiety and conflict, and they raise serious moral and political problems. Implementation of such policies may leave people dejected and inert, uninterested in social and economic advance or incapable of achieving it. Such outcomes have often been observed when people have been forced to change their mores and conduct.

There is one type of official policy that would tend to reduce population growth, extend the range of personal choice, and simultaneously promote attitudes and mores helpful to an improvement of the well-being of the population and also to economic advance. This policy is the promotion of external commercial contacts of people of LDCs, especially their contacts with the West. Such contacts have been powerful agents of voluntary change in attitudes and habits, particularly in the erosion of those harmful to economic improvement. Throughout the less developed world, the most prosperous groups and areas are those with most external commercial contacts. And such contacts also encourage voluntary reduction of family size. Thus, extension of such contacts and the widening of people's range of choice promote both economic advance and reduction in fertility. In these circumstances, the reduction in family size is achieved without the damaging effects of official pressure on people in their most private and vital concerns. Yet this type of policy is not on the agenda of advocates of the need for fewer children in LDCs.

It is widely agreed that the West should not impose its standards, mores, and attitudes on Third World governments and peoples. Yet, ironically, the most influential voices call for the exact opposite when it comes to population control.

4
Foreign Aid: Central Component of World Development?

In the United States, *foreign aid* has become the accepted term for the policy of official subsidies in the form of grants and soft loans from governments of relatively prosperous countries to those of less prosperous ones. In Europe, *development aid* is the term most often used.

Foreign aid and *development aid* are misleading expressions. To call official wealth transfers "aid" promotes an unquestioning attitude. It disarms criticism, obscures realities, and prejudges results. Who can be against aid to the less fortunate? The term has enabled aid supporters to claim a monopoly of compassion and to dismiss critics as lacking in understanding and sympathy. To paraphrase Thomas Sowell, aid is a major example of a policy which allows intellectuals and politicians to be on the side of the angels at a low apparent cost. The term also clearly implies that the policy must benefit the population of the recipient countries, which is not the case. If these transfers were generally known as government-to-government subsidies or subventions, terminology would encourage more systematic assessment.[1]

Unfortunately, the term *foreign aid* is now so widely used that it is not possible to avoid it in a book intended for both academic and wider readership. I shall use interchangeably the terms *transfers, subsidies,* and *aid,* and occasionally refer to *aid-recipient countries.* But it should be remembered that the recipients of official aid are always governments. They are not the poor, destitute, or starving people shown in aid propaganda.[2]

There are presumably also other reasons for the prevalent uncritical attitude toward the policy of official subsidies to governments of poorer countries. One is the familiar but facile identification of governments with the population at large. Perhaps more important is the belief that rich Western countries can readily afford to give away a small fraction of their income, which may do some good to the peoples of the recipients and cannot possibly harm their prospects. This latter belief ignores the political, social, and cultural repercussions of these subsidies.[3]

There are other forces favoring an uncritical attitude, such as a widely articulated feeling of guilt in the West, and the operation of political, administrative, and commercial interest groups. Altogether, a climate of opinion has emerged in which only supporters of these subsidies are regarded as expert, and dissenters can be readily dismissed as lacking in both understanding and compassion. The extension of these subsidies to Eastern European governments underlines the importance of a more thoughtful attitude to this policy.

Unquestioning support for aid helps to explain many anomalies. Western aid has gone to governments explicitly hostile to the West, such as those of Ethiopia, Vietnam, and Cuba; to governments at war with each other (which has enabled recipients to claim that the donors support their enemy); to governments whose policies have created refugees; and to governments of other countries who have taken them in, at high cost and with resultant tensions. Examples include the flow of refugees from Vietnam to other Southeast Asian countries, such as the Philippines, Malaysia, and Indonesia.[4] The governments of all these countries have received Western aid simultaneously throughout the relevant periods. A notable anomaly occurred at the height of the Falklands War in 1982, when Britain was supplying aid to the Argentine government under the United Nations Development Program at a time when that government was deploying expensive, sophisticated weaponry against British forces. This episode evoked no protest in Britain.

Aid has gone and still goes to governments that severely restrict the inflow of capital, the shortage of which is said to be the reason for aid. More generally still, these subsidies go to governments pursuing policies that plainly retard economic advance and damage the interests of their poorest subjects.[5]

"Foreign aid is the central component of world development." This was said by Professor Hollis B. Chenery in 1981 when he was vice-president of the World Bank in charge of economic research.[6] He could not have been right. Large-scale development takes place in many parts of the world without foreign aid, and did so long before this policy was invented some forty years ago.[7]

Though evidently not a central component of development, since the Second World War foreign aid has been the centerpiece of academic and public discussion on the economic prospects of Asia, Africa, and Latin America and on the relation between the West and these regions. Whatever its impact on development, foreign aid has had far-reaching results. For instance, it has brought into existence as concept and collectivity the Third World, also called the South. Foreign aid is the source of the North-South conflict, not its solution. The primary significance of aid lies in this important political result. It has also promoted the politicization of life in the recipient countries. These results have been damaging both to the West and to the peoples of the less developed world. The amount of money spent by the West in no way measures these effects.

Discussion on foreign aid envisages the world as being one-third rich (the West) and two-thirds poor (the Third World or South). In this picture, extreme poverty is the common and distinguishing characteristic of the Third World. But there is a continuous range in the per capita incomes of countries. The absence of a distinct break in the series undermines the concept of a Third World demarcated from the West on the basis of per capita incomes. The line of division between rich and poor countries is quite arbitrary. One could equally well say that the world is two-thirds rich and one-third poor.

The picture is misleading also in that many groups or societies in Third World countries, especially in the Far East, the Middle East, Southeast Asia, and Latin America, are richer than large groups in Western countries. Nor is the Third World stagnant. Both before and after the Second World War, many Third World countries grew rapidly, including South Korea, Taiwan, Thailand, Malaysia, Singapore, the Ivory Coast, Mexico, Venezuela, Colombia, and Brazil.

It is not sensible to lump together and average the incomes

of the very different societies of the Third World or South, which comprise at least two-thirds of mankind. What is there in common between, say, Thailand and Mozambique, Nepal and Argentina, India and Chad? Their societies live in widely differing physical and social environments and display radically different attitudes and modes of conduct. The Third World includes millions of aborigines and pygmies, and also peoples with ancient and sophisticated cultures, and others employing highly advanced methods of business and technology. It is both misleading and condescending to treat the richly varied humanity of the majority of mankind as if it were much of a muchness, an undifferentiated, uniform, stagnant mass, a mass, furthermore, that could not emerge from this state without external subsidies.

Nor is brotherhood a common characteristic of the Third World, as is evident from the persistent hostility and even armed conflict between many Third World countries, including India and Pakistan, Iraq and Iran, and many others, not to mention the numerous civil wars. It is not surprising that attempts at organizing economic cooperation within the Third World have failed, except for collective bargaining with the West over aid and related matters. Moreover, this collective bargaining is often organized and financed by the West.

*   *   *

The common characteristic of the Third World is the receipt of foreign aid and not poverty, stagnation, exploitation, brotherhood, or skin color. The concept of the Third World and the policy of official aid are inseparable. The Third World is merely a name for the collection of countries whose governments, with occasional and odd exceptions, demand and receive official aid from the West. This is the only bond joining its diverse and often antagonistic and warring constituents, which have come to be lumped together since the late 1940s as the underdeveloped world, the less developed world, the nonaligned world, the developing world, the Third World, or the South.

The Third World is, moreover, a progeny of the West. Aid was introduced and has always been organized by the West. It began with President Truman's Point Four Program of 1949. He urged bold measures to help the less developed countries, where,

he said, over half of mankind was living in sickness and wretch-
edness.

In creating the Third World, the West has created an entity
hostile to itself. Some individual Third World countries have
been neutral or even friendly to the West, but the organized and
articulate Third World is critical or hostile.

Foreign aid also encouraged the notion of the West (or North)
as a single economic decision-making entity, a homogeneous
aggregate with identical interests capable of imposing its will on
the Third World. In fact, Western governments do not cooperate
in setting market prices, and foreign suppliers compete for business in the Third World markets. Obvious examples include
suppliers of manufactured products such as cars, trucks, and
chemical products, and construction companies. Manufacturers
and traders compete vigorously in the purchase of exports from
the Third World.

Although the case for aid goes largely unquestioned, various
arguments are often heard, ranging from restitution of alleged
wrongs to preservation of the African elephant. The three most
persistently influential are the promotion of development, the
relief of poverty, and the political and economic interests of the
donors. Official Western aid is therefore envisaged as being
simultaneously a moral, political, and economic imperative.

Since its inception in the early postwar years, the central
argument for foreign aid has been that without it Third World
countries could not progress at a tolerable rate, if at all. In fact,
external donations have never been necessary for the development of any society anywhere. (As shown later in this chapter,
Marshall aid to postwar Europe provides no exception to this
statement.) Economic achievement depends on personal, cultural, social, and political factors, that is, people's own faculties,
motivations, and mores, their institutions, and the policies of
their rulers. In short, economic achievement depends on the
conduct of people and that of their governments.

It diminishes the people of the Third World to suggest that,
although they crave material progress, unlike the people of the
West they cannot achieve it without subsidies. Much of the
Third World progressed rapidly long before foreign aid—wit-

ness Southeast Asia, West Africa, and Latin America. Large parts of these regions were transformed in the hundred years or so before aid. There are, of course, Third World societies that have not progressed much over the last hundred years. This lack of progress reflects factors that cannot be overcome by aid, and are indeed likely to be reinforced by it. The notion that poor countries cannot progress without subsidies derives from the hypothesis of the vicious circle of poverty and stagnation, a major theme of development economics since the Second World War. It was concisely formulated by the Nobel laureate Paul Samuelson: "They [the backward nations] cannot get their heads above water because their production is so low that they can spare nothing for capital formation by which the standard of living could be raised."[8] This hypothesis is refuted by every individual family, group, community, or country that has emerged from poverty without subsidies, and that has often done so within a short space of time. Indeed, if the hypothesis were valid, the world would still be in the Old Stone Age.[9]

If a hypothesis conflicts with empirical evidence, this means that the model behind it is defective in that the variables specified or implied are either relatively unimportant as determinants or do not interact in the fashion implied. Both defects mar the hypothesis of the vicious circle. The growth of income does not depend on the volume of saving and investment, and poor people can save and invest sufficient amounts to emerge from poverty.

The argument for aid as necessary for development rests on the belief that possession of capital is critical for economic advance. If this were so, how is it that large numbers of very poor people could have become prosperous within a few years without donations, as they have done the world over? Evident examples include very poor immigrant communities in North America and Southeast Asia. To have capital is the result of economic achievement, not its precondition.

Poor people can and often do save and invest sufficient amounts to emerge from poverty. They can save enough from small incomes for direct investment in trading, agriculture, and other purposes. They can also work harder or longer or redeploy their resources more productively to improve their lot.

And much recent research by leading scholars, including Simon Kuznets, has confirmed that increase in capital played a minor role in the economic advance of the West in recent centuries.[10] Moreover, these findings refer to capital formation. They apply even more to the volume of investible funds because much spending, conventionally termed *investment,* does not result in productive capital formation. Furthermore, the findings refer to capital formation in societies where social and political conditions were helpful to economic achievement.

The contribution of capital formation to development can be secured without aid. To begin with, direct investment from abroad is likely to flow into areas in which capital can be employed productively. Externally financed plantation, mining, trading, and other commercial enterprises have been established in many parts of the less developed world in apparently unpropitious conditions in the absence of a hostile social and political climate. The inflow of this type of capital has been accompanied by an inflow of technical and administrative skills, and it encouraged new ideas and methods of production. As part of their operations these enterprises, notably banking and trading companies, have also financed small-scale local farmers and traders. Foreign direct investment played a large part in the economic progress and transformation of much of the less developed world in the nineteenth and twentieth centuries.

Moreover, enterprises and governments in the Third World capable of using capital productively can readily borrow commercially abroad as well as at home.

Both before the Second World War and since, the thousands of enterprises in the less developed world that advanced from very modest beginnings to considerable size and prosperity readily found the necessary capital. Even in very poor Third World countries, small-scale producers have had access both to domestic and to external funds. Western and Levantine trading firms routinely lend substantial amounts of money to trustworthy African borrowers, primarily traders, who in turn lend to farmers. Indeed, lending by trading firms to local people is generally a prerequisite for doing business. Ability to borrow does not depend on the level of income, but on responsible conduct and the ability to use funds productively.

Third World governments have also been able to borrow readily, even too readily, from international banks. This also applies to borrowing for facilities that do not yield a directly appropriable return. If such spending, often known as infrastructure spending, is productive, it increases national income (and thus taxable capacity) so that the loans can be readily serviced.

Since Third World governments and enterprises that can use funds productively and conduct their finances responsibly can secure external funds, it follows that the maximum contribution of aid to development cannot exceed the avoided cost of borrowing, that is, interest and amortization charges payable to creditors as a percentage of GNP. The most that aid can do for development is to reduce the cost of a resource that is not a major independent factor in the development process. For large Third World countries these benefits must be modest, even minimal, far too small to affect any macroeconomic aggregate. For instance, for India in the early 1980s this benefit would have been of the order of .25 to .5 percent of recorded GNP.

It may be thought that even such a modest contribution to development is worthwhile: the recipient countries must derive some benefit from the inflow of resources, while the donors can afford to give away a small proportion of their incomes. This prima facie plausible reasoning overlooks the adverse repercussions of official wealth transfers. Most of these repercussions arise because the subsidies go to the governments; some others would arise even if they went to the private sector.

Unlike manna from heaven, aid does not descend indiscriminately on the population at large, but goes directly to the government. Because aid accrues to the government it increases its resources, patronage, and power in relation to the rest of society. The resulting politicization of life enhances the hold of governments over their subjects and increases the stakes in the struggle for power. This result in turn encourages or even forces people to divert attention, energy, and resources from productive economic activities to concern with the outcome of political and administrative processes and decisions. This sequence provokes tension that often erupts in armed conflict, especially in countries comprising different ethnic, tribal, and cultural groups. Such sequences must inhibit economic advance because the deployment of people's energies and resources necessarily affects the economic performance of a society. Foreign aid has not been the sole cause of the politicization of life in the Third World, but it has contributed significantly to the process.

Foreign aid has also enabled many recipient governments to pursue policies that plainly retard growth and exacerbate poverty. The long list of such policies includes persecution and sometimes the expulsion of the most productive groups, especially ethnic minorities; suppression of private trade, and at times the destruction of the trading system; restriction on the inflow of foreign capital and businesses, depriving the country not only of capital but also of enterprise and valuable skills; extensive confiscation of property, including forced collectivization; takeover of foreign enterprises, which uses up scarce capital and deprives the country of valuable skills; price policies that discourage agricultural production; expensive forms of state support of unviable activities and projects, including uneconomic import substitution; and the imposition of economic controls, which, among other adverse effects, restricts external contacts and domestic mobility and so retards the spread of new ideas and methods often crucial for economic advance. Many aid recipients regularly pursue several of these policies simultaneously; the Ethiopian government has pursued all of them.

Such policies, when pursued singly, and much more so when pursued together, impoverish people and even cripple the economy. Vietnam, Burma, Ethiopia, Tanzania, and Uganda are conspicuous examples.

These policies often directly provoke conflict, even armed conflict, the effects of which are exacerbated by the neglect of public security and the protection of life and property, which in the Third World often goes hand in hand with ambitious, far-reaching policies.

Most aid recipients, possibly all, severely restrict private inward investment. This policy is both anomalous and damaging. It is evidently anomalous because shortage of capital is the basis, the rationale of official aid. The inflow of official aid makes it easier for governments to restrict inward private investment. These restrictions serve the political purposes of the government. They reinforce the hold of the rulers over their subjects, whose economic opportunities are extended by the inflow of private capital. The restrictions often also benefit special interest groups by shielding them from competition, and the beneficiaries are usually politically effective or useful supporters of the government. The restrictions on the inflow of private capital are very damaging because, as already noted, such investment from abroad is often accompanied by the inflow of administrative, technical, and commercial skills, the inflow of which in turn brings with it new ideas, crops, and methods of production.

Such policies are pursued because they accord with the purposes and interests of the ruling group, including promotion of governmental power, satisfaction of politically effective pressure groups, and provision of financial rewards to politicians, civil servants, and their allies. The pursuit of many of these policies is therefore not irrational according to the accepted meaning of the term, although if carried too far they may prove counterproductive and undermine the position of those in power. To describe them as irrational or misguided is to imply that the policymakers are engaged in the single-minded pursuit of increasing general economic and social welfare, so that policies which plainly go counter to this objective are only honest, well-intentioned errors. It is evident that the damaging, destructive policies pursued for years, even decades, cannot be attributed to well-intentioned mistakes. A number of governments pursuing such policies, most obviously in Africa and Asia, could not have survived without Western aid, which in some cases has even been increased substantially in the face of such destructive policies, notably in Ethiopia, Sudan, and Tanzania in the early 1980s.

This situation throws into relief a conspicuous and persistent anomaly. Recorded per capita income is a major factor in the allocation of much Western aid.[11] On this criterion, governments pursuing destructive policies can qualify for more aid. Paradoxically, aid allocated on the basis of per capita incomes rewards policies of impoverishment.

This anomaly applies evidently to program aid, that is, subsidies for the general purposes of government. But it applies also to project aid, that is, official subsidies for particular projects whether in the public or private sector. Such subsidies will be sanctioned by the recipient government only if the project fits with general government objectives. And generally it enables the recipient government to spend more in pursuit of its policies.

Actual or anticipated balance-of-payments difficulties also affect the allocation of aid. This criterion has also encouraged policies adverse to development. Confidence that balance-of-payments difficulties will attract further aid encourages financial profligacy, notably inflationary policies. These policies are often accompanied by exchange and other controls. Inflation, payments difficulties, and controls engender tension and insecurity, even a crisis atmosphere, thereby inhibiting domestic saving and productive investment and encouraging a flight of capital.

There are other untoward effects of aid. Official transfers have often biased development policy toward unsuitable external models. Subsidized import substitution, construction of petrochemical complexes, and state ownership of airlines are familiar examples. Adoption of external prototypes in development policy has often gone hand in hand with attempts at more comprehensive modernization. Such efforts have included attempts to transform people's mores, values, and institutions and have in turn invited backlash and conflict. Governments that engage in ambitious programs and projects of these kinds have simultaneously neglected the basic functions of government, including the protection of life and property.

The advocacy of official subsidies as necessary for economic advance also encourages or reinforces widely prevalent attitudes and inclinations in poor countries, especially in Asia and Africa, that are uncongenial to economic advance, such as belief that economic improvement depends on circumstances and influences outside one's control. These subsidies go to governments and encourage them to engage in beggary and blackmail rather than in exploring the potentialities of economic improvement at home. And such inclinations are apt to spread outwards from the rulers to the population.

The inflow of aid funds drives up the real rate of exchange and adversely affects foreign trade competitiveness. This effect can be offset to the extent that the subsidized transfers enhance the overall productivity of resources. For various reasons, in the case of official aid such enhancement is unlikely in practice. In any case, it can occur only after a time lag of years. Meanwhile the higher real exchange rate makes for continued dependence on external assistance. This effect of external subsidies applies whether they go to the government or to the private sector.

An indirect effect of these subsidies also damages the economic prospects of recipients. It is a familiar paradox that the donors erect severe barriers against imports from the recipients of their largesse. The granting of subsidies diminishes effective resistance to these barriers. The recipient governments are less inclined to protest for fear that the complaints may endanger the inflow of subsidies. And within donor countries, criticism of import barriers is muted because many people feel that they are doing enough for the recipients and do not wish to face the dislocation and opposition that accompany liberalization of imports. Since external trade and the contacts it promotes are important instruments in the economic advance of LDCs, the restriction of imports from these countries is correspondingly damaging. The subsidies serve to some extent as conscience money for the damage inflicted by the trade restrictions.

Trade restrictions are imposed because they benefit special interest groups in the donor countries. The subsidies also benefit important commercial, political, and administrative interests there. The presence of influential lobbies behind both the trade restrictions and the subsidies resolves the paradox of providing subsidies to LDC governments and simultaneously restricting the trading opportunities of the recipient countries.

Finally, the adverse effect of one type of aid needs to be noted. Official aid to Asian and African governments often takes the form of free or heavily subsidized food. Even in the absence of underpayment of producers by special taxation and the operation of government buying monopolies, this policy depresses farm incomes in the recipient countries and thereby promotes otherwise uneconomic migration from rural areas to the cities with attendant social, political, and economic costs.

Aid involves a double asymmetry in its effects on development. First, any favorable effect is on a resource that is not critical for development. The adverse effects, on the other hand, operate on critical determinants, primarily political and cultural determinants. Second, an amount of aid that is too small to benefit development appreciably can nevertheless bring about adverse effects. It is the relationship of aid to GNP that is relevant to the favorable effects, namely the reduction of the cost of investible funds. And because aid goes to governments, it is the relationship of aid to government receipts and to foreign exchange earnings (themselves readily subject to government control) that is relevant to the adverse repercussions.

Aid is necessarily much larger relative to tax receipts and foreign exchange earnings than it is to the national income of the recipients. Indeed, the differences in these ratios are striking. I calculated them for the year 1980 for India and Tanzania, leading aid recipients in Asia and Africa. For India, aid was 1.6 percent of recorded GNP, 16.8 percent of tax receipts, and 31.2 percent of export earnings. For Tanzania, the corresponding figures were 18.1 percent, 106.8 percent, and 152.8 percent. Thus, for both countries, aid as percentage of tax receipts and foreign exchange earnings was a large multiple of its percentage of GNP. The multiple becomes larger still when it is remembered that although statistics of tax receipts and foreign exchange earnings are reasonably reliable, the statistics much understate the GNP of Asian and African countries.

Thus, an amount of aid that, at best, could bring about an insignificant increase in income per head, could greatly increase the resources directly available to the government. And it is the latter increase that brings the adverse repercussions.

The plausible belief that external aid cannot damage the prospects of the population of the recipient countries has helped along the advocacy of this policy. In much the same way as the use of the term *aid,* this belief has promoted an unquestioning attitude. After all, even if aid is wasted no great harm results, because the donors can readily afford to give a small fraction of their incomes. A different attitude is likely to be adopted, at any rate by some compassionate people in the donor countries, if it is realized that the policy can inflict much harm on people in LDCs, especially through the politicization of life and by rewarding policies of impoverishment.

Recognition of the damaging consequences is also relevant to the adoption of possible reforms of this policy. Reform is the most that might be expected, since termination is not practical politics in the face of ongoing commitments, and of the formidable vested interests behind these subsidies. I have discussed elsewhere possible reforms of foreign aid to bring it closer to its declared objectives.[12]

The progress of the recipient countries is often instanced to demonstrate the effectiveness of aid. This evidence is in fact irrelevant. However substantial the progress of an aid-recipient country, the contribution of aid can never exceed the avoided cost of borrowing the investible funds as percentage of GNP. And the cost and volume of these funds are not critical for development. Moreover, the adverse repercussions still operate.

The establishment and success of individual projects financed by aid are also often instanced as evidence of its value. These, too, are irrelevant. When such projects promise to be productive they can be financed by government or private enterprise without aid, so that its contribution is again limited to the avoided cost of borrowing. The idea is unwarranted that such activities and projects could not have taken place without aid. Third World governments financed infrastructure projects long before foreign aid. Similarly, there were privately financed plantations, mining, manufacturing, and transport enterprises in many parts of Asia, Africa, and Latin America long before there was aid. And projects financed without aid are more likely to be productive because they are usually more closely geared to market conditions and to the surrounding social scene.

The oft-instanced analogy between the Marshall Plan and subsidies to Third World or Eastern European governments is misleading. After the war, the economies of Western Europe had to be revived not developed. As was clear from prewar experience, the personal, social, and political factors congenial to economic achievement were present in Western Europe. Moreover, recent research suggests that Marshall aid played at most a minor part in the recovery of the economy of the Federal Republic of Germany. In any event, Marshall aid to

Europe was terminated within four years of its inception, and Germany then became an exporter of capital and thereafter a major source of foreign aid. This experience contrasts with suggestions that official aid to the Third World will have to continue for generations.

Relief of poverty is the second major proclaimed purpose of foreign aid and one that most appeals to genuinely compassionate people. But aid does not go to the pitiable figures of its advocacy. It goes to governments, to the rulers, who are often directly responsible for the misery of their subjects. But even when this is not so, it is still the case that aid goes to the rulers, whose policies, including the pattern of public spending, are determined by their own personal and political interests, among which the position of the poorest is rarely prominent.

In most of the Third World there is no machinery for relief of poverty by the state. Even if a recipient government wanted to use aid to help the poorest, this could be difficult. Moreover, such help rarely accords with the priorities of the rulers and often conflicts with these, especially in multiracial, multitribal, or multicultural countries. For instance, an Arab-dominated Sudanese government will not help the poorest blacks in southern Sudan, hundreds of miles away, with whom it is in persistent armed conflict. In Sri Lanka, a Singhalese-dominated government is unlikely to help the Tamil poor.

In the context of development I have already recited a long list of damaging policies. These policies also exacerbate poverty. I have noted also that the allocation of Western aid rewards impoverishment. Indeed, the more damaging the policies, the more acute becomes the need, and the more effective become appeals for aid. Witness Ethiopia and the Sudan in the early 1980s. The poorest suffer most from such destructive policies as enforced population transfers, suppression of trade, and forced collectivization, and also by the civil wars and other forms of breakdown of public security. These policies and conditions have forced large numbers of people to rely for their existence on precarious subsistence production, as in Africa.

There are also many less extreme instances of damaging policies. The poorest do not benefit from brand-new capital cities such as Brasilia, Abuja, or Dodoma. And they do not benefit from the proliferation of state-owned airlines throughout the Third World in such countries as Burundi and Laos, where the vast majority of people do not use air travel, and local people cannot fly them. Many of these projects and enterprises promoted by foreign aid represent a drain on domestic resources and have to be subsidized by local taxpayers.

Spending on show projects and the presence of a number of very rich local people in LDCs where there are many extremely poor people make clear that the rulers, while demanding external donations in the name of relief of poverty and international redistribution, are not much interested in helping their poor. They seem to be interested in redistribution only if it advances their personal and political purposes, as for instance impoverishing their political opponents or politically unpopular groups.

Although external donations can do little or nothing for development or the relief of poverty, they can relieve immediate shortages, especially of imports. Governments can pursue even extremely damaging policies for years on end because this result of the donations conceals from the population, at least temporarily, some of the worst effects. Moreover, continued Western aid also tends to suggest endorsement of these policies, and thus confers spurious respectability on those who pursue them. It has been widely recognized that Western aid has kept afloat African rulers pursuing destructive policies, enabling these rulers to persist with such policies.

The obvious question arises whether donor governments could use aid to help the poorest either by influencing the policies of recipient governments or by channeling funds directly to the poorest.

Attempts by Western donors to influence the policies of the recipients have been half-hearted and ineffective. For instance, the governments of Ethiopia and the Sudan have successfully resisted the rather unenthusiastic attempts of Western donors to induce these governments to modify their harshest policies. In 1984 the government of Ethiopia stated emphatically that Western aid and voluntary charity must conform to their own policies. Third World governments have insisted that the distribution of aid must both conform with their own policies and remain under their own auspices.

The third major argument envisages aid as serving the political and economic interests of the West. This argument is insubstantial. About one-third of all Western aid is channeled through official international agencies. These organizations are not permitted to take into account the political interests of donors. Governments hostile to the West are represented in many international organizations and can thus affect the allocation of multilateral transfers. For instance, throughout the period of the Cold War, the Soviet Union and its allies were members of the United Nations and could influence the transfers under various UN programs, even when their own contribution was negligible. Practically all Soviet nonmilitary aid was then channeled to client states such as Cuba and Vietnam. These countries simultaneously received aid from the West.

The interests of the West are also largely ignored in bilateral transfers. Aid administrators are rarely qualified to know how to promote Western political interests and are often disinclined to do so. More generally, if official transfers were to serve Western interests, they would need to be geared both to the political or military significance of the recipient countries and to the conduct of their governments.

Many aid-recipient countries are of no political or military significance.[13] And many aid-recipient governments are openly hostile to the donors, whom they abuse and thwart as best as they can, at times to assert their independence from the donors. Some aid recipients are also hostile to the market system and sympathetic to the Eastern Bloc of controlled economies. Many aid recipients have since the earliest days of aid opposed and denigrated the donors, even when their own political survival has depended on these subsidies. The West feeds the mouths that abuse it. Many Third World rulers have derived their aid from the West but their ideology and political stance from the East.[14]

According to another variant of the political argument, the poverty and stagnation in LDCs, endemic without aid, would bring to the fore governments hostile to the West. This argument assumes first that foreign aid is necessary or helpful for development and relief of poverty, and also that support for anti-Western politicians depends on low levels of income and low rates of growth. Neither of these assumptions is valid, as is obvious from modest reflection and observation.

The proponents of the argument that aid promotes Western prosperity, or is even necessary for it, claim that this policy increases purchasing power in the Third World, advances growth there, and thereby promotes exports and employment in the West.[15] The argument would be invalid even if these transfers significantly promoted development, which they cannot do. Moreover, the argument would be invalid even if aid increased incomes substantially. Exports bought with the proceeds of foreign aid are given away. It is sophistry to argue that people who give away part of their wealth are better off because the recipients of their largesse are or will be better off. An enterprise does not prosper if its owners give away money to people who later may buy its products with this money.[16]

Similarly, aid will not alleviate unemployment, recession, and deindustrialization in the West. If such ills could be alleviated by government spending, spending at home would be more effective. Domestic spending is much more effective in maintaining employment than giving money to LDCs. Moreover, any assets created by domestic spending remain at home.

Often, spending on aid can aggravate domestic unemployment, for instance by diminishing the volume of productive investible funds, an outcome that reduces employment opportunities and incomes where these depend on domestic spending.

In sum, the idea that aid helps the economies of the donors simply ignores the cost of the resources given away.[17]

5
The Third World Debt Crisis: Can't Pay or Won't Pay?

With few exceptions, the flow of funds from the West to Third World countries has taken three forms: foreign aid, that is, intergovernmental grants or soft loans; direct and portfolio investment by Western firms and individuals; and sovereign borrowing by Third World governments. When this borrowing is on concessional terms it of course incorporates an element of foreign aid.

Since 1982, Third World sovereign debt has become a prominent international issue. Many debtor governments have failed to meet their contractual obligations. They have, in fact, defaulted in the proper, traditional sense of the word. Default has been accompanied by ad hoc arrangements, including writing off the whole or part of the debt, extending the repayment period, reducing interest rates, and extending further credit to finance partial debt servicing. The term default is rarely used in public discussion. Typically, the creditors do not term or treat as default the failure of debtors to meet their contractual obligations; the term default is reserved for formal repudiation of debt. In this essay, however, I use the term in the traditional sense of failure to discharge contractual obligations.

Public discussion generally portrays Third World sovereign debt as a major threat to the economies of much of the Third World and also of the West itself. The argument proceeds along the following lines. The honoring of debt obligations would impede economic improvement and even bring about significant deterioration in living standards in many Third World countries. Unless the obligations are canceled or greatly alleviated in favor of the borrowers, there is bound to be increased destitution, malnutrition, child mortality, unemployment, and deterioration of the environment. In the words of Mr. Jaime Lusinchi, president

56

of Venezuela: "The problem of foreign debt today strangles the economic and social development of the great majority of the world's peoples."[1] These results in turn undermine the economies of the West by reducing export markets and thus output and employment, and by threatening the stability of the international financial system. Furthermore, the economic and social repercussions of debt service in the Third World (including riots and a rise in political extremism) engender political destabilization and threaten Western security.

Widespread and influential acceptance of these views supports policies for partial or total cancelation of debts. Such measures are thought to be necessary to enable Third World countries to service their debt without severe hardship to their peoples and in line with their ability to pay.

When the Third World's creditors relieve the sovereign debtors of meeting their obligations wholly or in part, they in effect provide a form of foreign aid. Foreign aid involves a positive flow of funds to recipient Third World governments. Debt relief involves the avoidance of a negative flow. It is therefore not surprising that much the same arguments are advanced for debt relief as for foreign aid. Thus the relief of extreme poverty, the financing of development, the maintenance of employment in the West, and the promotion of Western political interests are the major components in the advocacy of both foreign aid and debt relief. Indeed, proposals for official or officially-organized debt relief on a large scale are typically accompanied by proposals for the granting of more foreign aid as well.

There are, however, some distinct features in the advocacy of debt relief. Thus it is argued that if the creditors were to try to enforce fulfillment of obligations, there would be massive open default, which would endanger the financial position of the creditor banks with serious knock-on effects on the international financial system. This contention is insubstantial. If, in the recent past, large-scale formal default would genuinely have threatened the solvency of creditor banks, they would have had to take measures to strengthen their asset bases. Western governments could have and almost certainly would have granted loans or subsidies to the exposed banks; and the banks themselves would have reduced dividend payments and called for additional funds from shareholders. In fact, most of the heavily exposed banks have been able to improve their financial positions without government help and in the face of extensive de facto defaults. They have been able to do so without major curtailment of dividend payments. The continued payment of dividends itself suggests that the creditor banks did not believe that their solvency was in jeopardy because of this exposure. In any case, if the creditor banks had needed rescuing by Western governments in order to avoid financial collapse, direct loans and subsidies to the banks would have been far more effective than channeling the money through debtor governments, which certainly would not have used all of it for servicing their debts.

It is sometimes urged that organized debt relief is warranted because some of the debts have resulted from irresponsible lending by the commercial banks, and that therefore they cannot expect full payment. Much of bank lending to Third World governments may well have been ill-advised and based on unrealistic expectations about debt repayment. The normal consequence of such imprudence by a lender is a voluntary agreement between borrower and lender to revise the terms of the loan. Although Western governments and the official international organizations (notably the International Monetary Fund and the World Bank) are naturally involved when they are the creditors, there is no reason why they should be drawn into the process of debt revision between creditor banks and their sovereign borrowers.

A review of the statistics of Third World debt is not warranted here, and the argument does not depend on the magnitudes involved. We may note in passing, however, that the statistics often cited in public discussion are much affected by what is included in the debt. The usual practice is to include only sovereign debt; but sometimes the estimated total of private debt is also included. The number of indebted countries covered also varies: sometimes the discussion refers to Latin America, at other times to seventeen (or occasionally fifteen) countries treated by the World Bank as highly indebted, at yet other times to all Third World countries; and there are many other variants as well. Again, the usual practice is to exclude debts owed by one Third World government to another, and to measure only sovereign debt to the West. Nevertheless, debts between Third World governments are sometimes included. Moreover, very different categories of debt are habitually lumped together in these figures. Thus the large disbursements made to many governments by the International Development Association (IDA) of the World Bank are included. These fifty-year loans, which are free of interest, are not indexed for inflation. They are, in effect, grants and not loans.

One statistic is often used in discussions of Third World debt. This is known as the debt service ratio: the sum of interest and amortization obligations (that is, debt service) expressed as a percentage of export earnings. This ratio may appear to be sensible and relevant as a measure of the ability of the debtor country to service its foreign debts. It is in fact an inadequate measure.

The debt service ratio does not indicate whether the debt service is large or small in relation to GNP. In fact, almost all of the seventeen countries now regarded as problem debtors are so-called middle-income countries with per capita GNP of well over $1,000.[2] The aggregate debt service payments of these seventeen countries in 1986 represented about 5 percent of their aggregate GNP, and debt servicing of this magnitude could not have caused any significant reduction in the average standard of living. It is worth noting that at the same time South Korea, not a problem debtor, had a higher ratio of debt service to GNP (7.6 percent) than Brazil (3.1 percent), Mexico (7.2 percent), or Venezuela (6.5 percent). The GNP figures in many cases are almost certainly substantially understated. According to Professor Deepak Lal (at the time research administrator at the World Bank), the burden of debt service of the problem debtors at the onset of the debt crisis was far from exceptional by historical standards. It was appreciably lower than it had been at some times in the past for Argentina (now one of the seventeen), when that country was rated as a first-class debtor.[3] A further inadequacy of the debt service ratio is that it takes no account of the liquid funds and other marketable assets of the debtor governments.

Although there are widely varying estimates of the external liquid assets of the major debtor governments, their para-statal organizations, and their private citizens (whose foreign assets could be requisitioned, as was done by the British government in the two world wars), the sums involved are undoubtedly large. In 1987 the government of Peru had externally held reserves of about $1.5 billion, at a time when it refused to pay a few million dollars on servicing its sovereign debt. According to the Bank of International Settlements, the increase in the external balances of residents of eleven Latin American debtor countries for the period 1978–87 "amounted to a very large proportion of, or even exceeded, their [the debtor countries'] debts to commercial banks."[4] Besides liquid assets, the major debtors also have other readily marketable assets. The large state-owned oil enterprises of Mexico, Venezuela, Brazil, and Nigeria are only the most conspicuous examples. Some of these para-statal organizations have in recent years bought large stakes in major Western enterprises.

The current Third World debt crisis erupted in August 1982 with the refusal of the Mexican government to service its external debt. At the time this debt was around $80–85 billion. The capital value of PEMEX, Mexico's state-owned oil monopoly, was about $40 billion if valued conservatively on the basis of six times 1982 pre-tax earnings of $6.7 billion. The sale or pledging of part of PEMEX might well have averted the Mexican debt crisis, or even the entire Third World debt crisis, as being evidence of the earnest of the government to meet its obligations. This is especially likely because, insofar as there is a debt crisis, it is one of liquidity not of solvency, arising from doubts about the willingness of the debtors to meet their obligations.

The debt service ratio has also diverted attention from the effects of government policies on export earnings. The preceding essay explained how Third World governments, including the problem debtors, have adopted policies that have wasted resources and damaged living standards and development. Several of those policies directly, promptly, and adversely affect export earnings. Obvious examples include underpayment of farmers of exportable crops, restrictions on certain exports, confiscation of private property, suppression of private trade, and overvaluation of the exchange rate.

Specific examples may be helpful. In 1940 the Gold Coast (now Ghana) supplied over a third of world exports of cocoa. By 1987 its share had fallen to under 15 percent. The tonnage exported from Ghana then was less than in 1940. World consumption had more than doubled, and exports from other countries had more than trebled. The principal factor has been the sustained and severe underpayment of Ghanaian farmers.[5] Another instance is the recent history of clove exports from Zanzibar. In the 1960s and 1970s the state buying monopoly severely underpaid clove producers, and the large estates were confiscated and handed over to inexperienced, previously landless people. Clove exports fell greatly, to about half what they had been in the years before the introduction of these measures. World consumption had increased substantially.[6] The relevance of government policies for export earnings is also reflected in the very different export performances of major debtor countries, of industrialized Far Eastern economies such as Hong Kong and Taiwan, and of primary producers such as Malaysia and Thailand.

The well-nigh universal restrictions on the inflow of private equity capital similarly reduce the availability of foreign currencies and, in the longer term, reduce productive capacity, and thus the capacity to generate export earnings. The familiar flight of capital from many debtor countries also affects export earnings adversely by reducing the volume of productive investment; and government policies are largely responsible for open and covert export of capital, the extent of which is reflected in the very large external liquid funds of citizens of the major debtor countries already noted.

Thus, to focus on the debt service ratio suggests inevitably, but mistakenly, that ability to service debt is something that depends on external factors and is outside the control of debtor governments.[7]

What is known as the debt crisis does not arise from the inability of debtor governments to service their sovereign debt without hardship to their peoples. It arises from the unwillingness of these governments to meet their obligations. In the present circumstances it is rational conduct for these governments to default.

Sovereign debt obligations cannot be enforced in the courts. Payment is therefore at the discretion of the debtor government, which in turn depends on the expected economic and political consequences of payment or default for the government and for the country as a whole. A government is likely to be concerned primarily with the consequences for itself. Potentially, the most important adverse consequence of default is a drying up of new flows of external finance, which could result in an economic crisis sufficiently serious to undermine the position of the government. In current conditions, the debtor governments quite realistically do not believe that failure to meet their obligations will bring about such a severe reduction in external finance as would threaten their position. They rightly believe that even if they default, they will nevertheless receive sufficient funds from the international organizations, Western governments, and commercial lenders to be able to sustain their position. There is therefore little inducement for them to service their debts in full or on time.

Default on sovereign debt has not caused the flow of external funds to dry up, even in the face of recurrent default. In fact, in important cases debtor governments have been receiving greatly increased flows of official aid. The Western governments have not applied the only effective sanction. The debtor governments correctly believe that the flow of aid will continue in the face of default and probably even increase. It is also realistic for some of them to expect that, before long, Western banks may be back in the market as suppliers of new funds, largely because they will find it difficult to continue to resist pressure on them from their own governments and the international organizations.

The flow of official funds from Western governments and the international organizations will continue to depend on the play of political forces in the West. And to repeat the relevant point, the play of these forces will not be affected substantially by the play of political force. Western governments habitually exert pressure on their banks to maintain or increase lending to the Third World.

In the light of the discussion here, it is worth some conjecture as to why most debtor governments have continued to meet at least part of their obligations. There may be several reasons. Some time had to elapse before the debtor governments could be reasonably confident that major creditors would be accommodating in the face of de facto default, and not react by discontinuing further flows. A government might have believed that a demonstration of willingness to meet some of its obligations could elicit larger current and prospective flows of funds than would have been forthcoming with a more complete default. Each debtor government might have considered itself as being in competition with other governments in securing additional funds. The formation of a debtors' cartel, if effective, would of course remove this limited incentive, which at present may serve to contain the number and extent of defaults.

Debt relief is a form of foreign aid in its effects on international funds to Third World governments. Its incidence does not reflect the usual criteria on which official aid purports to be allocated among recipient governments, namely the level of incomes per head and the development prospects of the recipient countries. The beneficiaries of debt relief are simply those governments that have decided not to honor their obligations and have been allowed to do so very largely unscathed. Western governments have condoned Third World default and have even encouraged it by insisting on forbearance by both official and commercial creditors in the face of default, including default on very soft loans. Such a stance may well lead to domestic repercussions in the West. In the United States groups of citizens have already asked why their municipalities should be asked to service their debts in full when their government does not ask Third World debtors to do so. It may well prove impossible for Western governments to reserve debt forgiveness for export only.

6
Marketing Reform: An Inventory of Intervention

Government measures to control or modify agricultural marketing, or to reshape the structure of trade in agricultural produce are in force in many parts of the world, and are of three broad types. First, there are measures designed primarily to raise the returns of certain classes of producers; these include monopolistic restriction of supply, differential prices, and subsidies. Second, there are various measures designed, at least ostensibly, to stabilize prices or incomes. These two types of measure have received considerable attention in the economic literature and are discussed in Essay 8. In addition, in recent decades a miscellany of measures designed to improve agricultural marketing have been introduced in many countries. These include reduction in the number of intermediaries, control of the channels of marketing, delimitation of the places where transactions may take place, and elimination of inferior grades of products. Advocates of these miscellaneous measures contend that they are in the interests of both producers and consumers. These measures have received little attention, and it is with their implications that this essay is concerned. Illustrative examples are taken principally from the history of some of the British colonies in Africa from the 1930s until their independence. The arguments advanced in support of the measures and the implications of the measures themselves stand out distinctly in LDCs. Moreover, since agriculture accounts for a large part of their output and exports, the effects of these measures are more important than those of their counterparts in more industrialized countries.

There is another reason why most of the examples here are taken from poor but developing countries. The activities of traders and the extension of marketing facilities and opportunities have, in the past, promoted the cultivation and harvesting of produce for home consumption and export and have helped to draw larger numbers of producers into the orbit of the money economy. They have extended the area of the exchange economy and have provided increasing numbers of people with the opportunities, means, and incentives to improve their material well-being. The measures under discussion bear upon the activities and numbers of traders and the nature of marketing facilities and opportunities available to producers.

For convenience of presentation this somewhat mixed group of measures is divided into three broad classes: measures that seem to be based on the view that the typical farmer or peasant cannot make a sensible choice among the available marketing opportunities, measures that reflect dissatisfaction with the effectiveness in practice of competition among traders and other intermediaries, and measures the advocacy of which does not postulate either the commercial incompetence of producers or the ineffectiveness of competition. There is also discussion of a feature of competitive marketing that, although it is not stressed or singled out for special discussion in the literature on marketing reform, may nevertheless explain some of the discontent with agricultural marketing.

It is a common complaint of marketing reformers that unnecessary categories of middlemen are able to interpose themselves between producers on the one hand and "necessary" middlemen and dealers on the other, and that the costs of marketing are thereby raised.[1] As a corollary, reformers advocate compulsory elimination of the supposedly redundant links in the chain of distribution.

The advocates of such measures generally fail to ask the relevant question why the so-called redundant intermediaries are not bypassed by those with whom they deal. For the services of an intermediary will be used only if the price (margin) charged is less than the value of service to the customer. The intermediary will be bypassed if no services at all are provided (that is, if the agent is redundant) or if the charges exceed the costs that would be incurred by customers if they were to provide these services for themselves. Thus redundant intermediaries and intermediaries charging excessive prices will be eliminated without official intervention. This result must follow unless the parties served by them are unaware that it is cheaper to bypass them or unless institutional arrangements prevent the more economical direct method from being followed.

The agricultural producer rarely sells his output directly to consumers. Usually there are several stages in the marketing process, and it is generally conceded that the middlemen are necessary in some of the stages. The supposedly redundant middleman must stand between another middleman and the producer, between a middleman and the final consumer, or between two middlemen. In each case, at least one of the parties served by an allegedly redundant middleman is a middleman himself. Now, even if it were true that the average farmer or peasant is unaware of other marketing opportunities or is unable to perform simple commercial calculations, a redundant middleman would not be used so long as his middleman-customer was able to see a profit or a saving in direct dealing. It is unlikely that dealers will fail to see an economic opportunity within their field of business or fail to take advantage of it. Hence the knowledge or capacity of the producer is largely irrelevant.

In any case, there is much evidence to suggest that the typical agricultural producer in LDCs knows the opportunities open to him (that is, he knows the difference between more and less). Low cash incomes and the often low opportunity costs (which are low because of the absence of other profitable opportunities) give the producer a strong incentive to market his output advantageously. This situation clearly applies in West Africa, where, no doubt as a result of the low level of incomes and the comparative lack of other more productive occupations, Africans will spend much time and effort to secure price advantages in selling their produce or in purchasing merchandise. Sellers of produce are distinctly sensitive to price differences. In the eastern provinces of Nigeria, for example, women selling palm oil will walk or cycle several miles to secure another penny or twopence on the sale of a beer bottle of palm oil or another shilling on the sale of a four-gallon tin of palm oil. In these circumstances, a redundant intermediary (that is, a dealer whose margin is higher than the value of his services to the parties served by him) would certainly be bypassed.[2]

The compulsory elimination of any class of intermediaries (such as itinerant buyers in country districts, market commission agents, or touts) will therefore mean that their services have to be performed on more onerous terms by one or another of the parties between whom they stand. It will involve an otherwise uneconomical measure of vertical integration and, at the same time, a reduction in the number of marketing alternatives open to the parties concerned. Both these consequences are likely to be serious in LDCs.[3]

Restrictive practices may prevent customers from bypassing middlemen whose services are redundant or, more frequently, whose charges are higher than the costs of the prohibited alternatives.[4] Such practices are against the interests of producers and consumers because they impede the competitive elimination of redundant middlemen and the competitive moderation of excessive charges. But improvement is not to be found either in the compulsory removal of the class of middlemen concerned or in the restriction of their numbers. Both these courses merely reduce the choices and opportunities available to producers and consumers.

It is sometimes contended that the producer in LDCs is not always free to use the most advantageous method or channel for marketing his produce: he may be forced to employ the services of a particular intermediary because he owes him money. This overlooks the fact that the producer has a choice among a number of lenders and trader-lenders, and that he will borrow from the source most advantageous to him. The terms of loans from trader-lenders may well be a combination of interest payments and the obligation to sell the produce to the lender, possibly on terms favorable to the latter. What in isolation appears to be a forced sale at a low price simply represents an indirect part of a payment of interest on the loan. Compulsory reduction of the number of trader-lenders simply reduces the sources of funds and so makes the terms of borrowing more onerous. To prevent traders from lending to producers on condition that the crop is sold to them would not improve the position of the borrower; the latter might secure an apparently better price on the sale of his produce, but only by being required to make correspondingly higher direct interest payments to the lender.[5]

The tacit assumption that producers are ignorant of their own interests and of the marketing opportunities open to them also underlies occasional proposals that producers be forced to take or to send their produce to specified markets or along specified routes.[6] These proposals imply that, without compulsion, many producers would drive their cattle along unprofitable routes or send their produce to unprofitable markets.[7] In fact, producers generally are well informed in these matters. In any case, even if producers were ignorant and undiscriminating, better-informed and specialized middlemen would buy up the produce and reroute it. Furthermore, marketing routes prescribed by authority will not easily be changed even if supply and demand conditions change. In underdeveloped territories, the prescription of permitted market places or of marketing routes may therefore seriously retard the opening up of new areas of production and the spread of the exchange economy, which in the past has often followed the activities of traders pioneering in new regions and along new routes.

Critics of agricultural marketing often state or imply that competition among middlemen works against the interest of producers. Sometimes it is said that there are too few competitors; in other cases it is said that there are too many.

In some markets or areas there are only a few buyers of agricultural produce. Almost necessarily, the number of operators declines as the distance from the main assembly, transport, or consuming centers increases. Hence some producers are confronted with only one or a handful of buyers in the immediate neighborhood of their farms or holdings. It is argued that in such conditions of monopsony or oligopsony the producers will be exploited. One type of proposal to improve the position of the producers requires the compulsory centralization of market transactions. The underlying idea is that the producer will be forced to take his produce to one of a limited number of markets, at each of which there will be a larger number of buyers than would otherwise visit his farm or buy in his locality. In this way competition among buyers is increased for the benefit of the producer.[8]

The essence of this type of proposal is to foster one kind of competition (the competition of more buyers in one place) by denying producers access to other opportunities for selling their produce. The idea that competition is stimulated by reducing the alternatives open to producers and consumers is here driven almost to its logical but absurd extreme.[9]

The proposal for compulsory centralization of transactions (that is, for standardization of one condition of selling) is only one among several suggestions intended to promote competition by compulsory standardization (by reducing the alternatives open to customers). Such proposals rest upon a misconception of the nature of competition and of competitive forces. From the narrow definition of perfect competition in static economic analysis, it is inferred that competition prevails only when the customers can choose among a number of *identical* alternatives, that is, among alternatives that are identical as regards quality, place and time of supply. In fact, when demand is not identical or uniform in these respects, competition is not promoted by forcing demand into a common mold by denying to suppliers the opportunity to adapt their product or service to the varying requirements and unstandardized desires of customers. Geographic differences are generally significant in bringing about unstandardized demands. In such circumstances, competition tends to take the form of making available to customers a range of alternatives adjusted to individual circumstances. Moreover, the offering of new services is a form of competition that may improve the terms upon which the customary services are made available.

Undue emphasis on the dangers of local buying monopolies in any area neglects the fact that such buyers, though appearing to have no competitors, nevertheless have to set their buying prices in competition with other buyers elsewhere; they cannot depress their own buying prices so low that producers (or other intermediaries) would be better off taking their produce to other, more distant buyers. Accordingly, if producers are readily able to get their produce to other markets, the prices they receive locally cannot be far below those obtaining in the more important market centers. In West Africa, for example, producers are sensitive to price differences, knowledge of which spreads quickly, and they are generally prepared to cover great distances to secure attractive prices. On the other hand, if producers are not in a position to undertake long journeys or to hold produce so as to reduce the number of journeys, the compulsory closure of local buying would cause otherwise avoidable loss and hardship. Such a measure would either deprive them of markets altogether or compel them to undertake costly journeys to markets when previously less costly methods of disposing of their produce had been available to them. This reasoning is borne out by the fact that buyers in outlying areas are voluntarily supported by sufficient producers to keep them in business. Closure of outlying trading posts would prevent some producers from selling their output and force them to remain subsistence producers.

The compulsory centralization of trading may itself promote monopoly practices. Where all dealers and transactions are concentrated, it becomes easier for dealers to form market-sharing or price agreements, provided that they are not too numerous and that entry of new competitors is not easy. Effective price agreements typically require a high degree of standardization of products and conditions of sale.

The proposal to defeat oligopsony by centralizing transactions extols competition and aims at improving it. Other reformers, recognizing that there may be few dealers in some areas, incline to the view that effective competition is impossible in the circumstances and propose that local monopolies be established to operate under strict government control. The view is that if there must be monopoly, it should be a controlled and supervised one. Similar proposals emerge from a quite different chain of reasoning. Such proposals are discussed later in this essay.

Reform of marketing is often urged on the grounds that there are too many competing middlemen and that their competition is not to the best advantage of the producers. This complaint is made not only against the competition of traders but also against that of the first processors of agricultural produce, such as the owners of slaughterhouses or of cotton ginneries. The argument takes two forms: first, if there are many competitors competition is too severe, and this situation leads to the payment of excessively or uneconomically high prices to producers; second, if there are many competitors competition is wasteful, and this situation leads to the payment of unnecessarily low prices to producers.[10] The two forms of the argument are often combined; moreover, each gives rise to the same proposals for reform, namely, that the number of intermediaries (dealers or processors) should be reduced in the interests of producers and that the margins for their services should be controlled.

In recent years it has been argued frequently and influentially that severe competition among intermediaries results, or may result, in bankruptcies among them, with adverse effects on the producers. This argument has been advanced in support of compulsory limitation of the number of intermediaries and/or prescription of minimum margins for the performance of their services.[11] Yet producers can only benefit from increased competition for their crop. If some buyers go bankrupt through paying excessively high prices, their bankruptcy cannot harm the producers who have received these prices.[12] Furthermore, as long as entry is free, there is no danger that the surviving merchants or processors will subsequently be able to exploit producers. There is no need to ensure a supply of the services of the intermediaries, either by protecting a number of them through statutory control of numbers or by prescribing minimum margins for their services. On the other hand, if the entry of new firms is difficult because of high costs of establishment or similar obstacles, there is no need for official measures to protect the established firms by erecting statutory barriers to new entry.

Compulsory reduction in the number of intermediaries to raise their returns increases the supply price of their services and thus harms the producers whose services are in joint demand with those of the intermediaries. In contrast, a reduction in the number of intermediaries as a result of competition implies the survival of those who offer the services at a lower supply price, which benefits producers.

The more common version of the case against so-called excessive competition is that each competitor is unable to obtain sufficient supplies to keep his plant operating at lowest average cost. As a result, it is argued that competitors are forced to pay producers less than the economic price, so that each can have a larger margin per unit of his limited output to meet the higher unit overhead costs brought about by unnecessary multiplication of facilities. It is not clear why this situation does not lead to a bidding-up of producer prices in the struggle of each competitor to get closer to his optimum rate or scale of operations, and why this should not lead to the elimination of redundant intermediaries. The events that usually give rise to demands for limiting the number of competitors tend to support the view that excessive competition serves to raise rather than depress producer prices.

Generally, if there were significant economies in the operation of fewer and larger buying establishments, abattoirs, or ginneries, the interest of traders or processors and the responsiveness of producers to higher prices would promote a market structure comprising a few large establishments, without the need for compulsion. If there were substantial economies, intermediaries operating on a large scale would be able to offer higher prices for produce. They would be prepared to pay the higher prices to attract supplies, even though their current rate of purchases might temporarily be below the rate at which the full economies were secured. They would be ready to absorb the costs of growth if substantial economies were in prospect. The action of intermediaries and producers would tend to bring about a situation in which economies of scale were balanced with evaluation by producers of the convenience of marketing and the opportunities open to them.

When competition is said to work against the interest of producers for the reasons discussed above, it it usually proposed that the number of competitors be reduced by state action. The extreme version of such proposals requires the establishment of purchasing monopolies (that is, monopsonies). Discussion of this limiting case will throw the issues into clear relief.

The establishment and supervision of purchasing monopolies raise problems of their own, which tend to negate the superficial

attractiveness that such systems present because of their ostensible tidiness, orderliness, and amenability to official control.
The spur of actual or potential competition will be absent, and
there will be costs and inconvenience of supervision.[13] In any
event, the consequent reduction in the facilities available to the
population will impose inconvenience and possible hardship on
some producers. It will also greatly increase customers' feelings
of dependence on whichever firm has been selected as the
monopolist.[14]

It will also be necessary for the government to attempt to
control the level of costs and profits of the monopolists. The
necessary calculations will pose difficult problems of assessment
and allocation of costs and revenue; for the calculations often
have to refer to a small part of the interrelated activities of large
organizations engaged in a great variety of geographically dispersed and dissimilar lines of business. In practice, even in the
simplest cases, official allowances for costs and profits tend to be
wide of the mark. The allowances are prone to be generous;
indeed, they cannot err on the side of underestimate, since the
desired services would then not be provided. Under competitive
conditions, overgenerous allowances are competed away in
favor of the parties between whom the intermediaries operate.
Under statutory monopolies, however, any additional profits or
savings in cost will not be passed on to customers but will be
retained by the monopolist.[15]

If the interests of producers are to be protected, the type of
service provided by the monopolist (especially the number and
spread of buying points) must be defined and its supply supervised. If this is not done, the monopolist may reduce his services
to cut his costs, even though this action would put a disproportionate burden of costs on the producers. This is more likely to
happen if government officials are prone to judge efficiency in
terms of the level of costs of the supplying organization. If the
type of service to be supplied is specified and controlled, marketing arrangements may become inflexible and fail to be
adapted to changing needs—particularly as producers with new
or changing needs will not be able to express their requirements
in the most effective manner, that is, by removing their custom
to more amenable suppliers. The dangers of a rigid system of

marketing facilities and the costs of inflexibility are likely to be high in territories in which the area of cultivation is still extending and in which large areas have not yet been integrated, or fully integrated, into the market economy. The cost, in terms of frustrated development, may not be visible or measurable. Finally, detailed official control of the type of service rendered by the monopolist cannot take account of the (possibly widely) divergent needs and requirements of different producers. Those who prefer more (or less) service at higher (or lower) prices are precluded from satisfying their needs or preferences.

Establishment of a statutory monopoly bears harshly on those whose entry into the monopolized activity is barred and who have to content themselves with less preferred ways of earning a living. In LDCs, the potential entrants into trade are likely to be farmers. The produce buyer or village trader is quite often the farmer who thinks it worth while to collect and market his neighbors' produce or to cater to their simple requirements. Trading intermediaries are often members or former members of the farming community. Thus the establishment of monopolies is likely to harm producers not only in their capacity as customers of the monopolist but also as potential entrants into trade.

It may seem that many of the difficulties enumerated above could be avoided if a producer organization such as a producer cooperative society were appointed as the monopolist. When a producers' organization is the monopolist, it may appear as if the interests of the producers and those of the trader or processor (monopolist) are identical. In practice, however, the harmony of interests is not easily established or maintained. Those managing the monopoly are likely to regard their organization as an end in itself, with interests possibly different from, and even antagonistic to, those of the majority of producers. The divergence of interests and outlook between the administrators of large organizations and their numerous and often uninformed constituents is a conspicuous feature in large-scale public and private enterprise and trade unions. It is all the more remarkable that this dichotomy of interests is so frequently disregarded in proposals for marketing reform in immature societies, in which the detailed and democratic control by producers over the administrators of the organizations supposed to be acting on their behalf is likely to be weak, and in which a check on the formulation of policy and economy of operations is likely to be absent or ineffective. When such organizations are endowed with statutory monopoly powers, a further check is removed in that dissatisfied constituents cannot transfer their custom elsewhere. At the same time, new entrants cannot expose the possible inefficiency of the organization or the feasibility of other more attractive price and marketing policies.

Moreover, the interests of all producers of a particular product are not necessarily the same. The producer-constituents of a marketing organization are likely to have conflicting views on many matters. These include the determination of prices for different grades of the same product; the question of whether each producer should bear his own transport costs or whether these costs should be averaged; the membership of the governing body; the timing of payments to producers; and the type of marketing service to be provided. The specific policies adopted by an organization are certain to affect some of its constituents less favorably than others; those who feel that their interests are more adversely affected than those of their fellow producers are unable to seek better treatment elsewhere.

Criticisms of so-called excessive competition among middlemen are often supported by the claim that such competition forces middlemen to cheat producers more scandalously. Abuses such as the use of false weights feature prominently in discussions of marketing reform; official supervision of transactions or the establishment of producer-controlled statutory marketing monopolies is recommended to protect the producer against such practices.[16]

The earnings of middlemen, whether from honest trading or from improper practices, cannot for long exceed the competitive level; competition among the existing traders or from new entrants soon erodes earnings above this level. Competition forces buyers to pass on the illicit gains to the producers; for example, if debased weights are used, under competitive conditions buyers will be forced to offer correspondingly higher prices per debased unit in their search for business.[17] From the producer's point of view the result is the same as if he had received payment for the full weight at a lower price per unit.

Whether producers (or, for that matter, consumers) themselves are familiar with standard weights and measures does not affect the outcome. The individual producer is concerned with sales of specific lots of produce, and he will endeavor to obtain price offers for such lots from itinerant traders and/or from traders at one or more trading centers. Even a producer who is ignorant of weights is able to judge which is the most favorable offer. The conclusion is not substantially affected in circumstances in which the producer does not receive several offers simultaneously for the same lot of produce; his knowledge of his trading opportunities is widened by his contact over time with different traders and the treatment and terms offered by each. The ability to make such comparisons and the competition of buyers ensure that producers tend to receive competitive prices for their produce, irrespective of apparent abuses or absence of standardized weights and measures.[18]

On the other hand, the producer is liable to exploitation if he has no choice of buyers and is forced to deal with a sole buyer or a concerted group of buyers whose monopoly position is protected from competition by barriers to new entry. Here again the question of abuses is largely irrelevant; for, by one means or another, the monopolist pays a price just sufficient to elicit the supply he desires. It is of little consequence whether this price is expressed in terms of standard or of debased weights. In both cases the returns to the producers will be less than the competitive returns.

Thus statutory measures to prevent specific abuses are unnecessary under competition and are likely to be ineffective under monopoly. In produce buying in LDCs the situation is usually a mixture of competitive and monopolistic elements. Accordingly, the statutory measures for the elimination of abuses are partly unnecessary and partly ineffective.

Measures to eliminate specific abuses postulate the establishment and maintenance of expensive supervisory and inspecting staff. Administrative costs can be reduced by requiring all transactions to take place at a limited number of centers at which the necessary supervisory services are provided. But in this case the costs are merely transferred to the producer or the smaller trader who has to travel greater distances to market. Moreover, the inspecting staff generally consists of large numbers of petty officials with extensive powers over traders and producers. They are therefore in a position to abuse their powers for their own profit. Such abuses, however, differ greatly from abuses in competitive markets, in that their benefits will not be competed away in favor of producers. And producers may not be able to obtain redress from higher authorities.[19]

In the preceding discussion the case for a variety of marketing reforms has been questioned on the ground, inter alia, that competition among intermediaries protects the interests of producers. It is necessary to look at this general proposition more closely and to deal with a specific omission.

At any given time the activities, offers and transactions of buyers in a competitive trade may be conceived of as forming part of a process of experimentation and movement leading toward the equilibrium price consistent with existing supply and demand conditions. Until this equilibrium is reached, competing traders may be offering different prices for the same goods in the same circumstances. Some price offers may be above or below the equilibrium price. Differences will tend to diminish as equilibrium is approached. But because the details of supply and demand change all the time, there is continuous scope for the emergence of differences.

Knowledge of alternatives and chance determine the particular point on the path to equilibrium at which a particular seller disposes of his produce. The producer cannot offer his goods to all buyers at the same time; he cannot know full details of the changing offers of all accessible buyers; and, having taken his produce to one buyer or place, he cannot, without cost, transfer it to some otherwise more advantageous alternative. Thus some producers receive overpayments and others underpayments relative to the (theoretical) equilibrium price. The spontaneity of price adjustments in theoretical models and the device of recontracting are absent in workaday agricultural markets. Although competition safeguards the average returns to producers as a whole, the returns to individual producers are affected by skill in marketing or by chance.

The significance of the differences between competitive price offers and the (theoretical) equilibrium price is likely to be greatest where short-period fluctuations in supply and demand are frequent, where producers are widely dispersed, and where transport and communications facilities are poor. The price differences are therefore likely to be prevalent in agricultural markets generally; in such markets in LDCs they are likely to be particularly common.

The practical question is how much weight should be given to the particular point raised here, as this point is not significant in an assessment of the general effects of competitive trading and with the drawbacks and dangers that attach to alternative systems of controlled or regulated marketing or statutory buying monopolies. This judgment applies with special force to conditions in LDCs, where the benefits of competitive trading and the drawbacks of regulated marketing are likely to be marked.

The price differences under discussion here effect a redistribution of a total return among the individual producers. The safeguarding or raising of the total would seem to be more important than the achievement of what may be thought, by some, to be a more equitable distribution of the total. Even where the price differences are greatest, their effect is canceled if the community of agricultural producers is considered as a whole. Moreover, the absolute magnitude of the differences and of their effects on individual producers is never likely to be great.[20] To the extent that the incidence of price differences is distributed by chance factors, the returns to the individual producer are little affected over time. To the extent that luck does not enter into the results, the superior marketing knowledge, skill, and effort of some producers give them higher returns than are enjoyed by other producers. There does not seem to be any good reason why these attributes should not be rewarded; in LDCs it is one way of encouraging the development of some of the qualities that are necessary if members of the rural population are to take a more active part in economic advancement. Moreover, the superior ability and effort of the successful producers indirectly help their fellows; for they improve the effectiveness of competition among traders and tend to reduce the magnitude and duration of the price differences.

There is another group of measures of intervention in agricultural marketing the advocacy of which is independent of alleged shortcomings in the operation of competitive markets. In effect, the advocates of this group of measures reject market prices as appropriate incentives to producers.

An informative example is the imposition of a system of control whereby all producers in a zone receive the same price for their produce, irrespective of the distance of the point of first sale from the consuming market(s). Uniform price systems are extensively used in statutory agricultural price and marketing control schemes.

Uniform price systems are superficially attractive because they appear to treat producers equally and equitably. Advocates of such systems claim that is is unfair that certain producers should receive lower prices merely because they happen to be farther away from the markets, and they suggest that the "burden of transportation" should be borne equally by all producers near or far. It is also contended that uniform prices encourage production by favoring marginal producers. Moreover, uniform price systems sometimes appear to be preferable on administrative grounds, as there are fewer prices for the administration to worry about. These arguments are not convincing.

Production in distant areas requires more transport (that is, the use of additional resources) to move the crops to the ports or to the markets; it does not seem inequitable, and it certainly promotes the husbanding of resources, to require that the additional costs be borne by the producers who cause the additional resources to be used and who benefit directly from their use. The suggestion that uniform prices stimulate marginal production overlooks the distinction between the intensive and the extensive margins. Producers near the markets or centers of communication can expand their output of the crops by more intensive effort, by more costly methods of production, or by diversion of effort and resources from other productive activities. Uniform price systems reduce the returns to nearby producers and so discourage these types of marginal production. Such systems may encourage the extension of cultivation in distant areas, but only by making expansion of cultivation less attractive in more favorable locations.

Support for uniform price systems may be less pronounced if it is realized that they result in the use of greater amounts of resources in transportation to yield a given total output of the crop and that they penalize some producers for the benefit of others. These considerations are particularly important in LDCs that are poor in capital equipment, especially in transport, and where producers, even those favorably placed near the main markets, are generally poor. If a government intends to develop outlying areas, it can do so much more efficiently by direct subsidy or grant than, covertly and wastefully, by uniform price systems.

The administrative convenience of uniform price systems is more apparent than real. If the transportation of the crop to the principal markets is undertaken in the first instance by intermediaries, they naturally have to be reimbursed for transport charges incurred. The marketing authority therefore has to deal with countless claims and to institute burdensome systems of checking, filing, and repayment. These costs of administration are additional to the extra demands on transport resulting from uniform price systems.

In several LDCs, the government or marketing organizations with statutory powers determine that produce that falls short of stipulated minimum standards or grades may not be exported. Such measures indicate that the authorities concerned do not accept world market prices as being relevant for production and export decisions; the minimum exportable qualities that are prescribed are always higher than the lowest qualities that are acceptable and have a price on world markets.

The prohibition of the export of inferior but commercially marketable qualities of produce necessarily affects adversely the interests of producers and of the economy as a whole. Such measures (1) frustrate the export of substandard output already produced, (2) induce the uneconomic expenditure of additional resources, or (3) deflect production into less valuable activities.[21]

First, whenever resources (including time and effort) yield a substandard output that is not marketed there is economic loss, both to producers and to the economy, of a kind that could have been avoided if the export of the produce had not been banned. Second, producers may attempt to raise substandard output to reach the minimum exportable level. Whenever producers are induced to devote additional resources in an attempt to raise the quality of their output merely because lower qualities may not be exported, the cost of the additional resources must exceed the increase in the commercially realizable value of the output; that is, there is a net loss to the economy.[22] Third, producers who are aware that substandard output may not be sold and that the improvement of substandard produce requires additional resources may be deterred from embarking on the cultivation of the product in question. Whenever producers transfer their resources to other activities because of restrictions on exports, the value of their output in the other activities is less than the commercially realizable value obtainable from the produce in question.

The insistence on minimum standards and the obvious pride of some marketing authorities in the improvement of quality of export produce exemplify the confusion of technical and economic efficiency.[23] If economic and technical efficiency were synonymous, it would be in the interests of the automotive industry and of the British economy to restrict the output of the industry to Rolls Royces or similar high grades of cars. Inferior products would disappear, and the quality of output and exports would be greatly raised. Yet nobody would argue that technically inferior but cheaper cars should not be exported when there is a very large and profitable demand for them in world markets. Similarly, there is no cause for refusing to allow the export of inferior grades of produce for which there is a demand at a lower price, simply because they do not conform to certain prescribed technical standards.

In some LDCs there are statutory organizations that have the sole right to buy for export, and to export, major agricultural products. They prescribe prices to be paid to producers. They often prescribe different producer prices for different grades of the same commodity; often the grade differentials are not the same as the differentials that prevail in the markets in which the organizations resell their produce.[24]

The prescription of grade differentials out of line with market differentials either encourages uneconomic expenditures and effort or discourages economic expenditures and effort. On the one hand, where the imposed differentials exceed the market differentials, producers are induced to spend additional effort and resources to raise the grade of some of their output that would not have been profitable to the producers if only commercial differences were paid. This means that some producers incur costs to raise quality that are in excess of the additional proceeds received by the marketing organizations on the sale of higher grades of produce.[25] If the marketing organizations are considered as the guardians of the collective interests of producers, the results are patently perverse; if, however, the organizations are considered by others or by their executives as something apart from the producers, then this policy might nevertheless be favored, since the extra exertions and expenditures of the producers would not fall upon the marketing organizations, whereas the higher receipts in world markets would obviously raise their sales receipts.

On the other hand, if the officially prescribed differences in producer prices are smaller than those prevailing in the market, the effect is to inhibit improvement in the quality of output. Producers are discouraged from improving quality whenever the additional costs exceed the increase in the producer price, even though they are smaller than the increase in market value. The inhibited improvement would be in the interests of producers and of the economy as a whole.

It is conceivable that arbitrarily wide producer-price differentials may result in some loss of production, somewhat analogous to part of the loss brought about by arbitrary minimum exportable standards.[26] Some producers may find that the price paid for the lowest grade is not sufficient to induce them to produce at all, and that the extra costs of qualifying for the higher grades (and therefore better producer prices) are beyond their reach for technical or economic reasons. This may affect the distribution of effort between different crops.

*   *   *

The policies of imposing minimum standards for export produce and of arbitrarily wide premiums and discounts for different grades of produce are sometimes defended on the grounds that the consequent improvement in the quality of export produce strengthens the position of the exporting country, particularly in unfavorable world market conditions. This view is untenable, for the buyers on world markets judge the produce they buy according to its quality in the light of market requirements. Since the policies under discussion stimulate expenditure of resources and effort in the exporting countries that exceed the additional value in world markets, the result is uneconomic.

It has sometimes been argued that, without restrictions on exports, severe competition among traders forces them to accept all produce offered to them, irrespective of quality, and that, in consequence, competition leads to a constant deterioration of the average quality of export produce, to the long-run disadvantage of producers. The argument was used to support the prescription of minimum export standards in Nigeria. The reasoning is invalid. Vigorous competition forces merchants to adjust the prices they pay for different qualities closely in accordance with market valuations. Competition does not cause a constant deterioration in quality; rather, it leads to increasing vigilance in seeking out supplies acceptable in world markets and in linking buying prices with world market values, which is to the advantage of producers.

The prescription of minimum export produce standards and of producer-price differentials for different grades requires a system of compulsory inspection of produce to check whether the minimum standard is reached or to determine the particular grade of the produce. The cost of inspection and grading services is likely to be onerous in poor countries where administrative talent is often scarce. In such countries, it is likely that the number of authorized buying or inspection posts will be kept small in order to reduce the costs or to raise the technical efficiency of the service; and this is likely to be inconvenient and costly to producers.

In LDCs, where many producers and small-scale traders are

illiterate and unaware of their legal rights, a system of compulsory inspection and grading may place them at the mercy of the inspecting officials. Thus in many parts of Nigeria petty tyranny and corruption in the operation of produce inspection have been widespread and oppressive. In 1949 and 1950 in many places in Nigeria there was a recognized scale of (illicit) fees payable to produce examiners to have the produce inspected and passed. Those who refused to pay were made to wait for such long periods that their produce deteriorated and fell below standard;[27] or they were forced to sell their produce uninspected to other intermediaries at less than its commercial value; if they were liable to have their produce downgraded by the examiners. Wherever possible, the traders or clerks tried to placate the examiners by paying the recognized tariff; and, indeed, they complained only when the exaction exceeded the conventional level that was regarded as reasonable.

The foregoing discussion does not imply that the grading of produce may not be a useful marketing device in appropriate circumstances. Accurate and acceptable grading facilitates commercial communication and reduces marketing costs. It is for this reason that systems of grading (and consequential arbitration of contract) have been freely developed in world commodity markets by those in the markets. However, such systems of grading are voluntary; and transactions in ungraded produce or in produce below the standard of the lowest recognized grades take place if it suits the parties concerned. From the point of view of producers and produce exporters, the market recognition of grade specification may be convenient, and they may voluntarily submit their produce for inspection and grading.

In export trades in which many shippers are small firms that are not well known or represented in world markets, difficulties arise when supplies are found on arrival to be below contract specification in quantity or in quality. Since consignments are normally shipped under a letter of credit, the importer has difficulty in obtaining redress because the exporter has by then received most of the contract price. In these circumstances, the additional risks of the importer may seriously retard the development of the export trade. In such cases, however, it is in the interests of both importers and exporters to devise methods to provide safeguards to traders. They are thus likely to support firms of cargo supervisors who can inspect consignments before they are accepted. Or the government can introduce a voluntary inspection system, financed by charges. Both the problem and the two types of solution are illustrated by developments in the Nigerian export trade in logs.

For many years African traders exported timber in the form of logs. With the influx of many new shippers after the war, there was a considerable increase in consignments of logs that, on arrival, were seriously below specified weight or quality. Importers became increasingly reluctant to place contracts with the smaller exporters. Eventually, one of the smaller merchant firms undertook to act as cargo superintendent. The services it provided were not regarded as sufficiently extensive; and in 1949 the Nigerian authorities devised a simple and practical scheme of voluntary inspection that proved an immediate success. The exporter on application could have his consignment inspected during the loading of the timber on the ship,[28] and an official certificate of quality and quantity was issued, which could be presented by the exporter to the bank with which the letter of credit was arranged. The actual amount paid out to the shipper under the credit depended on the contents of the certificate, a procedure that effectively safeguarded the overseas importer against loss. The scheme was widely publicized in the principal overseas markets for Nigerian timber, and importers generally insisted on this inspection certificate before arranging a letter of credit.

The scheme was voluntary and served to protect the interests of the trade without investing the inspectors with compulsory powers and without introducing arbitrary grading or quality standards. And yet it fulfilled all the essential requirements. Unless the overseas importer neglected to take advantage of this simple facility, he was effectively safeguarded against loss and needed to have no reluctance in placing an order with a shipper unknown to him.

The preceding example refers to external trade. Similarly, voluntary arrangements can develop to facilitate business transactions with an LDC between parties who are strangers to each other. Certain West African cattle markets provide an interesting example. So-called landlords act essentially as intermediating guarantors in transactions between cattle dealers from distant parts and local butchers, and in various ways make possible a mutually advantageous trade involving the extension of credit.[29] Analogous arrangements were common in medieval Europe.

7
Cooperative Societies in Less Developed Countries

The measures analyzed in the preceding essay are designed to remove certain specific real or supposed shortcomings in the marketing of agricultural produce. This essay addresses a wider issue, namely the case for government support of cooperative societies in marketing, including the provision of credit to farmers.

Government support of cooperatives is extensive in LDCs. It takes various forms, including the following: provision of advisory and supervisory services by a government department; official participation in the administration of the societies; financial assistance ranging from the guaranteeing of loans to the payment of subsidies and grants in aid; restrictions on or the prohibition of activities of competing private undertakings; and preferential treatment in the allocation of licenses or supplies. Quite often, government departments have in fact become partners in cooperative enterprises in which they are deeply involved. In these circumstances, cooperative societies are better seen as extensions of government departments rather than as independent organizations.

The case for government support of cooperatives is not obvious. In the absence of government involvement, a cooperative society is simply a form of business enterprise whose capital is provided and whose activities are organized by its suppliers (in the case of marketing and credit societies) or its customers (in the case of retail societies). A member of a cooperative society is both a part owner, and a supplier or customer of the society.

The principal economic or commercial services of cooperative societies, such as credit, marketing, or consumer societies, are similar to those supplied by private firms. When a cooperative society does not receive privileges, preferential treatment, or financial support from the government, its economic efficiency can be measured by its ability to survive and to satisfy the requirements of its members, who can always turn to private firms if they are not satisfied. The survival or expansion of the society implies that its members prefer its services to those of privately owned firms. Its advantages may stem from various sources, such as efficiency or a perception of commercial opportunities ignored by private firms. Or it may operate in a field where there is little competition among private firms, so that there is room for an independent supplier. Or the society may benefit from the loyalty of its members, or from its knowledge of their creditworthiness, or simply from the members' preference to deal with their own organization. But whatever the reasons for its success, this provides its economic justification, if it is gained without special privileges and support denied to private competitors.

When cooperative societies enjoy sustained and substantial government support, the simple tests of survival and progress no longer indicate their economic usefulness, because they enjoy advantages that arise from privileges created for them by the government. In fact, the assessment of their economic performance becomes difficult (except in the case of evident failure even with the benefits of government support). The difficulty of assessment is exacerbated when government support takes such forms as restrictions on the activities of competitors or preferential treatment for cooperatives in the allocation of licenses, trading sites, finance, or supplies. Cooperative societies that have received government subsidies enjoy further preferential treatment in that their affairs can be conducted with the expectation that, in the case of difficulties, the government cannot refuse to come to their assistance, particularly if the societies have acquired many members as a result of earlier government support.

It is often argued that cooperatives, especially cooperative trading and credit societies, should not be judged solely on the criterion of commercial effectiveness. Their activities are thought to be desirable on wider grounds, for instance by encouraging the virtues of self-reliance and thrift or acquainting producers with problems of organization and marketing. This may justify limited government assistance in the form of advisory service or technical assistance, but it can hardly serve as an argument for large-scale government assistance, which comes near to government participation. Such assistance and the expectation of its continuation undermine the self-reliance of the cooperators. Membership is valued not for its own sake but because of the government support enjoyed by the society. There is little or no educational advantage in cooperation in such conditions; rather the reverse, since any apparent success is in large measure the result of the special privileges granted to the society by government rather than of the ability to serve the needs of customers.

Certain special arguments are often urged in support of the cooperative principle and of government support to cooperatives in Africa: that cooperatives to some extent resemble the communal economic activity of tribal life and are thus particularly suitable to African conditions; that cooperation helps African farmers to secure loans on tolerable terms, chiefly because the management has personal knowledge of the debtor; and that cooperation redresses the inequality of economic strength between the farmer and the middleman. But in themselves these arguments do not justify government support for cooperatives. If cooperatives were so suitable to local conditions, it would not be necessary to subsidize them. Again, the individual producer is known also to the small trader and moneylender. The high rates on loans to farmers reflect largely the scarcity of capital, the high cost of administering small loans, and the high risks. High rates of interest may also sometimes involve an element of monopoly profits, although this factor is likely to be comparatively unimportant because of the ease of entry into small-scale trade and moneylending. But whenever there is insufficient competition between suppliers, the situation presents opportunities for *unsubsidized* cooperative enterprise. The same argument applies to the alleged inequality in bargaining strength between producers and moneylenders. If this inequality were a substantial factor affecting adversely the terms of trade of producers, to be redressed by cooperation, the resulting improvement in these terms would secure the adherence of producers without government support.

Wherever entry into small-scale trade or moneylending is easy (as is generally the case in Africa, especially because farmers themselves often act as traders and moneylenders), trading margins or the terms of loans are unlikely to be such as to yield excessive profits. This is so because the traders and moneylenders have to secure custom and therefore to offer terms that yield no more than competitive returns, regardless of differences in wealth, commercial skill, or sophistication between themselves and the producers.

It may be argued that such support is still required to overcome initial difficulties, even if ultimately the society becomes viable, a suggestion along the lines of the familiar infant-industry argument for protection. But this argument is irrelevant. It does not justify assistance to cooperative societies rather than to other forms of enterprise, to which the same reasoning could be applied.

The favorable attitude toward cooperative societies, especially in the former British Empire, in part reflected the misleading example of the success of British consumer cooperatives in the nineteenth and early twentieth centuries. This example is irrelevant.

First, the British cooperatives were not subsidized by government, a fact that in itself should suffice to dispose of the comparison. Second, the cooperative movement benefited greatly from the availability of latent managerial and administrative talent among the British working and lower-middle classes, for which in the nineteenth and early twentieth centuries there was little outlet in commercial or public life. This talent was therefore available relatively cheaply to the cooperative movement. In LDCs, however, the exact reverse applies. There is a dearth of administrative and managerial talent locally, and there is ample opportunity in government service or private commerce for this talent. Third, in the nineteenth century competition in retailing in Britain was often weak, a fact that helped the rapid progress both of the unsubsidized cooperative societies and, toward the end of the century, of various other new types of private retail organizations also.

It is often thought that government-supported cooperatives represent the best of both worlds in that they serve the public interest without the political and administrative difficulties presented by government operation. The truth seems to be rather the reverse. Such organizations are subject neither to the commercial or competitive test of the market, nor to the public scrutiny to which government agents or corporations are sometimes exposed.

8
Commodity Stabilization: Disguised Restrictionism

The market prices of many primary products fluctuate considerably, often widely within quite short periods such as a day or a week. Such fluctuations may seem to be haphazard and to serve no economic function: they may seem to be both irrational and avoidable. Hence there is a distinct intellectual appeal in devising governmental or intergovernmental schemes or instruments designed to moderate price fluctuations. These schemes typically involve some official agency or organization provided with funds so that it can buy the commodity in question when prices are thought to be low, and sell when they are thought to be high. The organization, in other words, is expected to act as a well-financed and farsighted trader. Further interesting analytical questions arise whether operations of this kind, *if successful,* would increase or reduce economic welfare (on the standard allocational criterion). As various analyses have demonstrated, it is by no means necessary that a successful scheme would increase economic welfare.

However, to be successful, the managers of such a stabilization scheme would need to know the future course of prices, that is, longer-term developments in the commodity's supply and demand. They would also need to assess whether the current market price is high or low in relation to the underlying supply and demand conditions. Their knowledge or foresight would need to extend to the ability to distinguish between a price movement that is temporary or aberrant and a price movement that is an appropriate adjustment to a change in the underlying supply and demand conditions. Now, any person who had this ability would be able to amass large wealth by buying cheaply and selling dear. It is primarily because prospective price movements are unpredictable, and actions based on mistaken judgments are costly, that market prices fluctuate frequently and widely. This unpredictability equally confronts the managers of a government price stabilization scheme designed solely to reduce price fluctuation. To put it neutrally, they are no more likely to reduce price fluctuations than to increase them; what is more, any losses arising from failure to predict correctly will fall on taxpayers, while the losses of private traders, including speculators, fall upon themselves.

We need not pursue further the pure theory of price stabilization. In practice, advocates of so-called stabilization schemes are not concerned simply with the moderation of price fluctuations. They are concerned either with raising prices in order to increase the income of producers or, in the case of certain national schemes, with reducing producer prices and incomes for the benefit of consumers of the commodity or the national treasury. Both types of scheme are usually referred to as price stabilization schemes. The former type of scheme involves monopoly, the latter monopsony. The former is designed to raise producer prices, the latter to depress them. The former type of scheme can continue in operation as long as the scheme has effective control over supplies of the commodity; the latter type can persist as long as producers have no other outlets for the commodity.

Since the early 1920s, stabilization has been invoked to justify both international and domestic commodity cartels designed to improve producer incomes by maintaining or raising prices above competitive levels. For this purpose restriction of supply and of the extension of productive capacity is necessary. Domestic cartels, such as those established in Britain under the agricultural marketing legislation of the 1930s, had to be supported by restrictions on competing imports and by officially-enforced restriction of production and of capacity. Government support is usually also necessary under international schemes in order to restrict both current supply and the expansion of capacity. Since the Second World War, international commodity cartels have, at various times, covered rubber, tea, tin, sugar, and coffee.[1]

In an international cartel, a central organization committee

or council determines the international quotas of each partici-
pating country, based usually on some assessment of productive
capacity or by reference to past performance, and subject to
review from time to time. The central organization also determines periodically the amount each country may export
expressed as a percentage of basic quotas. Each government in
turn assigns to the local producers shares in the permitted
national export total.[2] The central organization decides the price
or price band at which it aims, and determines the export quotas
in the light of market conditions. It takes account of such
diverse factors as the level of stocks, the reaction of users, the
expansion of supplies in countries outside the cartel, and the
emergence of substitutes. It also takes account of the reactions
of governments whose support is necessary for the continuation
of the scheme.

The history of rubber restriction illustrates some features of
the operation of so-called stabilization cartels. The Stevenson
Rubber Restriction Scheme (1922–1928) covered Malaya (now
Malaysia) and Ceylon (now Sri Lanka), at the time supplying
about 70 percent of world exports. It was introduced after the
prices had fallen in 1920–1921. The acreage established shortly
before and during the First World War reached maturity in
those years and coincided with what proved to be a short, sharp
decline in demand. After raising the price very substantially, the
scheme collapsed under the weight of a large expansion of supplies outside the scheme, chiefly from the Netherlands East
Indies (Indonesia).

In the early 1930s, the price of rubber had fallen greatly. The
drop partly reflected the general depression of the period, but
mainly the increase in supplies being produced on additional
acreage chiefly in the Netherlands East Indies established under
the impetus of the high prices under the Stevenson Scheme. (It
takes about five or six years for a rubber tree to reach maturity.)
A much more comprehensive cartel was set up in 1934, and this
time included the Netherlands East Indies and controlled over
95 percent of world exports throughout its existence. The International Rubber Regulation Scheme (IRRS) lasted until 1942
when Japan entered the Second World War.

The Stevenson Scheme failed to raise producer incomes for

more than a few years because it did not control enough of total supply. It did, however, aggravate long-term price fluctuations by raising prices substantially for a year or two, a development that in turn eventually elicited much larger supplies and produced a precipitous fall in prices. In the mid-1920s rubber sold at over four shillings a pound; in 1932 its price had fallen to below two pence.

The IRRS, which controlled practically all exports, maintained prices at highly profitable levels. The profitability is evident, for example, in the large profits reported by the quoted rubber-producing companies. These high profits were made in spite of the higher costs that inevitably accompany restriction of output under quota schemes. Although prices were highly profitable during most of the currency of the IRRS, they fluctuated widely. Price fluctuations were aggravated by wide variations in the level of permissible exports and therefore in actual production. The relevant committee repeatedly seriously misjudged demand even a few months ahead. The scheme thus secured monopoly profits but did not stabilize producer prices, incomes, or output.

The failure of the Stevenson Scheme to control supplies has been shared by other commodity cartels. For example, since the Second World War the tin, coffee, and cocoa cartels (called agreements) have broken down because high prices elicited additional supplies that could not be kept off the market, a sequence that brought about abrupt and disruptive changes in producer prices and incomes.

The second type of so-called stabilization method involves sustained depression of producer prices, in other words taxation of producers. State-operated export monopolies illustrate the process.

Marketing boards in British West Africa were first introduced for cocoa in 1940, and for other major West African export products in 1942 and 1943. They were all put on a permanent basis from 1946 through 1948. These government bodies had the sole right to buy the controlled commodities for export, and also the sole right to export them. They were therefore able to divorce the price paid to the producers from the world market price. Similar marketing boards were also established in East Africa and Burma. The West African experience, discussed here, was typical.

When the West African boards were put on a permanent basis, assurances were given officially that the boards would on no account serve as instruments of taxation. The boards would act as trustees for producers, shielding them from the disturbing effects of short-term price fluctuations by withholding part of the sale proceeds at times of high world market price, and disbursing them at times of low world market prices.

From their inception the boards became instruments of taxation. They withheld from producers a large proportion of sales proceeds. They continued to do so well into the 1960s, when some of them ceased to publish reports. The large surpluses made it easier for the government authorities to raise export duties and impose various other levies because these imposts merely diminished the surpluses of the boards and did not directly affect the prices paid by the boards to producers.

From the inception of the boards in the 1940s to the early 1960s, the combined surpluses of the Nigerian and Gold Coast–Ghana boards and the export levies exceeded £650 million. This represented very onerous taxation. West African producers with very small cash incomes, often only a few pounds a year, in effect paid taxes at rates that in Britain were levied only on the wealthiest taxpayers. They were also taxed much more heavily than their much more affluent citizens such as local businessmen, administrators, and professional people.[3]

Thus producer prices and incomes were severely depressed. Even though producer prices were far below world market prices (and therefore in principle more easily kept constant), in fact they fluctuated widely because of discontinuous changes in the prescribed producer prices. The changes were largely arbitrary. They tended to be dictated by the opinion of the boards about the extent to which they could safely underpay producers. Sometimes producer prices were changed in partial and belated recognition of changes in world market prices. No attempt was made to adjust the producer price in the light of the expected size of the forthcoming crop. Hence the pricing decisions were as likely to destabilize producer incomes as to smooth them.

The severity of the taxation affected adversely both current production and the maintenance and extension of capacity. These effects have been widely recognized.

Finally, the proceeds of taxation through the underpayment of producers were not used for the benefit of those producers. In fact, as is also well documented, the enterprises and projects financed by the marketing boards in West Africa as well as in Burma were unproductive and in many cases suffered large losses.

So-called stabilization schemes of the type discussed on pages 93–95 above have since the 1960s come to be regarded as instruments of aid from the West to the Third World, that is, as resource transfers from rich countries to poor countries. This is now a persistent theme of international organizations and conferences.[4] The acceptance of producer cartel schemes for this purpose has given them a considerable measure of respectability and approval. The notion of a cartel as a medium of resource transfers to the producing countries is, of course, altogether different from the notion of stabilization in the sense of the reduction of fluctuations of prices or incomes.

Third World countries exporting primary products typically are better off than countries that do not produce such products. Thus LDCs exporting commodities such as rubber, cocoa, coffee, palm oil, tea, and tin are relatively prosperous. Moreover, products such as copper, sugar, tobacco, and mineral oil are produced in rich countries in the West as well as in LDCs. Furthermore, within LDCs that export primary products the actual producers often are better off than many other people. The poorest LDCs and the poorest people in LDCs rarely produce for export.

Consumption of primary commodities and products made from them is not confined to the West, or to richer people in the West. Many primary products or products made from them are consumed in LDCs, and in many cases they import such products. In these countries the consumers of such products are not necessarily the more affluent, nor are they necessarily richer than the producers of the commodity in question. For example, some of the richest LDCs export rubber, which is used by poor people in LDCs importing rubber goods; and some of the producers of crude rubber are highly prosperous and include public companies with rich shareholders and employees.

It follows that the incidence of resource transfers effected by cartel schemes is haphazard and may well be regressive. Moreover, to be effective a cartel scheme has to restrict supply of the commodity. Restriction of output in turn involves restrictions on extension of capacity and, almost invariably, exclusion of potential producers. The excluded would-be producers are usually poorer, often much poorer, than their countrymen who benefit from the scheme. Thus the incidence of resource transfers through cartel schemes, though haphazard, in various ways tends to be regressive.

Export commodities are often the principal source or even the only source of cash income in many rural areas of the Third World. Their production has been a major instrument for advancing from subsistence production, and with it have come economic and social mobility and the widening of horizons. A cartel scheme denies would-be producers of the controlled product the opportunity to earn higher incomes and to participate in the process of economic and social advance. Exclusion from production is thus a severe, though concealed, penalty.

9
Wage Regulation in Less Developed Countries: On Not Helping The Poor

In most less developed countries wages are regulated in important sectors of the economy.[1] The principal instruments of regulation are: minimum wage legislation; promotion of binding wage arbitration; official insistence on, or promotion of, payment of wages above the supply price of labor, as for instance by fair wages clauses in government contracts and in protected industries; and trade union action, often sponsored or facilitated by government, notably by the granting of special legal rights and immunities. Regulated wages, when they are effective, are instruments of restriction, irrespective of the agency that has established them; their introduction implies the withholding from employment in the regulated activity of part of the labor supply available at the regulated wage or at lower rates. By thus curtailing supplies that can be offered, regulated wages create, and indeed are often designed to create, a situation that has been conveniently called a contrived scarcity in the regulated activity.[2]

Wage regulation in LDCs dates from the interwar period and has become very widespread since the Second World War. It is neither possible nor necessary to estimate its extent quantitatively. There are several reasons why specific quantification is not possible. These include the presence of much subsistence activity in most LDCs, frequent shifts between activities, and imperfect occupational specialization. Moreover, it is often difficult to discover whether a particular wage is above the supply price of labor (that is, whether it is a regulated wage) and also the extent and effectiveness of its enforcement. However, these difficulties do not affect either the general discussion or the confident general conclusion that regulated wages affect economic activity in much of the less developed world.[3]

Industrywide collective bargaining by trade unions is officially encouraged throughout the underdeveloped world, notably in Latin America, Asia, and the British Commonwealth.[4] In important and controllable sectors where collective bargaining is not yet effective, the government generally regulates wages either by statute or by the other measures already mentioned. Thus there is wage regulation either by official action or by industrywide collective bargaining. This is the pattern officially and explicitly promoted by the International Labour Organization (ILO), the British Colonial Office (now Commonwealth), and the Indian government. In most underdeveloped countries, official action is as yet more important than the activities of trade unions. There are statutory minimum ages in important sectors of practically every Latin American and Caribbean country, coupled generally with maximum hours and frequently with fines for discharging workers.[5] In Asia, statutory minimum ages are in force in several countries, including India, where they are supplemented by maximum hours, binding arbitration, and at times by compulsory bonuses varying with company profits. In many African countries there are statutory minimum wages as well as compulsory arbitration, and their establishment elsewhere is proposed or foreshadowed.

The comprehensive labor legislation in India (which provides, among other matters, for minimum wages, maximum hours, compulsory and binding arbitration, and enforced profit sharing), affects the interests and prospects of vast numbers of people. Some of this legislation dates from the interwar period or, very exceptionally, from before 1919, but the bulk, including the most important items, has been introduced since 1948. The legislation applies to the whole of India, and the minimum wage rates are prescribed for entire states with populations up to sixty million. There is ample evidence that in unregulated activities the wages earned are much lower than statutory minimum wages.

Regulated wages are not always effectively applied and observed; there are significant differences both between countries and between different sectors within a single country. They apply to the large enterprises and are usually observed by them. The smaller local enterprises are often legally exempt. Sometimes wage regulation applies nominally to all employers but is unenforced or even unenforceable over large sectors. Such a situation presents opportunities for corruption and extortion, as many people are always technically in breach of the law.

Many of the reasons behind the spread of restrictionism in the labor market of underdeveloped countries are familiar from experience elsewhere. The forces behind it include the organized employee beneficiaries; established employers, especially the largest, who benefit from such measures if they impede actual or potential competitors more than themselves; people who favor a more closely controlled economy; the vested interests in the organization and administration of wage regulation; and humanitarians who habitually ignore the serious adverse effects of these measures on the poorest people. Moreover, these pressures are rarely counteracted effectively, partly because those who are most adversely affected are seldom aware of the causal sequence, and are in any case unorganized and politically impotent.

There is a further major factor operative in this particular sphere of restrictionism. This factor is an international emulation effect that suggests to politicians, administrators, and others that their country is backward unless it has labor legislation and organization modeled on those of the most advanced industrial countries; that is, that the introduction and extension of wage regulation and other labor controls (for instance, of hours and conditions of work) are evidence of modernization.

This influence operates pervasively in the less developed world. It is amply illustrated in the statements of several prominent Indian spokesmen. Thus, according to N. M. Joshi, an Indian labor leader, "India's desire to prevent being classed at the International Labour Conference as a backward country in matters of social policy has led to the initiation of labour measures which might not otherwise have come up for consideration at all."[6]

This emulation effect is both recognized and magnified by the ILO. According to one of its publications, "Every State . . . now knows that the measures by which it applies the Convention's provisions will be closely scrutinised by authorised bodies at

Geneva, and that any serious discrepancy will in all probability be discussed in public debate."[7] And a commentator has concluded justifiably, "It may not then be far-fetched to attribute to the ILO a decisive role in accelerating Indian labour legislation if one realizes that, in the days immediately after the First World War, the ILO possessed the incomparable prestige of the international organization in Geneva."[8] A further example of this influence is mentioned in another ILO publication: "As a sequel to technical assistance provided to Burma by the International Labour Organization, the first wage council, for the cigar and cheroot manufacturing industry, was established by the Government in 1953. This council has prepared proposals for fixing minimum rates of wages . . . the Government of Burma plans to extend the system progressively to other industries and other parts of the country."

The relative abundance of manual labor in relation to capital, developed natural resources, and administrative and technical skills is a general characteristic of LDCs. Indeed, the possession of — or access to — comparatively cheap labor is among their few economic advantages in relation to more developed and richer countries. Wage regulation raises the price of labor and endows it with some element of contrived scarcity, and thus reduces this advantage and injures these countries' prospects of economic progress. This conclusion applies generally, because labor costs affect the establishment of economic activities and their scale of operation. A few examples will demonstrate the relevance of this obvious consideration to the less developed world.

The history of the rubber-growing industry and of its impact on Southeast Asia is an outstanding example of the attractive power of cheap labor. Cheap labor was the principal force that brought the industry to Southeast Asia; this fact has been widely and explicitly recognized from the time the industry began.[10] The rubber tree (*Hevea brasiliensis*) was not indigenous to Southeast Asia. Until the beginning of the century the small amount of rubber exported came from South America. The hardy rubber tree thrives practically anywhere in the tropical rain forest. Cheap labor is important in this industry, the main phases of which are labor intensive (labor costs are about two-thirds of production costs) and have not yet been mechanized even on American-owned estates. Most of the labor supply that attracted the industry to Southeast Asia was not in the principal producing territories but in other countries, which themselves were less suitable for rubber cultivation but from which labor could be obtained. Cheap labor in turn attracted to Southeast Asia large amounts of capital and specialized administrative and technical skills. Rapid economic development and pervasive social changes resulted from the interplay of these forces. Had cheap labor not been available, this development would have been obstructed or prevented altogether.

The very high profits of the few rubber companies in the early years of the century, especially from 1908 to 1912, greatly stimulated expansion. The total planted area, which was about 8,000 acres in 1900 (almost all of which was still immature), increased to about 250,000 acres in 1906 and to about 2.25 million acres in 1914. The high profits were secured by a small volume of capital on a small output, about 2 percent of present production. If wages had been raised greatly, either directly or by compulsory profit-sharing systems such as are now operated in many Indian industries, the incentive for rapid expansion would have been greatly reduced. Wage regulation and related measures obstruct the flow of capital into industries the expansion of which would be economic, and which would raise labor incomes generally.

A large and elastic supply of cheap and efficient labor has been a major factor, probably the major factor, in the emergence and growth of Hong Kong as a producer and exporter of manufactures. This tiny country has practically no raw materials, fuel, hydroelectric power and only a very restrictive domestic market. In spite of these limitations, often said to be crippling to development of manufacturing in LDCs, unsubsidized manufacturing industry has advanced rapidly in Hong Kong. Cheap labor has also been important in the growth of the cotton textile industries of India and Pakistan.

Low labor costs also played a major part in Japanese industrialization. For instance, the textile industry relied extensively on young girls from rural areas who accepted industrial employment at very low wages for a few years before marriage.

Although the introduction of comprehensive labor legislation in India is relatively recent (chiefly in the 1940s and 1950s), the merits and implications of the imposition of maximum hours and minimum wages have been discussed for about a century. Factory production of textiles in India began in the 1850s and developed rapidly. Beginning in the 1870s, the establishment of minimum wages and particularly of maximum hours for Indian industry (especially textiles and jute) was frequently proposed by manufacturing interests in Britain. These proposals were resisted in India, where it was often pointed out that they were designed to reduce the effectiveness of Indian competition by inflating industrial costs. Indian manufacturers and effective public opinion were well aware of the relevance of labor costs for attracting capital, securing markets, and providing employment.[11] It is ironic that under the influence of the international emulation effect and of special interest groups, the measures that were resisted fifty years ago, and the implications of which were then so clearly realized, are now vigorously espoused. These effects and implications remain the same. The deliberate inflation of industrial costs is paradoxical in view of the insistence in Indian economic planning on accelerated industrialization. Such contrived barriers to industrialization are seriously damaging in India because of the poor quality of the soil, the pervasive rural poverty, the social obstacles to economic mobility and to the raising of agricultural productivity, and the barriers to emigration.

The economic analysis of the results of regulated wages is straightforward. Unless it is either redundant or evaded, wage regulation raises wage rates in the industries in which it is introduced. This effect reduces the volume of employment in the regulated industry and raises the prices of its products relative to what they would be otherwise. These effects depend on three factors: the readiness of the consumers of the product to turn to alternatives (elasticity of demand); the readiness of the other productive resources employed in the regulated activity to withdraw from that activity if their rewards are reduced (elasticity of supply); and the ease of substitution of other productive resources for labor when its cost is raised (elasticity of substitution).

The proportion of labor costs to total costs is also relevant. The role of this factor has been familiar since Alfred Marshall, although his treatment has been corrected substantially by J. R. Hicks and Joan Robinson. If the elasticity of demand for the product is higher than the elasticity of substitution between labor and other factors, then the elasticity of demand for labor varies directly with the proportion of labor costs to total costs; and it varies inversely with that proportion if the elasticity of substitution between factors is higher than the elasticity of demand for the product. It follows that the burden of wage regulation falls on those consumers and on those factors of production that cannot turn readily to other lines of production consumption.

In practice, the effects of wage regulation on employment are often obscured by concurrent changes in other factors. Thus an increase in the demand for the products of the regulated activity reduces the impact on employment; in fact, employment might even increase. Similarly, government subsidies to the regulated industry will mask the effects of wage regulation. And, in most cases, the reduction in employment manifests itself gradually, not instantaneously, because it takes time for cooperant enterprise, capital, and other resources to be withdrawn, even if their returns have been reduced as a result of wage regulation. As is well known, factors of production that cannot be redeployed readily (including categories of specialized labor) are exploitable.

But all this does not detract from the conclusion that effective wage regulation reduces employment and raises prices in the regulated industry, above what they otherwise would be. And, of course, raising the price of labor through wage regulation also discourages new activities in which that type of labor has to be used; indeed, expectation of the introduction of wage regulation or of an increase in regulated wages can discourage the establishment of new activities. In the nature of things, these latter effects of wage regulation are not readily observable.

At this point it is necessary to take cognizance of a category of situations in which wage regulation need not, in principle, contract employment and raise product prices and in which the cost falls entirely on employers. This is the case of monopsony, that is, monopoly buying in the purchase of labor, whether exercised by a single dominant firm or by a group of firms acting in concert.

When a monopsonist is confronted by a rising supply curve of labor, the wage rate can be reduced by decreasing the amount of labor employed, and up to a point the monopsonist's profits increase.[12] In these circumstances, regulation may raise wages without increasing the marginal cost of labor (because the employment of additional labor no longer raises wage rates) and thereby secure more employment and higher wages.

Monopsony is not unknown in labor markets. The arrangements in the recruitment, wage determination, and allocation of labor in the South African mining industry are an example. Somewhat similar arrangements have been in force at various times in other activities in LDCs, such as plantation industries relying on organized immigration for their main labor supply. However, wage regulation is unlikely to be the most effective remedy for monopsony. For instance, there is the difficulty of setting and adjusting the dose, that is, of determining the wage that transfers monopsony profits without affecting employment adversely. Moreover, it does not affect the source of monopsony, which is the absence of accessible employment alternatives for the workers. The development of a wider range of such alternatives is more appropriate.

Although not absent, monopsony is as exceptional in LDCs as elsewhere. The high degree of concentration in an industry or trade often encountered in underdeveloped countries does not imply even effective monopoly power, since such power is also affected by ease of entry of competing firms and access of customers to alternatives, and these are not measured by the degree of concentration. Moreover, monopoly in the product market does not indicate monopsony in the labor market, since industries producing widely different commodities compete for the same factors of production, so that a monopolistic industry may have no monopsony power whatever. Again, wide disparities in wealth, knowledge, literacy, or commercial sophistication between employers and workers are not evidence of monopsony or of differences in bargaining power that might result in exploitation. Liability to exploitation results from lack of independent competing alternatives, and not from differences in wealth or commercial sophistication. Workers who are both poor and illiterate are paid what they are worth to their employers when those employers can obtain their services only by competing for them.

Monopsony is absent in most of the sectors in LDCs in which wages are regulated. Wages have been regulated in many highly competitive industries into which entry is easy and in which producers act independently, both in the purchase of labor, which is relatively undifferentiated and occupationally mobile, and in the sale of the products. They have also been introduced in regions in which there are many forms of employment. Minimum wages have been established in India in agriculture, cotton and leather manufacture and simple food processing; in Burma in the manufacture of cigars and cheroots; and in Latin America in many small-scale industries, including handicrafts. In these activities there is no monopoly and no monopsony.

The irrelevance of monopsony to wage regulation as practiced in LDCs is evident from the literature of the ILO, the British Colonial Office, and the Indian government. Monopsony is rarely mentioned. On the contrary, this literature often deplores the absence of employers' organizations on the ground that the multiplicity of independent employers obstructs the introduction of industrywide collective bargaining, and even the establishment of statutory wage determination. In fact, such measures often bring about the formation of employers' associations, the influence of which may extend beyond the labor market.[13]

Wage regulation creates contrived scarcities. These contrived scarcities result in uneconomic allocation of resources and thus diminish aggregate output. Besides this effect on current production, regulated wages and similar measures retard the growth of output by reducing the national income and thus the volume of investible resources, and also by reducing the flexibility and adaptability of the economy.

In LDCs, special factors reinforce these results of regulated wages. The diversity of supply and demand conditions of labor is one of these. Such diversity does not generally, or even primarily, stem from institutional barriers to movement, but rather from differences in aptitudes, resources, and customs, and also from the underdeveloped state of transport facilities. Within apparently undifferentiated unskilled labor there are wide differences in attitudes, adaptability, skill, and productivity that are reflected in wide differences in earnings of workers on piece rates in particular enterprises, as for instance the earnings of rubber tappers on estates. These earnings differ widely even within the same ethnic group, and much more so among workers of different ethnic groups, such as Chinese, Indian, and Malay tappers. Again, the efficiency of newcomers to town and industry from rural and tribal areas is usually far lower than that of more experienced workers.

The supply price of different types of unskilled labor also differs widely. For instance, the supply price of migrant labor from rural to urban area varies with distance, family circumstances, the length of stay envisaged, agricultural prosperity, employment opportunities of dependents and other factors.

In these conditions, the compulsory standardization implied in regulated wages is wasteful in terms of both the allocation and the growth of resources. For instance, it prevents the migration of prospective newcomers to industry and their acquisition of skill, because in view of their inexperience they are not worth the prescribed wage. Thus the incomes of the would-be migrants are depressed, and they are also disqualified from improving their condition.

The adverse economic results of regulated wages are likely to be pronounced in LDCs. Moreover, wage regulation affects the factor of production, the relatively ample supply of which is among the few economic assets of these countries.

We have seen that wage regulation reduces the number of jobs in the regulated activity below what it would be otherwise. As a result, those workers who would have taken jobs in the regulated activity but for wage regulation are forced to seek less advantageous employment.

In LDCs, workers excluded from activities affected by wage regulation are generally forced into activities such as part-time employment, underemployment, or virtual unemployment; or are denied the opportunity of moving out of subsistence or near-subsistence agriculture. Thus, earnings in these occupations, which in any case would tend to be among the lowest, are further depressed as a result of wage regulation covering other activities.

The very low incomes in the overcrowded activities have been widely reported in altogether different conditions. For instance, the 1956 ILO study *Problems of Wage Policy in Asian Countries* quoted several official Indian and Indonesian reports to the effect that regulated wages exceeded by more than 300 percent the wages and earnings of similar labor in unregulated activities in the same region. This gap cannot be explained by differences in skills and aptitudes; if this were the reason, wage regulation would not be necessary. The extremely low incomes in unregulated activities are often attributed to the absence of wage regulation, and its extension is urged accordingly. The legislation of several Latin American countries, including Argentina and Uruguay, specifically provides for the extension of minimum wages to cottage industry at rates comparable to those in the corresponding factory trades. Such measures, if they could be carried to their logical conclusion, would deny all sources of earned income to those who fail to secure employment at regulated wages; they would be reduced to the cold comfort of public relief or private charity, or would have to face starvation.

Thus wage regulation in LDCs does not improve the condition of the poorest; indeed, it aggravates their situation. In principle, wage regulation could ameliorate their condition only if otherwise they were subject to monopsonistic exploitation. Effective monopsony is generally rare; and it is highly unlikely that the poorest would be affected by it. The prospects of improvement for the poorest do not depend on wage regulation or similar restrictive measures. They depend on the growth of the markets for their labor. In South Africa, wage regulation was used to protect white labor at the expense of black, and it achieved that end. At the same time, the general growth of the economy over many decades inexorably increased the demand for black labor and improved the living conditions of large numbers of black people.[14] The same two opposing influences were in operation in the American South.

*　　*　　*

In conclusion, I consider two further arguments in support of wage regulation. It is sometimes urged that the adverse effects of regulated wages on development are offset by benefits resulting from the adoption of more capital-intensive methods induced by raising the money cost of labor, notably by the impetus this provides to technical change. This reasoning ignores the slowing down of technical change in the activities in which wages are depressed as a result of overcrowding brought about by the curtailment of employment opportunities in the regulated activities, the effect on investment resulting from the reduction in the current national income, and the reduced flexibility and mobility resulting from institutional wage determination. Although criteria based on the allocation of resources may conceivably be inadequate guides for policy designed to promote their growth (especially in the field of public finance), it does not follow that deliberately raising the money cost of labor somehow promotes the growth of resources that would offset the wasteful allocation it brings about.[15]

Some arguments in support of wage regulation may be noted in passing because of their popularity. One is that such measures maintain or increase purchasing power. In fact, they only transfer purchasing power from some individuals and groups to others and do not increase it. They necessarily diminish aggregate demand because they affect adversely the total national income, the ultimate source of real purchasing power.

The suggestion that the prescription of higher wages increases the productivity of undernourished workers ignores the effect of wage regulation on the incomes of those excluded from the regulated activity. These generally are people poorer than those protected by wage regulation, and their low incomes are depressed still further by it. Since wage regulation tends to diminish the total national income, and especially the incomes of the poorest people (that is, those excluded from the regulated activities), it is unlikely to improve general nutritional standards.

Wage regulation is frequently advocated on the ground that it is required to protect the welfare of poor, illiterate workers in LDCs. In fact, wage regulation generally harms rather than benefits the poorest sections of the community, whose employment opportunities it restricts. Nor are illiterate workers ignorant of available opportunities. For instance, in the early decades of this century hundreds of thousands of South Indian laborers migrated from the rural areas of Madras to Malaya and Ceylon. The volume and direction of this migration responded promptly and markedly to changes in economic conditions in those distant countries. Throughout the underdeveloped world there is much detailed evidence that poor and illiterate people are aware of differences in economic conditions and in net advantages of different occupations, and are ready to respond to these differences.

10
Price Control in Less Developed Countries: Unexpected Consequences

In Western Europe, North America, and Australasia, wartime and postwar price controls were largely dismantled in the 1950s. But in many parts of Asia, Africa, and Latin America they have been retained or reimposed. In certain conditions these price controls are more effective at one stage of distribution than at others.[1] The problems and situations discussed here have been suggested largely by the experience of West Africa and India, and to a lesser extent Pakistan and Cyprus in the 1940s and 1950s. But the analysis applies more widely.

There are distinctive characteristics of the economic scene in LDCs that affect the outcome of price controls.

In many LDCs much trading activity is conducted by people who are seen by the local population as being different from themselves. These differences may take the form of nationality, language, religion, color, or ethnic grouping. Sometimes the relevant differences, though of concern to the local people, may go unnoticed by external observers. This is true for instance, of membership of different African tribes or of religious groups in the Middle East.

Foreigners or strangers in this sense are especially prominent in the external trade and wholesale trade in LDCs. Their prominence reflects such factors as skills, commercial aptitudes, capital and business knowledge, and contacts. These factors are particularly significant in long-distance trade, notably external trade, and they help to explain a high degree of concentration in external trading, and to some extent in internal wholesale trade. However, such concentration does not secure monopoly profits for the participants. Sustained or substantial monopoly profits are unusual in private trading in LDCs because competitors can enter readily, and market-sharing agreements tend to be unstable or ineffective in the absence of state measures protecting the established traders. Situations in which trading activity is conducted largely by ethnically distinct groups are often described as monopoly; for instance, it is habitually said that Chinese in Southeast Asia and Indians in East Africa have a monopoly on trading. The use of the term *monopoly* in this context is misleading. Common membership in a distinct group does not confer monopoly power or profits; it does not mean that the numerous members of the groups will not compete, or that they can restrict entry.

In the external trade of LDCs foreigners—that is, members of ethnic groups different from the indigenous population—are especially prominent. They generally operate on a larger scale than traders who operate only locally.

In this essay, importers are referred to as merchants; they are the first stage in the internal distribution system. In this context they include wholesalers who obtain supplies at controlled prices from producers, from the government, or from other domestic sources. Firms and individuals operating in the distributive chain between the merchants and the ultimate consumers are termed intermediaries. Reference to traders may be either to merchants or to intermediaries, according to the context.

Effective rationing at the final consumer stage is rarely possible in LDCs, partly because the majority of consumers are illiterate (and so the use of ration cards causes difficulties), and also because the ideas behind rationing often conflict with the values and customs of the community. As a result, the ultimate consumer almost invariably pays the higher market-clearing price, that is, the price at which the quantity on offer and the quantity demanded balance. The market-clearing price, known colloquially as the black market price, may be much higher than the official controlled price. Most of the transactions after the stage of sale by the merchants to their customers (usually the larger intermediaries) are at the market-clearing price, that is, either at the price paid by the final consumer, or at a price differing from that price only by the costs of transport and distribution to the point of final sale. This fact is occasionally acknowledged by the

authorities in that controlled prices are not announced for transactions beyond the wholesale stage. But the existence or nonex-
istence of formal price control beyond the wholesale stage rarely
affects the prices actually paid by the majority of small-scale
intermediaries or final consumers.[2]

The dispersal of consumers and the poverty of the individual
consumer bring it about that ultimate retail transactions are on
a very small scale. For these and certain other reasons, there are
a large number of successive stages in the distributive process,
and a large number of traders at each stage (see Essay 2). Most of
the sales by merchants are made to intermediaries, especially to
large intermediaries, who are a small proportion of the total
number of intermediaries in the economy. This situation arises
partly because consumers and the smaller intermediaries often
buy in smaller individual quantities than the minimum quantities that it is economic for merchants to sell; and also because
many of the consumers are far from the merchants' establishments. Some of the merchants' sales, however, are to final consumers, especially to certain categories whose position is considered in the last section of this essay.

Since 1939 there have been frequent, rapid, and substantial
changes in the supply of and demand for imports in many
LDCs. Many of these changes bring about discontinuous sharp
increases in the local market-clearing prices of imported commodities. Such situations have resulted from either a sharp contraction in supply, an expansion of demand, or both.[3] The principal reasons for these changes are familiar. During the Second
World War and the first postwar decade they included the temporary eclipse of certain sources of supply; enforced reliance on
higher-cost sources of supply because of licensing of foreign
exchange or scarcity of shipping; longer delivery dates for
imports, especially from sources not subject to licensing; and
discontinuous variations in producer prices subject to official
determination. Since about 1955, domestic inflation and
changes in import licensing and exchange control policies have
been the principal factors bringing about discontinuous changes
in the supply-demand relationships of imported commodities in
LDCs. The resulting sharp increases in the local prices of im-

ported commodities have often affected adversely the interest, notably the standard of living, of influential groups of consumers.

A rise in the local market-clearing prices of imported commodities may or may not be accompanied by abnormally high profit margins of merchants. A higher price may simply reflect a general rise in the cost of imports (that is, a shift of the supply curve to the left) without abnormal profits. This situation does not raise issues of analytical interest, nor does it usually issue in the imposition of price control.

But a change in supply may take certain forms under which the new equilibrium price will secure abnormal profits to merchants, which may be more than accidental or short term, since there are few or no elements of self-correction in the situation. Such instances of so-called short supply have been frequent since 1939; and although they all belong substantially to one genus, for the purpose of this discussion they may be considered under two headings.

There are arrangements under which a certain amount of the goods is made available at a given import price, and additional supplies are unobtainable. This occurs when the volume of the commodity to be imported is fixed by direct control or, indirectly, by control of the issue of foreign exchange or the allocation of shipping space. This situation is referred to as case A.

Case B is a variant. Certain strictly limited supplies are available from some sources, while additional supplies are obtainable at higher cost from other sources.

During and since the Second World War both types of arrangement have been frequent in the import trade of many LDCs. Locally, their counterpart is a system of licensing or allocation of supplies among merchants, usually on some basis of past trading performance. Frequently, however, a proportion of licenses or of supplies is reserved for members of the local population who had not previously been merchants. Usually the favored individuals are drawn from the ranks of intermediaries.

Both cases A and B imply that merchants who obtain supplies at a cost (including their own selling expenses) below the new local market-clearing price will secure abnormal profits, and these may be very large. In both these cases the abnormal profits have their roots in the system of allocation or licensing of supplies, or, in other words, in the inability or unwillingness of the original sellers, the authorities, or both to raise the cost of these supplies to the merchants or to impose or raise taxes to equate supply and demand at the merchant stage. Such profits arising from the difference between the supply price and the market-clearing price constitute windfall profits. This term seems more appropriate than monopoly profits, abnormal profits, or scarcity rents.

In LDCs, licensing of supplies and price control are affected by the differing degree of effectiveness of price control over the various categories of trader.

To start with, price control is likely to be partially effective when applied to the transactions of merchants, both to their sales in bulk and to their sales in smaller quantities. Merchants generally are substantial firms who keep regular accounts and employ large staffs. Thus control of their activities is comparatively easy. Evasion is more likely to be detected or denounced, and the political risks of evasion are likely to be great, because merchants often are foreigners or strangers who tend to be politically unpopular and vulnerable. These considerations apply much less to the transactions of local traders specially promoted to the status of merchants by the allocation of licenses to them.

But price control is often not fully effective over the transactions of the merchants. One reason is that employers and authorities find it difficult to achieve effective control over the actions of the employees of merchants. However, there is another and more important reason. The bulk of the sales of merchants (including sales through stores as well as out of warehouses) are to intermediaries, that is, to customers who are themselves resellers and not final consumers. These reseller customers of the merchants dispose of the commodities at market-clearing prices, since, for reasons stated above, price control is usually inoperative beyond the stage at which the merchants operate.[4] Because their customers resell in markets in which price control is inoperative, merchants and their employees are strongly tempted to evade price control. Indeed, pressure by their customers for the allocation of supplies at controlled prices may be so insistent that evasion of price control may be well-nigh unavoidable. Even when it is avoidable, evasion might involve merchants in less trouble and unpopularity than observance. Strict observance involves informal rationing by the merchant, since by definition there is excess demand at the controlled price. Informal rationing entails unpopularity in that not all customers can be satisfied. The more strictly a merchant adheres to the controlled price, the more subject he is to customer pressure and unpopularity because the windfall profits to the favored or fortunate buyers are correspondingly larger.

Evasion of price control by merchants (and also by subsequent traders) often takes the form of conditional sales. Sales of the price-controlled commodity are confined to buyers who undertake to purchase another commodity or range of commodities, which otherwise they would not buy, or at least not at the prices they are required to pay. This type of evasion is generally difficult to prove formally. Moreover, because merchants usually sell a range of imported commodities in their normal course of business, it is easier to subject their customers to conditional sales than it would be if trading were more specialized. The profits from conditional selling, as indeed from other types of evasion, often accrue to the employees of the merchants rather than to the merchants themselves. When these employees belong to the local population, their interest in the imposition and presentation of price control is plain.

Generally, merchants can secure only a part of the total windfall profits. The balance is shared between the employees of the merchants and the intermediaries who buy below the market-clearing price and sell at that price. The distribution of the total windfall profits among the three groups may be difficult to determine and does not affect the analysis. It is evident that these groups benefit from licensing and price control.

The likelihood that merchants receiving licenses will be able to secure some of the windfall profits, especially if they are members of the local population, attracts applicants for licenses to obtain controlled supplies. For this reason intermediaries not normally engaged in the import trade are likely to clamor for inclusion among the recipients of licenses.[5]

*   *   *

Thus, the windfall profits inherent in cases A and B are likely to result in demands for licenses to obtain supplies, demands for the imposition of price control over merchants, and demands by intermediaries and others for supplies from merchants at controlled prices. As many intermediaries operate on such a small scale that they cannot hope to secure import licenses (even given preferential treatment of local people). their demands tend to be largely for price control and for supplies from merchants; and these demands may be more vocal than demands for import licenses.

Since, there can generally be no effective system of rationing, merchants have to ration the price-controlled commodities informally. This trend in turn brings about an inflation in apparent demand, a speculative shift in the demand curve; that is, customers of the merchants overstate their requirements in order to secure larger quantities than they would obtain otherwise. For several distinct reasons this phenomenon tends to emerge much more readily and to be quantitatively more important in LDCs than in more advanced countries. As already stated, many of those who benefit from the difference between the controlled price and the market-clearing price are likely to be resellers, who make a profit on supplies acquired at less than the market-clearing price. The demands of resellers, unlike those of consumers, have practically no saturation point at the controlled prices. Furthermore, these gains are riskless and are a cash gift. The opportunity for sharing in these obvious gains attracts large numbers of applicants for supplies of the price-controlled commodities.[6] The apparent excess demand at the controlled price is greater than the actual excess of effective final consumer demand.

Such a situation conduces to political tension. The merchants are likely to be accused of evasion of price control, conditional selling, and of favoritism to particular individuals and groups, especially intermediaries and those of their own nationality or race. In the circumstances there are many disgruntled traders and would-be traders.

The effects of price control on the ultimate consumers are altogether different from what is usually implied by those demanding its imposition. In case A the great majority of consumers do not benefit. They buy at the market-clearing prices, which are not reduced by price control, however effective or ineffective it may be at earlier stages.

Certain categories of consumer, however, are likely to secure supplies at controlled prices. These include civil servants, members of the police force, politicians and public figures generally, and also employees of the merchants. These favored consumers, together with the intermediaries who obtain controlled supplies from the merchants, are generally a small proportion of the total population. But politically, socially, and administratively they are influential groups. Since they benefit appreciably from price control, they are likely to favor it, even though market-clearing prices are unchanged. Their advocacy of price control is not likely to be affected by its political and social consequences.

Under case B the reasons and motives of demands for price control are likely to be similar to those under case A: a sharp rise in the local prices of imported goods and the emergence of large profits for some merchants. And most of the results of the imposition of price control are similar to those observed in case A: excess of demand over supply, inflation of demand, informal rationing by merchants, and an obvious discrepancy between the market-clearing prices and controlled prices.

But there is one significant difference. Under case B, market-clearing process will be higher than it would have been without price control. The supply of imports is now not completely inelastic; additional supplies can be obtained from higher-cost sources. Unless price control over the operations of merchants is completely ineffective, some merchants will not be able to realize such high average prices as they would otherwise, and it will therefore not pay some merchants to tap certain high-cost sources that they would have tapped had their resale prices not been controlled.

Price control in LDCs will not help the general run of consumers of the price-controlled goods, or may even damage their interests. At the same time it sets up political tensions and conflicts that can be severe, especially in multiethnic societies. This outcome raises the question whether the emergence of windfall profits can be avoided, since it is those profits that provoke the conflicts.

It may seem obvious that the windfall gains can be eliminated by the imposition of indirect taxes on merchants' sales of the controlled commodities. In LDCs this measure would not affect prices paid by consumers, except those favored groups referred to above. This line of approach is likely to be resisted not only by the favored consumers but also by merchants (who make some sales above the controlled prices) and intermediaries. Those affected by the imposition of the taxes are likely to be vocal and influential. Moreover, it will be difficult to adjust the tax rates in line with changes in demand and supply conditions. Sometimes the remaining windfall profits will be so high as to arouse suspicion and tension. At other times, the tax rates are so high that merchants and intermediaries will curtail their operations, and consumer prices will thereby be raised.

Another possible measure is for the state to intervene directly and to assume the role of merchant, importing the affected goods and reselling them to intermediaries—or even to the final consumers through state shops—at market-clearing prices. Such a measure involves clearing prices, and also patent political disadvantages. In addition to politicizing economic life, state trading in LDCs has been inefficient, often corrupt and a burden on producers and consumers of the commodities affected. These effects in both LDCs and centrally planned economies are now notorious.

A third possibility is a policy of reduction in aggregate monetary demand to diminish the gap between the intended controlled prices and market-clearing prices. This approach would call for appropriate monetary or fiscal measures. It would be relevant only if the control of prices is intended to cover a large proportion of consumer expenditure rather than a limited number of items in temporary short supply. Such a situation is frequent in LDCs in which government policies have resulted in high inflation. Indeed, in such situations price controls, though often instituted, are ineffective even if, as sometimes happens, a few traders are executed either for so-called hoarding or for selling at above the controlled maximum prices. Only general deflationary measures will be appropriate. But such measures are grossly extravagant for dealing merely with situations of the kind analyzed here.

Another possible measure is the auctioning by the state of licenses to deal in the controlled commodities, whether imported or locally produced. This device would skim off all expected windfall profits unless there were collusion (which would be difficult to organize effectively). This method has been used occasionally in some LDCs, in the form of the auctioning of foreign exchange. It has not been more widely adopted, presumably because it does not suit influential interest groups in both the public and the private sectors. It is sometimes contended that auctioning is undesirable because it would reinforce or extend existing concentration in trade or would underpin the prevailing prominence of certain ethnic groups in trade. In fact, auctioning is as likely to help as to hinder newer firms and new entrants. It is a regime of licensing and price control that will preserve the status quo unless the authorities deliberately favor firms and individuals other than those already established in the trade. However, a regime of unrestricted auctioning deprives the authorities of opportunities to dispense windfall profits to favored individuals or groups.

A government could, of course, deal with short-supply situations by doing nothing about the windfall profits (except through the operation of general taxation of profits). However, such inaction can bring in its train social and political tensions, even civil disturbances.

Economic analysis does not throw any light on the choice among these available approaches.

11
Industrialization and Development: Nigeria

Since the Second World War, industrialization in the sense of state support for manufacturing activity has been a major plank of development policy and planning in many less developed countries. There is a voluminous academic, official, and popular literature on the subject. However, few studies of industrialization combine a firm grasp of economic analysis with close familiarity with the implementation of policy and with the political and economic scene in which events take place. Professor Peter Kilby's book on industrialization in Nigeria is such a study. It therefore provides a suitable vehicle for an examination of the principal issues involved.

In his substantial monograph, *Industrialization in an Open Economy: Nigeria 1945–1966* (Cambridge, 1969), Professor Kilby reviews the establishment and growth of manufacturing industry in Nigeria since about 1945, and examines at length the official policies designed to promote industrialization. He is knowledgeable, and brings to his task an unusual combination of qualifications. His temperament and outlook are scholarly, and his intellectual integrity is apparent throughout. He attempts to do justice to opinions that differ from his own, and when he notices evidence or opinions inconvenient to his position he does not attempt to minimize let alone to conceal them. He is at home in those parts of macro- and microeconomic theory usually deemed relevant to development economics. He knows Nigeria well, and he understands the value of direct observation and the use of primary sources. These qualifications have resulted in a book of considerable general interest.

Kilby's distinctive insights and contributions lie in the description and analysis of specific aspects of the process of industrialization. His primary concern is with the establishment of various manufacturing industries in Nigeria to supply the home market, mostly in replacement of imports and chiefly behind high tariff walls; and with the establishment of manufacturing facilities in Nigeria for the processing of agricultural produce, mainly for export.

Professor Kilby computes and emphasizes the high level of protective tariffs that shelter several major industries. He correctly notes that it is effective rates of protection that matter rather than nominal rates. The effective rate expresses protection as a proportion of the value added domestically, whereas the more usually quoted nominal rate relates the tariff to the value of the product: in measuring the extent of the effective assistance to domestic manufacturing activity, the value of imported raw materials and imported intermediate goods (which are usually admitted duty-free, or attract duty at much lower rates than the final product) needs to be deducted from the value of the output. Kilby shows in an interesting table (p. 48) that in several textile-manufacturing activities the rate of effective protection in 1961 exceeded 100 percent; this means that the domestic value added (at world prices) was less than the value of the domestic resources used (similarly calculated). He shows that conventional tariffmaking, which focuses on nominal rather than effective rates, ensures that "the shallower manufacturing processes receive a proportionately larger protective subsidy than do industries contributing a greater net output" (p. 47). The conventional pattern of tariffs favors assembly operations and the provision of finishing touches to consumer goods and can obstruct the subsequent establishment of intermediate and capital goods industries.

Much of the discussion in the theoretical literature on the welfare effects of tariffs, including the various arguments for tariff protection, assumes that the tariff makers are well informed about the relevant costs, markets, and production possibilities, and also that they determine tariff structures in a disinterested manner, designed somehow to maximize some nebulous social welfare function. These assumptions are unrelated to reality. Thus Kilby shows that in Nigeria, as elsewhere, the protective subsidies to encourage new industries were over-generous, partly at least because government was unable to check the claims of interested parties. Moreover, as is usual else-where too, there was generally intense political pressure to push through the project from the region of its prospective locations. Kilby notes that "it is a reflection of the intensity of regional political pressure for industrialization that an impartial tariff commission or similar technical body, first proposed in the mid-1950s, has not been established or even seriously discussed" (p. 49).

Kilby shows that before the late 1950s few industries were developed to meet domestic demand in Nigeria, although the market was often large enough to support a number of medium-sized factories. But from about 1958 there was a marked increase in private investment in local industry, notably by overseas manufacturers and local merchants who had been sup-plying imported goods. This occurred at a time when the general economic and political climate was deteriorating, with increased political uncertainty and a decline in public adminis-tration stemming from "internal political problems connected with tribalism and regional separatism, and the rapid expansion of government services coupled with an even more rapid Nige-rianization" (p. 54).

Kilby explains this increased investment largely as a response to the increased competitive pressure that faced overseas sup-pliers (that is, both foreign manufacturers and the merchants who distributed their products), chiefly as a result of the greater attention given to the expanding Nigerian market by an increasing number of foreign suppliers. He considers that "posi-tive entrepreneurial response" to threats to one's market "is to protect one's stake in the market by going into local manufac-ture. The competition from other sellers is eliminated by virtue of the protective tariff" (p. 55). Thus he suggests that the promi-nence of established suppliers of imports in local manufacturing reflects not only such familiar advantages as knowledge of the market, established contacts, and possession of capital, but also and particularly the operation of a market strategy stemming from the desire of local merchants and overseas suppliers to pro-tect their share of the market. Kilby does not argue that the first entrant into a manufacturing industry in Nigeria necessarily scooped the whole market; others might follow suit. But presumably because of economies of scale and possibly because of restrictions imposed by government (for example, on the number of expatriates allowed to work in the country), the number of suppliers established behind the high tariff would be materially smaller than the number of suppliers who would otherwise be willing and able to export to Nigeria. "For the price of an industrial investment . . . a seller can transform the competitive market he currently faces into a monopolistic (or oligopolistic) market . . . Hence for both the overseas manufacturer and the distributing merchant firm, the optimum solution to mounting competition and threatened markets will often be the establishment of a local factory" (p. 55).

Kilby develops and discusses his hypothesis with considerable skill and extensive reference to particular industries and firms. He does well to present and emphasize the point, which is often overlooked, that industrial development in an LDC can serve to transform a competitive market into one of oligopoly or monopoly. At times he does not argue his case in sufficient detail, and he may have stretched his hypothesis too far. He does not specify precisely enough why other suppliers do not take advantage of the protective tariff, nor does he examine possible motives (other than the market strategy he emphasizes) for former suppliers to establish local operations. Some suppliers of imports may have considered that the advent of complete political independence in 1960 would make local manufacturing an economic or political necessity for their continued operation, or would in various ways present exceptional opportunities for locally established producers, even in the uncertain situation that was developing. But on the whole, Kilby's account of the motives behind the establishment of local manufacturing activities by former suppliers of imports is convincing; at the very least it draws attention to the importance of market strategy.

He notes two important corollaries of his hypothesis. First, to the extent that income tax concessions were designed to induce new investment in industry, they may have been largely gratuitous, since the motivating force for many new investments was different from that envisaged in such legislation. Second, competition in the affected industries tends to be nonexistent or weak; indeed, this situation often provides the inducement for local investment by a pioneering firm. Hence some of the most adverse effects of overgenerous tariff protection are not even partially offset by the subsequent development of internal competition. Kilby observes further that policies designed "to promote maximum employment and training of Nigerians" have included highly restrictive immigration quotas for expatriate employees. These restrictions have "prevented new exporters to Nigeria from establishing sales offices prior to a possible industrial investment" (p. 133) and have weakened the incentive to new entry otherwise provided by high protective tariffs. Here, as frequently elsewhere in the book, Kilby's description and analysis show how one type of policy measure impedes or renders impossible the achievement of its ostensible objectives or those of other policy measures.[1]

Kilby himself does not suggest that all investments in import-substituting manufacturing activities were induced by threats to the market of established importers. He refers to several other industrial investments for which "the motive was the classical attraction to a profitable market opportunity rather than the compulsion of competition" (p. 72). In several instances the investing firms already had business interests in Nigeria. In other instances the entrepreneurs had no previous activities in that country. The latter category includes "reputable, long-established manufacturing companies seeking an outlet for redundant equipment." The "outstanding case" in this sub category was an American textile firm, Indian Head Mills, which "promoted a £2.4 million textile venture at Aba to which it contributed £72,000 in cash and forty-year-old machinery officially valued at £688,000 in return for 70 percent of the equity" (pp. 76–77). Unlike many others, this venture has been successful.

There is an informative account of the activities of machinery merchants as investors and of the resulting projects, known as "turnkey projects." Kilby describes the "rash of machinery-sale public-investment projects," in which the merchants had a small equity interest associated with a big sale of new (if not up-to-date) machinery. He explains that the public investment projects were mainly political in their motivation, and that their results were seriously damaging: "The drawbacks of this type of public investment are the extensive promotion of political and personal corruption, inflated capital costs (by 100% or more), serious external debt-servicing problems, and money-losing investments" (p. 78). And as was to be expected, the selection of the projects and of their location was made on political grounds, with little or no regard to economic efficiency; and the machinery merchants, unlike those manufacturers of machinery who have interested themselves in industrial projects, were unable or unwilling to supply or ensure on a continuing basis the necessary co-operant managerial and technical skills (or were not requested to do so). According to Kilby, this lack was the "key factor in explaining why not a single turnkey project in Nigeria was earning a profit as of December 1966" (p. 79).

The discussion of the turnkey projects covers a large part of the industrial activities of state enterprises. Kilby reports that "the regional Development Corporations, the agencies responsible for government-run industrial enterprises, reveal similar tendencies for public undertakings initiated during the 1950s, whether managed by Nigerians or hired expatriates: excessive over-staffing, sluggish response to competition, unresolved technical problems, profitless operation" (p. 79). He points out that this result contrasted markedly with the performance of joint ventures with foreign firms that undertook the management of the ventures and took a large part of the risk. Kilby's treatment is so austere, however, that he fails to note the unconscious irony of the designation "Development Corporations"- most of whose investments "are earning negative returns" (p. 168).

Apart from manufacturing industries that produce goods (largely substitutes for imports) for the domestic market, there are industries that process domestic products for export. Professor Kilby focuses largely on the production of palm oil.

Kilby provides a brief history of the palm oil industry in Nigeria and describes the various methods used in the extraction of the oil from the fruit. He sets out the changes in the composition of different grades of palm oil exported in the 1950s, which, in accordance with common Nigerian usage, he terms "a spectacular improvement in quality" (p. 154). He then shows that, contrary to what is sometimes claimed, the introduction of the Pioneer oil mills (one of the four methods of palm oil extraction now available in Nigeria) had little to do with this improvement.[2] He rightly attributes the change to the operation of the price incentives introduced by the Oil Palm Produce Marketing Board in paying producers grade differentials much wider than those obtaining in export markets (where the board resold the oil bought locally). This practice was made possible by the fact that the prices paid by the board to the producers were far below world market prices: because the board had the sole right to export, it was able to divorce both the level and the structure of producer prices from those ruling in the export market. Kilby notes also that the underpayment of producers reduced total output and export earnings: "Total proceeds to Nigeria from palm oil exports would undoubtedly have grown faster under a regime of higher producer prices and smaller [grade] differentials" (p. 156).

This observation is correct. The sustained underpayment would have had the adverse effects indicated by Kilby, besides other adverse effects not noted by him, even if the money withheld from producers had been used more productively than in the financing of projects, political parties, and persons favored by influential politicians and administrators. Kilby himself notes the negative returns of the bulk of the projects financed by the various organizations supported by the marketing boards. And although he shows that palm oil exports, and thus export earnings, were affected adversely by the underpayment of producers, he does not emphasize that this example, as well as others in the book, makes clear that the volume and value of exports (and also of imports), and hence the balance of payments, depend heavily on government policy and are not the inevitable consequences of forces outside the control of government.

The contrary view is implied or asserted in much of the development literature. The alleged lack of control by the governments of LDCs over the volume and value of their primary exports is adduced as the basis for the necessity of a variety of restrictive government policies. Indeed, much of the current development literature urges that substantial development of less developed countries is bound to involve balance-of-payments difficulties, a view that carries the implication that a country that is not experiencing such difficulties is growing less fast than it might otherwise do. Yet many less developed countries, as well as those now regarded as developed, have had long periods of effective growth without balance-of-payments difficulties; and, of course, many countries have had balance-of-payments difficulties without experiencing economic growth. Kilby himself accepts at times the insubstantial notion that development involves balance-of-payments difficulties, as for instance when he writes that the petroleum industry in Nigeria can free Nigeria from the "binding constraint" of "deficient foreign exchange earnings," an allegedly "growing-attenuating" constraint that is "typically the lot of developing economies" (pp. 15–16).

Kilby does, however, illustrate neatly a little-known implication of the marketing board's policy. He carefully examines the economics of the four different methods of palm oil extraction and explains why "the native method continues to be the predominant technology employed in palm oil extraction throughout Nigeria" (p. 154). The explanation is as follows. The technically more advanced methods extract a higher proportion of oil from the fruit than the more labor-intensive native method. The prices for palm oil that prevail in Nigeria are determined by the producer prices set by the marketing board, and these are far below commercial values in the world market. At the lower levels of price prevailing in Nigeria it does not pay processors to use the technically more advanced method that extracts more oil, although it would pay to do so if the prices obtainable for oil were the commercial values, that is, the export price minus cost of transport and distribution. Kilby emphasizes that there is a loss to the economy with regard to both export earnings and domestic consumption . . . of thousands of tons of palm oil left in the discarded fruit pulp each year" (p. 165), and the estimates that at the level of output in 1965, the volume of what he calls "recoverable" oil lost to the economy was about 61,000 tons against total exports of 156,000 tons.

*   *   *

Kilby's chapter on indigenous enterprise in manufacturing ranks among the most comprehensive surveys yet published on manufacturing industry in Africa. It is, however, strongly weighted toward the activities of government agencies. One would have preferred to read more about individual local entrepreneurs, whether stories of success or of failure. Most of the chapter is a review of the activities of various official agencies that assist indigenous enterprises, primarily by heavily subsidized loans or grants. The story is largely one of failure. Money was available for the promotion of subsidized enterprises, but various elements indispensable for their successful operation were not, such as adequate management of the labor force, separation of personal and business expenditures in the conduct of private enterprises, adequate provision for future contingencies, and systematic investigation of market conditions. Assistance was often granted for political reasons.

Kilby puts forward quite definite views on the general reasons for these failures, although he expresses them in a somewhat convoluted form. "The development of certain requisite entrepreneurial characteristics, relating to performance in the organizational and technological spheres, is being impeded by traditional socio-cultural factors common to all of Nigeria's ethnic groups" (p. 341); and again: "the weight of the evidence points to lack of absorptive capacity on the part of the aid-recipients [recipients of official subsidies] as the principal bottleneck" (p. 336). He also notes, more directly, that what he has been analyzing is "an important instance of homely truism that economic development involves far more than mere economic change" (p. 342).

This emphasis on socio-cultural and personal factors is welcome. But it is probable that in Nigeria (as in other former British dependencies in Africa) the process of development, and especially the emergence and spread of attitudes, conduct, and institutions required for the progress of the exchange economy, would have been both eased and accelerated if the incomes of agricultural producers had not been so drastically reduced over decades by the policies of the various statutory marketing boards. The surpluses of these boards—in effect export taxes—provided much or most of the resources of the so-called development boards and corporations. And the general politicization of economic life, to which the policy has contributed greatly, has reinforced the operation of sociocultural factors impeding development.

There is much of interest in Kilby's emphasis on sociocultural factors, and in his often illuminating account of the operation of certain institutions designed to enlarge the scope and improve the performance of manufacturing activity, such as the formal education system and applied industrial research. His account of the operation of these institutions is again a recital of well-nigh uniform failure of the officially sponsored transfer of methods and institutions which have functioned well, or at least tolerably, in the West, but which in the wholly different conditions of Nigeria have proved ineffective at best, and more often harmful. Thus there is a brief but perceptive discussion of the high costs and damaging effects (some of which will be lasting) of the extremely rapid expansion of formal primary education.

A chapter entitled "Industrial Relations and Wage Determination: Failure of the Anglo-Saxon Model" discusses at length the failure of the Nigerian trade union movement, governed by an ordinance drafted by a British expert on trade union affairs:

> The absence of an environment and a set of felt-needs similar to those which produced the Anglo-Saxon model has far-reaching implications for its institutional transfer. The sustained loyalty and discipline required of union members, which was built up in an earlier era only after long years of struggling for recognition, cannot be generated when the antecedent goals pursued by the trade union lose their primacy . . . The development sequence—the learning process—required to make collective bargaining viable as a technique for determining wages is denied to present day underdeveloped countries. (p. 302)

Kilby recognizes that "under existing circumstances in underdeveloped countries" labor organization serves as little more than "a political instrumentality for channelling the protest of privileged wage earners" (p. 303, who are "already a highly privileged minority" employed in the public sector, and by the large foreign-owned firms (p. 301). He notes the economic consequences of the "politicized Anglo-Saxon model." Wages in some sectors have been substantially increased, thereby reducing the volume of employment there below what it would otherwise have been. The widening of income differences between town and country has "aggravated the rural exodus and urban unemployment (with all of its political ramifications." And, compared to the "pre-existing non-unionized situations the politicized Anglo-Saxon model has resulted in worsened, rather than improved, industrial relations" (p. 303).

The results and implications of the expansion of the formal education system and of the attempted establishment of Western-type trade unions are specific instances of a wider range of problems, namely the extreme difficulty, or at times impossibility, of transferring institutions between societies profoundly different in historical background and experience, values, and customs. It is easy to transfer the name and form of an institution, but not the spirit and experience that animate it. Failure to recognize this important fact is common in much of the development literature and often derives in part from an unduly foreshortened time perspective of both the background of and prospects for economic development in LDCs. Such a foreshortening lies behind the belief, or at least the frequent statements, that most less developed countries can reach a Western level of material attainment in a few years or decades.

Inappropriate use of statistics is another pitfall involved in attempts to apply Western methods and concepts to the conditions of LDCs. Kilby recognizes some of the difficulties but fails to draw the requisite conclusion. Thus he notes that Nigerian population statistics are subject to wide margins of error; and he explains why he prefers his estimate of 37.1 million for 1963 to the official census figures of 55.6 million (p. 4). Yet at times he presents detailed statistics that are misleading, such as percentage changes in total gross domestic product and in gross investment, expressed to the nearest fraction of one-tenth of one percent, or statistics of the numbers of the school population or of employment in certain activities expressed to the nearest digit. In fact, the statistics of national income and of capital formation in Nigeria, as in other LDCs, are subject not only to vast inaccuracies of compilation but also to large biases and errors reflecting certain problems of concept and measurement that affect the orders of magnitude of the figures and often result in errors of several hundred percent.

In his last chapter, Kilby draws on two decades of experience of industrialization and considers the "costs and returns of alternative ways of deploying resources between industrial and non-industrial production and between different uses within the industrial sector" (p. 345). There is much of interest and value in this discussion, but it is nevertheless marred by a failure to see the problems and prospects of industrialization in historical perspective.[3]

Kilby begins from the position that the "great majority of underdeveloped countries will have to place major emphasis upon import replacement" if they wish to increase the extent of their industrialization (p. 346). Much of the chapter is about ways of achieving such industrialization most efficiently in terms of costs and benefits. He disposes effectively of two major strategies for import substitution encountered in the literature on development economics. These are based on the theories of balanced growth and unbalanced growth and are associated with the names, respectively, of Ragnar Nurkse and Albert Hirschman.

His examination of the two theories leads him to reject the two strategies and to suggest a "wiser policy," which in effect amounts to the prescription that measures should be taken "to increase productivity and to reduce cost." He rightly says that "cost reduction widens the markets for those industries that achieve it; their expanded output, conjoined with increasing agricultural production (particularly exports), progressively generates the growth in income which enlarges all markets." Granting the need to reduce costs and raise efficiency, he asks what "criteria should be used when selecting imports for domestic replacement." The general answer is that the criterion should be a "slightly qualified comparative cost principle." One should choose products "whose potential domestic unit cost is lowest relative to the duty-free import price," allowing, however, for such factors as "the estimated increase in factor productivity which results from the transfer of technology and organization [from the protected industry] to other industries" (pp. 351/353).

This may not strike the reader as amounting to much of a strategy for industrialization, especially since Kilby does not examine the problems of forecasting future costs of imports and of domestic production. However, it is a merit of his treatment that he resists the blandishments of taking over elegant and elaborate theoretical constructs and arguments for protection as if they were obviously applicable to the circumstances of and conditions in the country in question, and readily capable of being translated into practical policies and decisions. And in developing his proposed strategy, Kilby makes several important points.

He considers at some length the case for deliberately introducing more capital-intensive methods in manufacturing industry, although less capital-intensive methods are economically more efficient—a case argued on the grounds that, on certain assumptions, the choice of the former promises "a larger capital stock and higher consumption at some future time" (p. 354). He comes out strongly against this case and concludes that "cost-minimization should take primacy over all other criteria" (p. 361). He convincingly questions the conventional assumptions behind the choice-of-technique analysis. In particular, he scrutinizes the crucial "assumption that of the income generated by a particular investment, a substantially larger share of profits is likely to be reinvested than of wages," and concludes that although the assumption is "correct in its narrow formulation, the situation appears quite differently in its institutional setting, at least in Nigeria" (p. 360). He points out that in Nigeria the capital-intensive industries are likely to be foreign-owned companies or state enterprises; and he examines various disadvantages of relying on these categories as sources of productive saving. He also observes that small-scale labor-intensive industries in Nigeria have attracted many indigenous private firms, thus eliciting savings for investment in these activities. He also correctly notes a point familiar to economic historians but neglected or even denied in much of contemporary development economics, namely that productive saving and investment do not necessarily depend on the level of income.

Kilby explains also that capital-intensive enterprises have tended to remain "technological enclaves" (p. 358) with little or no effect on the quality of indigenous entrepreneurship, management, or industrial skills. He contrasts their limited influence with that of the "small, modestly financed, individual or family-owned concerns (predominantly Levantine)" in which men are substituted for equipment. The example set by such firms has given rise to "hundreds of Nigerian firms" in such activities as the manufacture of soap and umbrellas as well as sawmilling, rubber crêping, and metalworking (p. 358). He argues, in consequence, that "the encouragement of smaller-scale, labour-saving foreign investment (probably Levantine) will maximize the technological and managerial carry-over from the foreign sector" (p. 362). It is refreshing to find the advocacy of such a realistic but unpopular policy: it is unrealistic only in the sense that it is unlikely to be implemented. It is equally refreshing to find the final sentence of the book rejecting nostrums still widely canvassed as indispensable for the progress of LDCs in the face of much contrary evidence: "There is good reason to believe that a shift in emphasis in the development effort from maximizing public investment and the savings ratio to improving organizational efficiency will yield a higher rate of economic growth in the short run, and create necessary conditions for the absorption of new technology over the long run" (p. 364).

Professor Kilby rightly refuses to accept widely held views about economic growth and the means for achieving it. Nevertheless, his treatment is sometimes less careful than might have been expected from his generally cautious and critical approach.

Kilby agrees with "virtually all students of the subject" that "a certain amount of industrialization is likely to be a necessary condition for successful economic development" (p. 345). But the statement is invalid, however many students of the subject might agree with it. To begin with, Kilby does not specify what phase or period of development he has in mind. And again, although manufacturing is often a concomitant of certain phases of economic development, it is neither a generally necessary nor a sufficient condition for it. Moreover, as Kilby's own survey of

industrialization in Nigeria amply shows, the growth of subsidized manufacturing industries is more likely to retard economic development than to promote it. There is nothing in the
nature of manufacturing activities to suggest that enlargement
of the manufacturing sector will by itself result in economic
improvement, when the required resources have to be diverted
to it by a subsidy from other activities.

Kilby adduces, albeit rather briefly, three reasons for the
unwarranted presumption in favor of subsidized industrialization. These stem from supposed drawbacks in reliance upon primary production: "a low income elasticity of demand for primary products, possible disruptive instability in export earnings
and, most important, limited transmission of technological and
organizational stimuli from primary production to other sections of the economy" (p. 345). His advocacy of subsidized
industrialization rests primarily on the third of these arguments.
We begin with a brief consideration of the first two points.

A low-income elasticity of demand would not warrant
transfer of resources to less productive activities, unless it were
not only low but also negative.[4] If the income elasticity of
demand is low but not negative, it means no more than that
these activities will not be as advantageous as they would be if
the income elasticity were higher. A negative elasticity would
not imply that an early transfer of resources out of primary
products would be economic without a consideration of such
factors as comparative costs and market conditions of different
activities, of cost of the transfer of resources, and the advantages
of continuing for a while with primary production.

The principal exports of primary products from Nigeria, as
from many other LDCs, are industrial raw materials (such as
petroleum) and relatively high-grade foodstuffs (such as cocoa),
for which the income elasticity of demand is unlikely to be low,
and is certainly not negative. But even if the income elasticity of
demand for these exports were negative, such a situation would
not warrant subsidized industrialization. It might warrant
expenditure on increasing the flexibility of the economy to facilitate shifts of resources out of primary production, if and when
the market were to contract.

Fluctuations in export proceeds may serve as a reason for accumulating reserves in periods of prosperity and drawing on them in periods of depression. But they do not represent a valid ground for subsidized industrialization, which implies the taxing of other activities, so long as the income from the taxed activities exceeds that which could be secured over a comparable period from manufacturing. And this is the condition implicitly assumed in the argument that, to be viable, manufacturing needs to be subsidized at the expense of the rest of the community. Moreover, expenditure on increasing the flexibility of the economy would seem a more appropriate policy than the promotion of subsidized manufacturing.[5]

Elsewhere in the book (pp. 44–46 and 352) Professor Kilby refers explicitly to two other arguments for state-sponsored manufacturing: first, that factor prices do not reflect opportunity costs (especially that wages in organized activities often much exceed social opportunity costs); and second, that manufacturing industries yield pervasive external economies (that is, cost reductions in some activities brought about by expansion of other activities). He considers these arguments inapplicable to Nigeria. They can, however, be rejected on wider grounds also.

The first argument implies that wages in manufacturing exceed the economic cost of labor to the community, measured by the productivity in alternate employment. But such a situation would call for a revision of the methods of wage determination rather than for state assistance to manufacturing, especially since wages are often institutionally determined in various other activities as well (for instance, large-scale commerce as well as public employment and construction work), and also because manufacturing is already subsidized by the pattern of government expenditure in LDCs, which almost always favors urban communities and tends to benefit manufacturing. And, even if there were surplus labor in agriculture in some clearly defined and pertinent sense (which is by no means generally true in LDCs), either as a result of institutionally determined wages or for some other reason, it would not follow that subsidization of manufacturing, especially for import substitution, would provide more employment than, say, encouragement of agriculture or improvement of communications. The presumption is the other way.

The second argument is also defective. There are few authen-
ticated instances of genuine external economies yielded by manufacturing. In any event, subsidized industrialization implies
the contraction of the taxed activities, with a loss of potential
external economies stemming from those activities. It would
need to be established that the external economies yielded by
the subsidized activities exceed those lost in other directions.
For instance, even if subsidized import substitution would yield
appreciable external economies, these may well be outweighed
by external economies lost by the curtailment of export activities, including the processing of agricultural products for export;
and the latter categories are likely to be more suitable for the
conditions of many LDCs.

At one point Kilby writes that there is only "one viable justification for protection—to subsidize an infant industry during an
initial period in which it is achieving cost reductions as a result
of learning" (p. 45). However, this argument begs the question
why businessmen would not cover the cost of the learning process. Thus the validity of this argument depends critically on
unspecified externalities. Moreover, there is no reason why cost
reductions resulting from learning should be more pronounced
in manufacturing than in commerce, transport, or the production of cash crops.

Kilby's advocacy of assisted industrialization in Nigeria is
based primarily on the contention that there is a limited transmission of technological and organizational stimuli from agriculture to the rest of the economy, contrary to what he expects
from manufacturing industries. In his discussion, however, he
has taken an unduly restricted view of the interaction between
agriculture and the rest of the economy and, partly for this
reason, fails to note major implications of subsidizing manufacturing at the expense of agriculture, especially for export.

In several places Kilby comments that subsidization of manufacturing in Nigeria has been made possible by the substantial
and sustained underpayment of farmers, and that, in addition,
the prices of manufactured goods bought by them have been
raised as a result of government policies. Although Kilby notes
at times that these policies have retarded the expansion of

capacity and of agricultural production, he nevertheless neglects major economic results of these policies.

Kilby's treatment ignores the implications of the incomplete penetration of the Nigerian economy by the money economy, and by the attitudes and institutions appropriate to it. This matter is particularly relevant to Nigeria, where much agricultural activity is still largely subsistence or near-subsistence production. The emergence from subsistence or near-subsistence agriculture is critical for economic progress, including the development of viable manufacturing activities. The factors Kilby has omitted in his discussion of subsidized industrialization are almost certainly more important than the factors he has stressed, notably the advance of technology and organization.

The effects of the underpayment of agricultural producers in Nigeria have been compounded by the restriction of the supply of cheap imported manufactures through high protective tariffs and restrictive licensing, especially of imports. Many of the products affected are major inducement or incentive goods. The role of such products in the expansion of agricultural output is familiar, or at any rate should be familiar.

The heavy taxation of farmers has also restricted the market for manufactures, and it has obstructed the progress of industries processing agricultural products both for the domestic market and for export; that is, the development of types of manufacturing particularly appropriate to an economy such as Nigeria. Kilby has noted how official policies have curtailed such development. In the case of palm oil processing the price policies of the marketing boards have retarded the adoption of capital-intensive methods readily accessible to indigenous entrepreneurs. He could have added that the exceedingly heavy taxation of export crops has greatly restricted the scope of saving and investment, both in agriculture and outside it, and has also inhibited the extension of trading activity, which in Nigeria, as in many other LDCs, has often served as a training ground and as a basis for subsequent development of viable industrial enterprises.

In both the title and text of his book, Professor Kilby describes Nigeria as an open economy. He uses this term to indicate that the policies adopted in Nigeria ensured "that Nigeria's internal price structure has been fairly closely related to world prices," and that "the absence of extensive state intervention contributed to an open, market-orientated economy" (p. 1).

This characterization is astonishing in view of Kilby's frequent references to the policies of the marketing boards in keeping producer prices of the major export crops well below world prices. In fact, over the period reviewed by Kilby, the producers generally received only between one-third and two-thirds of the commercial value of their crops. Practically all agricultural exports were handled by state export monopolies. The establishment of industrial, commercial, and transport enterprises was subject to official licensing; imports were closely controlled; manufacturing industry was widely and heavily protected; and favored activities and enterprises received lavish cash subsidies.

So far from there being little state intervention in the economy, state control was so extensive that it amounted to large-scale politicization. This politicization of economic life has greatly exacerbated political tension and conflict in Nigeria, a country that is a collection of different societies and peoples with substantially different backgrounds and cultures. In fact, political conflict erupted into the large-scale civil war of 1966–1969. It is true that Kilby often refers to instances of corruption, large-scale misuse of funds, political and personal favoritism, and crass inefficiency in the operation and financial transactions of official organizations. But he does not link these phenomena to the extent and closeness of state control of economic life. Such pervasive state control and the concomitant politicization of economic life are not confined to Nigeria.

12
Policy and Progress: The Hong Kong Story

How would you rate the economic prospects of an Asian country which has very little land (and only eroded hillsides at that), and which is indeed the most densely populated country in the world; whose population has grown rapidly, both through natural increase and large-scale immigration; which imports all its oil and raw materials, and even most of its water; whose government is not engaged in development planning and operates no exchange controls or restrictions on capital exports and imports; and which is the only remaining Western colony of any significance? You would think that this country must be doomed unless it received large external donations. Or, rather, you would have to believe this if you went by what politicians of all parties, the United Nations and its affiliates, prominent economists, and the quality press all say about less developed countries. Has not the vicious circle of poverty, the idea that poverty is self-perpetuating, been a cornerstone of mainstream development economists since the Second World War, and has it not been explicitly endorsed by Nobel laureates Gunnar Myrdal and Paul Samuelson? Have not the development economists at the Massachusetts Institute of Technology said categorically about LDCs that "the general scarcity relative to population of nearly all resources creates a self-perpetuating vicious circle of poverty. Additional capital is necessary to increase output, but poverty itself makes it impossible to carry out the required saving and investment by a voluntary reduction in consumption"?[1]

According to mainstream opinion on the subject, foreign exchange shortages are inevitable concomitants of reasonable development of poor countries, and rapid population growth and colonial status major or even insurmountable obstacles to material advance. Indeed, according to respected academic figures in development economics and representatives of world opinion, even one of the half-dozen characteristics listed above would ensure persistent poverty.

If instead of following fashion you think for yourself and go by obvious evidence, then you will know that Hong Kong, the country in question, has progressed phenomenally since the 1940s, when it was still very poor; and also that it has become such a formidable competitor that leading Western countries erect barriers to protect their own domestic industries against imports from this distant country. If you inquired further, you would know that incomes and real wages have risen rapidly in Hong Kong in recent decades.

If you suspected all along that the established opinion on these matters was patently unfounded, you will welcome a short but instructive monograph, *Hong Kong: A Study in Economic Freedom* (Chicago, 1979), by Dr. Alvin Rabushka. Rabushka, an American political scientist turned economist, knows Hong Kong well, and his wife is Chinese.

Rabushka reviews the processes and methods by which, in less than 140 years, uninhabited barren rocks grew into a major industrial trading and financial center of about five million people. He ascribes this economic success story to the aptitudes of the people and to the pursuit of appropriate policies. Enterprise, hard work, ability to spot and utilize economic opportunities are widespread in a population 98 percent Chinese engaged in singleminded pursuit of making money day and night. Many are immigrants who brought skills and enterprise from the People's Republic of China, especially Shanghai.

The policies emphasized by Rabushka are fiscal conservatism; low taxation; the charging of market prices for specific government services; liberal immigration policy, at least until recently; free trade in both directions; unrestricted movement of capital into and out of the country; and minimal government involvement in commercial life, including refusal to grant privileges to sectional interests. There are no special incentives or barriers to foreign investment and no insistence on local participation in foreign-owned enterprises. There are no tax holidays or other special concessions to foreign investment, but equally, there are no restrictions on the withdrawal of capital or on the remission of profits. These liberal policies, notably the freedom to withdraw capital, were designed to encourage the inflow of productive capital and enterprise, which indeed they did.

Lack of natural resources together with colonial rule encouraged both official economic nonintervention and fiscal conservatism. The lack of natural resources has encouraged an open economy with a large volume of exports to pay for the necessary imports. Such an economy requires a wide range of competitive exports, and also competitive domestic markets. Government assistance to particular economic activities diverts resources from more productive uses and undermines the international competitive position of the economy. Moreover, in an economy as open as Hong Kong, the wasteful results of such subsidies become apparent sooner than elsewhere. Thus the very absence of natural resources has assisted material progress by discouraging wasteful policies.

In the traditional British colonial accounting system colonies were not permitted to run sustained budget deficits, and this tradition was continued after fiscal autonomy in 1958. The absence of election promises, together with an open economy and limited government, has much reduced the prizes of political activity and hence the interest in organizing pressure groups. These circumstances encouraged fiscal conservatism (that is, low taxation), balanced budgets, and the charging of market prices for specific public services. The wish to attract foreign capital, the business outlook of a traditional trading community, and the general preoccupation with moneymaking also worked in this direction.

Official policies and the aptitudes and habits of the population have brought about an economy capable of rapid adjustment. This adaptability has enabled Hong Kong to survive and even to prosper in the face of numerous restrictions against its exports, often imposed or increased at short notice. For social reasons, the principle of charging market prices for specific government services has for some time been subject to major exceptions. Large-scale provision of subsidized housing for the poor, and the rationing of water by cutting off supplies for certain periods rather than by charging higher prices for a continuous supply, are the two most important exceptions. They were introduced after much heart searching and with an eye to local social conditions. The subsidies, moreover, are largely confined to the really poor. In addition to these subsidies in kind there are substantial cash subsidies to the poor to ensure minimum incomes, and there are also various disability and infirmity grants. Comprehensive compulsory primary education, in fact as well as in name, and extensive public health services have operated for many years.

Rabushka's unashamed admiration for Hong Kong, its people, and its market economy pervades his book.

> Dare I reveal my boorishness by saying that I find Hong Kong's economic hustle and bustle more interesting, entertaining, and liberating than its lack of high opera, music, and drama? East has indeed met West in the market economy. Chinese and Europeans in Hong Kong have no time for racial quarrels, which would only interfere with making money. This prospect of individual gain in the marketplace makes group activity for political gain unnecessary—the market economy is truly color-blind. (P. 85)

There is some oversimplification here. For instance, pursuit of moneymaking can readily accompany racial strife in state-controlled economies. In closely controlled economies, moneymaking often goes together with taking advantage of controls: it is rent seeking, to use a currently fashionable term.

The crucial factor is not moneymaking as such but limited government.

Apart from the main themes, Rabushka provides much informative and unexpected detail. For instance, who would have thought that in 1843, soon after Hong Kong became a British colony, that the then British foreign secretary would have insisted that if as a result of the creation of a free port, large numbers of immigrants were to come to Hong Kong, the consequent rise in land values should accrue to the government.

The outstanding lesson of Hong Kong is the overriding importance of personal attributes and motivations, social mores, and appropriate political arrangements for economic achievement. Access to markets is also important, but less fundamental. Other countries also have had access to outside markets and supplies without having produced such an economic success story.

The experience of Hong Kong shows again that economic achievement does not depend on the initial possession of money or the presence of natural resources. Utilization of natural resources depends on people's economic policies and the policies of their governments.

In certain market conditions or political situations the possession or acquisition of natural resources can bring windfalls, even large windfalls; witness the gold and silver of the Americas in the sixteenth century and the operations of OPEC in the twentieth. But hitherto at any rate such windfalls have not led to lasting economic progress, much less to such sustained and spectacular advance as that of Hong Kong. Nor is economic success without natural resources anything new. Conversely, backwardness in the midst of abundant natural resources is evident in large parts of the present Third World, where many millions of extremely backward people live in the midst of unlimited cultivable land. As Tocqueville wrote more than 150 years ago:

> Looking at the turn given to the human spirit in England by political life; seeing the Englishman, certain of the support of his laws, relying on himself and unaware of any obstacle except the limit of his own powers, acting without constraint ... I am in no hurry to inquire whether nature has scooped out ports for him, and given him coal and iron. The reason for his commercial prosperity is not there at all: it is in himself.[2]

Hong Kong's success demonstrates that population increase is not an obstacle to progress, that suitably motivated people are assets not liabilities, agents of progress as well as its beneficiaries. It shows also that economic performance owes little to formal education. In Hong Kong as elsewhere in the Far East, the economic performance or success of hundreds of thousands or even millions of people has resulted not from formal education but from hard work, enterprise, thrift, and ability to use economic opportunity. This fact is disturbing to professional educationalists, who like to market their wares as necessary for economic achievement.

Hong Kong is unpopular with the aid lobbies and the politicized charities. These groups are hostile to people who can dispense with their ministrations. Hence the bad press that Hong Kong has in the West and the hostility it encounters from the great and the good. The achievement is ignored or underplayed, and the shortcomings, whether real or alleged, avoidable or inevitable, are prominently featured. Overcrowding and child labor are examples. In all these respects Hong Kong compares very favorably with the rest of Asia. For instance, real wages are the highest in Asia except for Japan. If a government tries to run a socialist economy, or at any rate a largely state-controlled one, Western politicians, writers, academics, and journalists are apt to present hardship or even suffering there as inevitable, or to commend the policies that contribute to those regrettable conditions. But if the government relies on a market economy, then these *bien-pensants* will condemn any deviation from arbitrary and Western-inspired norms as a defect or even a crime.

The experience of Hong Kong confirms once again that political sovereignty has nothing to do with personal freedom. This fact is blindingly obvious and yet often overlooked. The newly independent African states are habitually termed free, meaning by this that their governments are sovereign. But the people there are far from free, much less so than when they were under colonial rule. They are also much less free than the people of Hong Kong. Hong Kong is a dictatorship in that people do not have the vote. But in their personal life, especially their economic activities, they are far freer than most people in the West, not to speak of the Third World. Hong Kong should remind us that a nonelective government can be more limited than an elected one; and that for most ordinary people it is arguably more important whether government is limited or unlimited than whether it is elective or nonelective.

13
Import Capacity and Economic Development: India

It is often argued that a limited capacity to import is a special factor obstructing economic development, additional to and distinct from a low productivity of resources, that is, a limited capacity to produce; and that therefore developing countries are bound to run into serious or even crippling balance-of-payments difficulties. There is an interesting expression of this influential point of view in an article by Dr. S. J. Patel in the *Economic Journal.*[1] Patel's primary concern was with India, but he considered that his analysis and policy conclusions applied generally to underdeveloped countries. In a later issue of the *Economic Journal*, Professor Anne O. Krueger examined some of Patel's arguments that apply especially to India.[2] Here I discuss the more general aspects and implications of Patel's reasoning, which reflects a widely adopted approach, especially in the fields of international trade, deficit financing, and development.

Patel regarded the stagnation of exports, in conjunction with rapidly rising import requirements (which he considered as a corollary of development efforts), not only as an obstacle to economic development in India and elsewhere but also as the cause of the Indian foreign exchange crisis in the late 1950s. He attributed this stagnation of exports to the allegedly stagnant demand of countries with predominantly private enterprise economies. He supported his argument by reference to the stagnant volume of exports to the West from South Asia, especially India. Moreover, according to Patel the increase in the domestic output of the principal Indian export products, and also the response of jute exports to the Korean boom, showed that the stagnation of the volume of exports reflected stagnation, or even saturation, of demand: "The brief review of the four major commodities that figure in India's exports indicates that in all cases domestic supply has increased and can be increased even more over a period of time if there was an adequate demand."[3] This type of reasoning identifies changes in supply from a particular source with changes in the conditions of demand. Yet changes in the volume of exports from one country are quite different from changes in the conditions of demand for the goods in question in international markets. Most of Patel's presentation failed to distinguish between demand and supply, and between world exports and exports from one country. It further neglected the effects of prices on the quantities demanded. It also ignored the effects of the level of internal demand on the volume of imports as well as on the conditions of supply of exports.

Indian exports, which are largely or wholly standardized products, are only part of the world exports of these commodities and, of course, an even smaller part of total supply. Hence, even if world consumption of these commodities had remained constant or declined, it would be invalid to conclude that the market for Indian exports was saturated. On Patel's own showing, Indian exports of groundnuts were only about 12 percent of world exports, and only about 2 percent of world production; and they were an even smaller proportion of world exports and production of *all* oils and oilseeds, which are largely substitutable. And world production and consumption of oils and oilseeds had increased greatly in recent decades. Indian exports of groundnuts had declined because larger supplies had been diverted to internal consumption. Substantially the same argument applies to some of the other major Indian exports.

Patel did not discuss the effects of price changes on the quantities demanded and thus did not consider the elasticity of demand for Indian export products. For several of these the (price) elasticity of demand is necessarily large. The elasticity of demand for the exports of one country depends on the elasticity of demand for the product as a whole, the share of the particular country in world exports, and the elasticity of supply from rival sources, including home production in importing countries.

Patel instanced the decline of exports relative to domestic sales in India in support of the argument that exports had been limited by foreign demand. But this demonstration was and is irrelevant. It ignored both the level of internal demand and the prices at which Indian products were available for export. Information on India's share of world exports of particular commodities would have been more nearly relevant. An increase of this share in a constant or declining total volume of world exports would more nearly have supported his thesis. In fact, Patel did not produce this information, and the actual development was the opposite: there was an increase in the volume of world exports of these commodities but a decline in India's share.

The Indian exchange crisis emerged independently of the level of demand for Indian exports. It was principally a result of the massive deficit finance of the Second Five-Year Plan. In India as in many other less developed countries, deficit finance refers to the excess of government spending over receipts from taxation, loans from the public, and drafts on government reserves; that is, to a government deficit financed by the creation of money. It does not refer simply to a budgetary deficit. Patel himself wrote that from 1950 through 1956 Indian export earnings paid for 90 percent of imports, whereas since 1956 (the beginning of the Second Five-Year Plan) the proportion had declined to two-thirds. This drastic change was not the result of any long-term trend in export demand, but of the large-scale creation of money of the Second Plan.

In an open system with a fixed exchange rate, large-scale money creation tends to set up a deficit in external payments by increasing the money demand for goods and services, including both imports and potential exports, without a corresponding increase in output (save in certain conditions of general unemployment of resources inapplicable to India). By putting pressure on domestic prices, the process further discourages exports and attracts additional imports, thus further increasing the payments deficit. These results would not follow if the money creation did not exceed the amount necessary to finance expansion of output at stable prices. Indian deficit finance in the late 1950s far exceeded this level. The foreign exchange gap reflected a deficiency in real resources, of which the volume of deficit finance was another manifestation. It reflected the difference between the resources used in India for current investment and consumption and the value of current output, the inflow of foreign capital, and the draft on foreign exchange reserves beyond the rate considered safe.

Patel's analysis of the foreign-trade experience in India is an example of economics without prices and costs. It disregarded major determinants of the volume and value of Indian exports. His approach to the problem of long-term forecasting was similar. Throughout the discussion, prices, costs, exchange rates, and the level of internal demand were disregarded. This is an instance of the tendency to attempt to make long-term forecasts while ignoring the primary relevant factors amenable to economic analysis.

Neither in developed nor in underdeveloped economies is there particular merit in directing resources toward exports or import-saving activities instead of simply trying to ensure that they are deployed to contribute most to present or future output. The distinction between activities yielding or saving foreign exchange and other activities becomes material only if the national currency is overvalued in the sense that the foreign exchange earned or saved, expressed in local currency, understates the contribution of these resources to the flow of income. In the absence of an overvaluation of the exchange rate in this sense, any increase in national output makes the same contribution to available goods and services, regardless of destination. Thus it follows that the capacity to export or to import does not set up obstacles to development distinct from those stemming from the limited capacity to produce.

The concept of a saturated demand for exports, as often found in the development literature, is not clear. If it refers to a price elasticity of demand of less than unity, it would imply a situation in which a country could increase its export earnings by reducing exports and thereby, incidentally, also saving resources. Clearly this is not what is envisaged; nor is such a situation likely to be practically important.[4] Another possible interpretation is a low income elasticity of demand. Again, the practical importance of this type of situation is doubtful, as is suggested, for instance, by variations in international demand between more and less prosperous years.[5] But even where such a situation exists, the situation itself does not represent an additional or peculiar barrier to economic growth, that is, a barrier distinct from or additional to that resulting from a low productivity of resources in the economy. The situation would be analogous to that in a closed economy with resources yielding diminishing value returns in particular activities.[6] The value productivity in turn depends on physical returns and on their value. It is the value productivity of the resources that matters, regardless of whether the output is sold at home or abroad.

There is also no empirical or logical foundation for the suggestion that LDCs necessarily find themselves in chronic balance-of-payments difficulties. There is no support for this view in the earlier history of developed countries or in the experience of many LDCs that have advanced rapidly in the last few decades.

Balance-of-payments difficulties accompany economic development (with or without formal development planning) only when the money demand for resources for consumption and investment exceeds the value of current output, the inflow of foreign capital, and an acceptable rate of draft on reserves. Such conditions are not necessary for economic progress, rapid or otherwise. In both developed and less developed countries rapid progress can occur, and often has occurred, without balance-of-payments difficulties. And conversely, such difficulties can occur, and often have occurred, in stagnant economies, whether rich or poor.

14
Price Response: Cocoa and Palm Oil in Nigeria

There are well-known and serious difficulties in measuring the degree of responsiveness of producers to price changes. There are the familiar problems arising from the usual absence in the real world of anything resembling closely the *ceteris paribus* of the theoretical formulations of functional relationships in economics. There are further difficulties created by time lags between changes in agricultural capacity and changes in output and also by the effects of uncertainty about the permanence of absolute and relative price changes. The problems of testing a hypothesis or of measuring the strength of a functional relationship make it difficult to reach objective assessments, and rival hypotheses are likely to flourish side by side, often deriving from opposing policy preconceptions and sometimes giving rise to opposing policy prescriptions.

There is, therefore, some general interest in the policy of some of the statutory marketing authorities in Nigeria of raising the quality of certain agricultural produce by offering price incentives to peasant producers.[1] This policy was explicitly premised on the hypothesis that peasant producers responded to price differences and would appropriately adjust their behavior as producers to the incentives provided by the authorities. The results of this experiment support the hypothesis. The explicitly formulated hypothesis, the introduction of the measures, and the consistent results closely resemble the methods of observation and experimentation in the natural sciences.

From 1947 to 1954, all major agricultural exports of Nigeria were handled by statutory export monopolies (marketing boards). Two of the marketing boards, the Nigeria Cocoa Marketing Board and the Nigeria Oil Palm Produce Marketing

Board, prescribed wide differentials in the prices paid to producers of cocoa and palm oil for various grades of these products, in order to encourage the production of higher grades. These differentials in producer prices greatly exceeded the grade differentials in the market in which the boards sold the produce. The producer prices and grade differentials were announced before the opening of each season; and the licensed buying agents had to buy all supplies offered to them at not less than the announced prices. The producer therefore knew the additional returns for improving his output by more careful tending of the trees, gathering of the produce, and preparation for sales to the boards.

In their annual reports, the two boards frequently discussed the reason for prescribing wide price differentials between grades, and the outcome of this policy. One extract from the annual report of the Nigeria Cocoa Marketing Board (season 1948–49) reported:

> It is quite certain that, given an adequate cash incentive and the necessary instruction, the Nigerian farmer is capable of producing well-fermented cocoa. That he has not always done so in the past is attributed largely to the fact that the premia offered were too low, for it should be remembered that the fermentation process involves a loss in weight in comparison with beans which are dried only and not fermented.[2]

And in 1951 it stated: "That the Board's policy of offering a premium on first grade quality cocoa has resulted in an ever increasing effort to produce good quality cocoa, is illustrated by the progressively increasing percentage of the total annual tonnage of cocoa marketed in the first grade."[3]

Similarly, in 1954 the Nigeria Oil Palm Produce Marketing Board reported:

> Undoubtedly the major factor in the progressive improvement which has taken place in the quality of Nigerian palm oil over the past five years has been the board's producer price policy which has offered considerable financial inducement by way of price differentials in favour of the production of the higher quality grades. Under this incentive, the fruit has been harvested quicker and more care has been taken in its prepa-

ration. Higher prices have encouraged the greater use of hand-pressing machines which tend not only to improve quality, but also have a more favourable extraction rate than that obtained by traditional methods, and therefore increase production.[4]

Tables 14–1 and 14–2 show the results for cocoa and palm oil, respectively. The producers' responsiveness to the price incentives emerges clearly. Thus, the proportion of Grade I cocoa in the purchases of the Cocoa Marketing Board increased from 47 percent in 1947–48 to 98 percent in 1953–54; and, when purchases of the two lowest grades dwindled to very small quantities, the board discontinued them. Indeed, the increase in the proportion of Grade I cocoa under the stimulus of the price incentive was greater than appears from this series, which begins with the 1947–48 season. Until 1947, under the West African Produce Control Board (the predecessor of the Nigeria Cocoa Marketing Board), the premium of Grade I over Grade II cocoa was only £2.5 per ton, and in 1946–47 Grade I cocoa accounted for only 23 percent of total purchases. The Nigeria Cocoa Marketing Board made a deliberate early decision to substitute three new grades for the previous Grade II and to widen the differential between the Grade I price and the prices of the two lowest grades to £5.5 and £15, respectively; the proportion of Grade I cocoa rose to 47 percent in the 1947–48 season.

From its first year, in 1949, the Nigeria Oil Palm Produce Marketing Board widened the differences in prices paid for the different grades of palm oil. The producer prices paid by the predecessor West African Produce Control Board in 1948 ranged from £32.25 per ton for Grade I to £26.25 for Grave V, a spread of £6 per ton. The new board widened the spread to £16.5 in the first two years of its operation. This measure had little effect on the composition of the board's purchases. The board increased the differentials more markedly in 1951, which was also the first entire year in which the board bought the Special Grade of oil at a special premium price. The extent of the improvement in the produce bought by the board is apparent in the statistics. Thus in 1954, purchases of the Special Grade constituted as much as 60 percent of all purchases, and, as was the

Table 14-1. Nigeria Cocoa Marketing Board producer prices for cocoa and composition of purchases by grades, 1947–1954[a]

Year	Grade I		Grade II			Grade III			Grade IV			Total purchases (1000s of tons)
	Producer price (£ per ton)	% of total board purchases	Producer price (£ per ton)	Difference from Grade I price (£ per ton)	% of total board purchases	Producer price (£ per ton)	Difference from Grade I price (£ per ton)	% of total board purchases	Producer price (£ per ton)	Difference from Grade I price (£ per ton)	% of total board purchases	
1947–48	62.5	47.0	60.0	−2.5	24.7	57.0	−5.5	21.3	47.5	−15.0	7.0	75.0
1948–49	120.0	76.0	115.0	−5.0	21.2	105.0	−15.0	1.8	90.0	−30.0	1.0	109.0
1949–50	100.0	89.4	95.0	−5.0	10.5	75.0	−25.0	0.1	Grade no longer purchased			99.1
1950–51	120.0	95.1	110.0	−10.0	4.9	Grade no longer purchased						110.3
1951–52	170.0	96.0	155.0	−15.0	4.0							107.9
1952–53	170.0	95.0	155.0	−15.0	5.0							109.0
1953–54	170.0	98.2	155.0	−15.0	1.8							97.4

Source: Nigeria Cocoa Marketing Board, annual reports, 1948–1954 (Lagos).

a. Grades were differentiated on the basis of proportions of unfermented or insufficiently fermented beans and of defective beans. The producer prices refer to those paid for main-crop cocoa, which accounted for over 90 percent of total supplies. The small quantity of light-crop cocoa, harvested earlier in the season, was subject to a discount of 5 per ton for all grades (somewhat smaller in 1947–48), until parity of treatment was introduced in 1953–54.

Table 14-2. Nigeria Oil Palm Produce Marketing Board producer prices for palm oil and composition of purchases by grades, 1949–1954

| | Special Grade | | | Grade I | | Grade II | | | Grade III | | | Grade IV | | | Grade V | | | |
| | Producer price (£ per ton) | Difference from Grade I price (£ per ton) | % of total board purchases | Producer price (£ per ton) | % of total board purchases | Producer price (£ per ton) | Difference from Grade I price (£ per ton) | % of total board purchases | Producer price (£ per ton) | Difference from Grade I price (£ per ton) | % of total board purchases | Producer price (£ per ton) | Difference from Grade I price (£ per ton) | % of total board purchases | Producer price (£ per ton) | Difference from Grade I price (£ per ton) | % of total board purchases | Total purchases (1000s of tons) |
Year																		
1949	No special price			42.75	66.4	37.13	− 5.62	14.5	33.0	− 9.75	12.7	29.63	−13.12	6.0	26.25	−16.5	0.4	161.5
1950		+10.25	0.2	42.75	61.3	37.13	− 5.62	17.8	33.0	− 9.75	14.4	29.63	−13.12	5.8	26.25	−16.5	0.5	158.7
1951		+16.0	6.3	55.0	70.8	43.0	−12.0	11.4	34.0	−21.0	7.5	30.0	−25.0	4.0	Grade no longer purchased			135.2
1952		+19.0	29.6	61.0	56.3	47.0	−14.0	7.4	35.0	−26.0	5.2	30.0	−31.0	1.5				178.5
1953		+17.5	50.4	58.0	38.0	45.0	−13.0	7.2	34.5	−23.5	4.4	Grade no longer purchased						205.0
1954		+15.0	60.8	50.0	29.9	38.0	−12.0	4.4	33.0	−17.0	4.9							205.0

Source: Nigeria Oil Palm Produce Marketing Board, annual reports, 1949–1954 (Lagos).

Notes: Grade differences: The original five grades were based on the free-fatty-acid (f.f.a.) content of the oil, ranging from 0 to 9 percent f.f.a. content for Grade 1 in equal increments to 36–45 percent f.f.a. content for Grade V. This classification was maintained, except that in 1952 the permissible range for Grade IV was narrowed to 27–33 percent. The Special Grade refers to "edible" (as distinct from the other "technical") oil, with a low f.f.a. content (up to 4.5 percent).

case for cocoa, purchases of the two lowest grades were discontinued once they had fallen to small quantities.

Another feature of the boards' operations also showed clearly the producers' awareness of economic opportunities and their readiness and eagerness to take advantage of them. Whenever higher prices were announced or even generally anticipated for the following season, producers and intermediaries withheld supplies in the closing months of the previous season; and when a reduction was announced or anticipated, supplies were rushed forward. This response was reflected in statistics of monthly purchases by the boards and was sometimes mentioned in their annual reports.

15
Competition and Prices: Groundnut Buying in Nigeria

Assessment of the relationship between the number of firms and prevailing market prices faces various difficulties. Most of these arise from the familiar problem of finding situations in which all other factors are constant except the one under investigation. A special difficulty is that of defining and delimiting a particular market and of counting the number of firms operating in it; buyers and sellers in a given geographic area may (and indeed usually do) have access to sellers and buyers outside the area. The numerous obstacles probably explain the apparent paucity of statistical studies of this aspect of price behavior despite its wide relevance for economic theory and policy.

In the course of a general study into the economics of trade in British West Africa it emerged that the organization and circumstances of the groundnut trade in Nigeria presented an exceptional opportunity for a systematic statistical inquiry into the influence of the number of firms on market prices. This essay collates information about the numbers of groundnut buyers and the prices paid for groundnuts in different regions and centers, and analyzes the findings.

Groundnuts in Nigeria were produced in two geographically distinct regions. At the time of the inquiry, during the 1949–50 season, about 95 percent of the groundnuts for export were produced in the Kano or so-called Northern area, while the balance came from the Rivers (or Upper Niger–Benue) area. The two areas are separated by large and thinly populated stretches of country. In the period covered by the investigation, groundnuts were not moved from one area to the other by either producers or traders. The produce of both areas was exported by the Nigeria Groundnut Marketing Board, a statutory monopoly, and bought on its behalf by trading firms that acted as its licensed buying agents. In the season 1948–49 there were seventeen licensed buyers operating in the Northern area, and twenty-one in 1949–50. In the Rivers area there were only two firms buying for the board; both of these firms also operated in the Northern area.

The buying agents made their purchases either through middlemen acting for them on a commission basis or through their own clerks, who generally were remunerated partly by salary and partly by commission. The middlemen had their own network of submiddlemen. The clerk and the middlemen or their submiddlemen might be in competition with one another, although ultimately they were buying for the same firm. Most clerks were in charge of retail stores as well; at outstations, produce buying was merely one of their activities. The buying "establishments" of middlemen were generally very simple and often temporary. In the Rivers area the two buying agents purchased through clerks only.

Each season the marketing board prescribed statutory minimum prices to be paid for purchases at a large number of designated markets (gazetted stations) throughout the groundnut-producing areas. In the Kano area the structure of minimum prices pivoted on the uniform price prescribed for all railway stations.[1] In 1949–50 the railway line price was £21 4s. per ton. In the Rivers area the structure pivoted on two basic prices payable along the rivers; the difference in the two Rivers prices (£1 per ton in the period under review) was designed to allow for the approximate differences in the cost of shipment to the ports. In 1949–50 the two basic Rivers prices were £20 and £19 per ton.

At buying stations away from the railway line or the rivers (that is, at road stations), lower minimum prices were prescribed to allow for the cost of transport to the railway or river stations; the difference was known as the transport differential. In a number of road stations in the Kano area the gazetted minimum prices were fixed at higher levels in relation to the basic price at rail stations than would be warranted by the officially calculated transport differentials. This measure was intended to encourage production in outlying areas. For purchases at these subsidy stations the buying agents received so-called transport subsidies from the board designed to cover what otherwise, on official calculations, would have been losses to them.

The buying agents received from the board no more than the relevant minimum prices for the tonnages bought. They also received certain tonnage payments known as "block allowances" to reimburse them for their expenses and to remunerate them for their services. In 1949–50 this block allowance was £4 10s. 6d. per ton for the Kano area, and £4 17s. 9d. for the Rivers area. The principal items included the cost of bags, interest, insurance, and other finance charges, an allowance for overhead expenses, middlemen's commission, and the agents' remuneration. The middlemen's commission allowed on all purchases in the Kano area was 14s. a ton. There was no similar item in the Rivers area because there were no middlemen; but the overhead allowance was raised by more than 13s. in recognition of the fact that all purchases were made through the salaried clerks of the trading firms. The agents' remuneration was 8s. 6d. and 7s. 8d. per ton in the Kano and Rivers areas, respectively. This was 2 percent of the basic price. There was no item for transport costs in the block allowance, since the transport differentials and subsidies were deemed to cover the transport expenses of the firms from the road stations to the railway line or the rivers.

The block allowances in the two groundnut areas were settled by negotiation between the marketing board and the buying agents. There is no reason to believe that they were less generous in the Rivers than in the Kano area. The absolute level was higher in the Rivers area in acceptance of the claims of the buying agents that their costs were higher. Within the total allowance the overhead items were both absolutely and relatively larger in the Rivers area.

Although a fair number of buying agents operated in the Kano area, the organization of the trade might suggest that little buying competition would have taken place there. First, in 1948–49 sixteen of the seventeen agents were members of a confidential market-sharing syndicate; in 1949–50 sixteen out of twenty-one were members. In both 1948–49 and 1949–50 the combined share of members of the syndicate in total purchases was over 90 percent. Members of the syndicate were allotted quotas (shares), and those who purchased more than their quotas made penalty payments to those who underbought.[2] Second, there was a marked degree of concentration in groundnut buying; three of the licensed buying agents, who handled between one-half and three-fifths of total purchases, were financially linked, although their operations locally were largely independent. Third, with very few exceptions all licensed buying agents were European and Levantine (that is, non-African) firms or traders who operated with substantial capital and who possessed a large measure of commercial skill; in many cases their middlemen were non-African also. They bought from customers (producers and small African traders) who in the majority of instances were illiterate, had little capital, and were geographically dispersed.

It might be thought that in the Kano area, price competition, or indeed any form of buying competition, would have been negligible despite the apparently large number of licensed buyers; and that buying competition in the Kano area would not have been materially different from that in the Rivers area, where there were only two buyers.

The reasons for the small number of traders in the Rivers area are fairly clear. The region was sparsely populated, comparatively poor, undeveloped, and backward. It was therefore not an easy market for traders to enter. A further difficulty was that river shipping, the cheapest method of transport, was owned by the two trading firms established in the area. It would have been costly and possibly impracticable for a new trading firm to develop its own river-shipping services.

In fact, there had been a substantial measure of buying competition in the Kano area for many years past, even during the war, despite the existence of confidential buying syndicates and despite an officially established and administered system of buying quotas with fines for overpurchases; moreover, new firms were not allowed to buy produce. The statutory minimum producer prices, which from 1942 to 1946 ranged from £6 to £16 per ton at rail stations, were frequently and increasingly exceeded. At first, such overpayments were of the order of a few shillings per ton, but by 1946 overpayments of 40s. and 50s. per ton were frequent in outlying road stations, where the minimum prices were appreciably lower than those fixed for rail stations. These overpayments were particularly large in areas where there were wide transport differentials or where transport subsidies were paid.

For the two seasons 1948–49 and 1949–50, prices paid to producers were officially recorded at thirty-two road stations in the Kano area. From these statistics, weighted average prices have been calculated. In both years the gazetted minimum prices were exceeded at every station. The highest over-payments were recorded at road stations where the gazetted minimum prices were lowest and where, therefore, the transport differentials, usually augmented by subsidies, were greatest. In 1948–49, overpayments of £3 10s. were frequent at stations where the minimum prices were slightly over £13 per ton. In 1948–49 the overpayment at all thirty-two road stations aver-aged just over £1 per ton on an average price of just over £18; in 1949–50 the corresponding figures were just over £1 5s. on £20 8s.

The presence and the extent of the overpayments were them-selves significant; and they become more notable when con-trasted with the situation in the Rivers area, where there were only two licensed buying agents. With one picturesque excep-tion, no overpayments had been recorded or reported during the war or since.[3] The statutory minimums were observed but nowhere exceeded. The reason was undoubtedly the absence of competition and not the lack of available margins, which, had there been competition, would have been competed away in favor of sellers. In the Rivers area, four-fifths of the tonnage was bought in 1949–50 at buying stations at which only one or other of the two firms was operating. In this large portion of the area informal market sharing was in effect in force.

It would have been interesting to investigate the correlation between the extent of overpayments and the number of buyers at road stations in the Kano area. But the available data cannot be used for this purpose. The amount of the overpayment depended not only on the extent of competition but also on the margin available. This margin was not the same at each road station, principally because it was affected by the difference between the officially recognized transport differential (and subsidy where this applied) and the actual transport costs incurred.[4] Sufficiently detailed information of actual transport costs incurred in the two seasons was not available.

There is some information, more limited in scope but of considerable interest, on prices paid in 1949–50 at nine buying stations on the railway line.[5] It is unlikely that any errors they may contain would significantly alter the conclusions they suggest.

In 1949–50 24,000 tons were bought at these stations; this amount was about 15 percent of total purchases in the Kano area and 45 percent of total purchases at rail stations. At all these stations the gazetted minimum price was £21 4s. per ton. As there were no transport differentials or subsidies, the prime costs of buying groundnuts were about the same at each station; hence the margin available for overpayments was also much the same at each station. The major influence vitiating the comparability of overpayments at different road stations was absent.

Table 15–1 summarizes information on buying operations at the nine railway stations. There were overpayments at six of the nine markets along the railway line. Moreover, the data suggest very strongly that the extent of overpayments was much influenced by the number of traders present.[6] There were only one or two buying agents represented at the three stations at which no overpayments were recorded. At the other extreme there were three stations at which six or more buying agents were represented, and two of these had the largest overpayments.

Numbers of traders alone do not give a full picture of the degree of buying competition at the different stations. It may be expected that, apart from numbers, the intensity of competition would depend upon various other factors. These would include the presence of newcomers trying to find their way into the trade generally or into the particular trading center, and the presence of firms outside the buying syndicate. An additional factor could be the presence of firms without extensive organization that might therefore have had to rely to a greater extent on price inducements to secure supplies.

A heterogeneous group of traders comprising Europeans, Levantines, and Africans was likely to behave more competi-

Table 15–1.   Groundnut purchases and overpayments at nine markets
on the railway line, Northern Nigeria, 1949–50

Station	Number of licensed buying agents	Average overpayment in shillings per ton	Tonnage bought	Average tonnage per buying agent
A	1	0	1,196	1,196
B	2	0	666	333
C	2	0	1,412	706
D	2	10	1,968	984
E	3	11	3,107	1,036
F	4	6	1,975	494
G	6	16	2,885	481
H	7	6	2,756	394
I	10	20	8,967	897

Source: Produce Department, United Africa Company, Kano, Nigeria

tively than a homogeneous group of the same size, as the contacts between members were likely to be less continuous and smooth. In addition, Levantine firms tended to be more individualistic in outlook and behavior.

The influence of competition on prices becomes clearer when the figures in the table, instructive by themselves, are subjected to qualitative analysis. Thus station D, which at first sight appears to be an exception, falls into place; for here a newcomer who was not in the syndicate had entered the market in that season, and had moreover to contend with the difficulties of a late start in the season. At E, a recently established Levantine firm with no extensive organization, again not a member of the syndicate, entered the market. At F and H, where overpayments were modest, only syndicate firms were present. The situation at I was one of some interest in that all ten firms that operated there were members of the buying syndicate, four of them small firms, including three Levantine enterprises. Substantial overpayments occurred even though all buyers were members of the syndicate.

A study of the average tonnages per buyer, in the last column of the table, suggests that differences in overpayments were independent of the scale of operations as measured by average volumes handled. There was evidently no correlation between the average tonnage purchased per firm and the size of overpayment.

These statistics suggest several conclusions. They confirm that the emergence of competition under apparently unpropitious circumstances resulted in substantial overpayments; and they suggest that these overpayments were largely a function of the intensity of competition. They suggest that the number of firms was an important element in the competitive situation and that even small numbers could result in a substantial measure of price competition. But numbers alone do not provide a full explanation; qualitative assessment is also necessary. Here the role of new entry and the composition of the group of competitors appear to have been important.

The heaviest overpayments since 1942–43 (when they were first recorded) occurred in the remote Bornu province. In 1949–50 the overpayments at the principal buying stations in that province were of the order of £3 to £4 per ton on a basic minimum road station price of about £16. The officially calculated transport differentials and subsidies were high and in effect provided the main source from which competition was able to produce overpayments. The actual transport rates between the principal Bornu buying stations and the railway line tended to be far lower than the figures assumed in the calculation of differentials and subsidies. In 1949–50 the officially calculated transport costs from the principal buying stations to Kano were of the order of £10 per ton, whereas the actual costs were about £4 per ton. The main reason for the low actual costs was the cheap rate quoted by owners of trucks returning with little cargo from the Lake Chad area, to which large consignments of merchandise had been conveyed.

The groundnut producers of Bornu were generally illiterate and among the most backward sections of the peasantry of northern Nigeria. Their groundnuts were bought by or on behalf of a handful of generally well-financed and organized alien traders, frequently acting in concert. Yet so far from being exploited, competition among buyers secured for them prices far in excess of the minimum laid down for their protection.

16
Economic History as Theory: An Unrealistic Prospectus

Sir John Hicks's *A Theory of Economic History* (Oxford, 1969) is the most ambitious attempt by a twentieth-century economist to present a theory of world economic history. The scope of the endeavor and Hicks's stature must command serious attention for the book and warrant careful scrutiny and analysis. The book by this Nobel laureate in economics also presents an opportunity to examine yet again the potentialities and limitations of general theories of history.

In the opening chapter Hicks defines his task and the methods by which he intends to pursue it. He proposes to "treat the Economic History of the World as a single process—a process that (at least so far) has a recognizable trend" (p. 7). The inquiry is to span "the whole world" and "the whole span of human history, from . . . the earliest ages of which anthropologists and archaeologists have given us some fragmentary knowledge, right up to . . . the present day" (p. 1).

Instead of using "bits of theory to serve as hypotheses for the elucidation of some particular historical processes," he seeks to apply economic reasoning conceived broadly, on a grand scale, "so that the general course of history, at least in some important aspects, can be fitted into place" (pp. 2–3). By means of a theoretical scheme rooted in economic reasoning he intends to explain the process by which one state of society succeeds another.

Hicks's unifying theme is the transformation of the market in successive economic states of society, from time when the market emerged from what he calls revenue or custom economies up to the present day. He proposes to generalize about this evolution by means of a general "theoretical enquiry . . . the

166

more general the better . . . to classify states of society, economic states of society . . . to look for the intelligible reasons for which one state should give way to another" (p. 6). Such a program requires clear definition of the successive states of society and of the process by which one such state succeeds another. In Hicks's book, however, neither the different states nor the different phases of the process through which they succeed one another are clearly specified or defined. Indeed, the distinguishing characteristics of the economic states of society, that is, the crucial entities, are nowhere identified or defined.

The wide scope of the major theme and of the subthemes is circumscribed by hedging qualifications. Thus Hicks writes, "it is only a *normal* development for which we are looking, so it [the theoretical schema] does not have to cover all the facts; we must be ready to admit exceptions, exceptions which nevertheless we should try to explain" (p. 6). But the reasons why a particular development is to be considered the norm are nowhere presented, and exceptions are not stated, much less pursued.

It may seem as if these difficulties are met by Hicks's references to statistical uniformities in history. "Every historical event has some aspect in which it is unique; but nearly always there are other aspects in which it is a member of a group, often of quite a large group. If it is one of the latter aspects in which we are interested, it will be the group, not the individual, on which we shall fix our attention; it will be the average, or norm, of the group which is what we shall be trying to explain" (p. 3).

It may at times be useful to classify historical events and changes into groups. Demographic phenomena and sequences are an example. But Hicks does not proceed in this manner. He does indeed often present individual episodes, but he does not explain or establish, by enumeration or otherwise, why his examples are normal or typical in a statistical, or some other, sense. Nor does he explain by what criteria or on what grounds his "states of society, economic states of society" are amenable to informative classification.

Thus the avowed organizing principle of the inquiry is not applied to the record of history. The author's approach to the historical process is casual in the extreme. His procedure is mainly to consider why one situation, or state of society, can give way to another; and he does this almost exclusively by examining implications rather than by narrating and analyzing historical events and sequences. The references to averages and statistical uniformities suggest extensive reliance on statistical evidence, perhaps even a largely inductive method. But another passage proposes a procedure that is almost exclusively deductive: "My plan is that we begin with this transformation [the Rise of the Market], that we seek to define it, and then see, so far as we can, what logically follows from it. We shall look over our shoulders at the historical record, so as to see that we do not put our logical process into a form which clashes with the largest and most obvious facts. (This is only the first stage of fitting, but it is as far as we shall go.) As we continue with the implications, many things, we shall find, will fit into place" (pp. 7–8). This deductive method is adopted practically throughout. References to the historical record are confined to casual glances, to ensure no more than that the results of logical inference do not clash with the "largest and most obvious facts." However, since the declared concern is with the normal and the average, even this rough checking procedure is of very little use, because Hicks does not tell us how to establish an average or a norm, or how to decide whether an inconvenient fact is an irrelevant abnormality or a refutation of the theory.

Hicks's concept of the underlying trend poses similar problems. His theory is supposed to explain how the economic states of society logically succeed one another. And yet, "we are not to think of our normal process as one which, on being begun, is bound to be completed" (p. 6). But again he does not say how we can discern or define the underlying trend or normal process.

Though described by him as a theory of history, Hicks's theory cannot be checked by confrontation even with "the largest and most obvious facts," as he does not tell us how to distinguish the normal from the abnormal, the average from the atypical. And although he claims that his theory explains the course of economic history up to the present, he explicitly doubts whether it can predict the future (p. 8). Thus, future events will not be able to refute the theory either, even though it claims to explain an underlying (albeit unspecified) trend.

In his concluding paragraph, Hicks writes (p. 167):

I have tried to exhibit economic history, in the way that the great eighteenth-century writers did, as part of a social evolution much more widely considered. I have tried to indicate the lines that connect the economic story with the things we ordinarily regard as falling outside it. But when one becomes conscious of these links, one realizes that recognition is not enough. There are threads that run from economics into other social fields, into politics, into religion, into science and into technology; they develop there, and then run back into economics. These I have made little attempt to follow out; but I am in no way concerned to deny their existence.

This passage confirms again that Hicks does not offer a coherent theory that can be assessed rigorously. It is absolutely impossible to distinguish systematically between failure of the theory to explain what it claims to be able to explain, and inability of the theory to explain what lies outside its apparently restricted scope as delimited by the author.

Hicks claims to interpret economic history broadly, to note the findings of cognate disciplines, and to acknowledge the influence of institutions. But at least from the phase he terms the rise of the market he envisages institutions and institutional change as emerging from economic activity, as serving its purpose, and thus in effect as being only dependent variables. Apart from one or two quite perfunctory remarks which refer mostly to preclassical antiquity, neither religion nor any other belief is mentioned as influencing either conduct or social institutions. Religion and religious differences are ignored as influences on conduct, as agents of history, and as parameters of economic life.[1] In general, in Hicks's account the causal relationship runs almost exclusively from economics to the other social fields, and not in the reverse direction.

Hicks explicitly disclaims affinity with Spengler and Toynbee. He does not intend to present "a grand design of history." His theory "will be a good deal nearer to the kind of thing that was attempted by Marx, who did take from his economics some general ideas which he applied to history, so that the pattern he saw in history had some extra-historical support. That is much more the kind of thing I want to try to do" (p. 2). The theories of history of Marx, Spengler, Toynbee, and Hicks all exhibit instances of considerable insight. Economists may prefer Marx and Hicks to Toynbee and Spengler either for political reasons or because of their emphasis on economic factors. But all four share the basic flaws of the use of ill-defined concepts and an arbitrary choice of examples and periods.

It is not possible systematically to examine Hicks's theory of economic history, because he does not in fact pursue his own declared objective. What he regards as a theory of economic history is not susceptible to methodical review. My discussion must therefore focus on the specific major issues and events he introduces in support of this theory.

Whatever the shortcomings or limitations of *A Theory of Economic History*, it contains, as one would confidently expect from Sir John Hicks, several insights and penetrating observations. There are three matters on which his discussion is especially useful.

Hicks envisages economic history as a series of transformations of the mercantile or market economy. The process begins with the custom-command economy from which the early market emerges, and extends to the modern phase, in which the market is in retreat before new types of command and revenue economies. This approach may prove a fruitful way of organizing and (possibly) of interpreting much of the material of economic history, and may serve to provide a pattern of its course over large time spans and areas. It seems distinctly preferable to systems of interpretation that emphasize the role of single variables such as technology, entrepreneurship, social class, or capital. Hicks's system can accommodate the phenomenon of economic decline, which some of the familiar models cannot do.

In general, Hicks does not trace the interplay between economic forces and political developments. However, he has a thought-provoking discussion of the impact of the transformation of the market economy upon political centralization. Thus he writes (p. 100):

The Mercantile Economy, in its First Phase, was an escape from political authority—except in so far as it made its own political authority. Then, in the Middle Phase, when it came formally back under the traditional political authority, that authority was not strong enough to control it. It might destroy, but it could not control. In the Modern Phase, into which we have now passed, that is changed. Largely because of the internal evolution of the Mercantile Economy, control over it has become immensely easier. This is so, whatever is the political structure, and whatever are the ends of the controllers. Their powers will serve them alike for War or Peace, for the solving of social problems or for smothering them.

Hicks reformulates Adam Smith's celebrated maxim that the division of labor depends on the extent of the market by saying that it depends on the concentration of demand. Adam Smith's dictum is indeed invalid if the term *market* denotes organization for the voluntary exchange of goods or the volume of voluntary exchanges. There can be much highly specialized activity when there is no market in this sense, as is evident both from the relics of antiquity, especially in Egypt, and from the experience of present-day command economies, such as the Soviet Union. Hicks's reformulation is more than a semantic one. The market in the sense of organization for voluntary exchange is but one method of achieving the necessary concentration of demand. Hicks's concept of the revenue economy likewise is illuminating as a summary description of conditions that make possible the emergence of highly sophisticated specialization, reflected for example in magnificent structures, works of art, and artifacts, in periods when most people are very poor.

In Sir John Hicks's exposition, the city-state system is crucial for the development of the mercantile economy[2] and "is the principal key to the divergence between the history of Europe and the history of Asia. The reason . . . is mainly geographical. The city-state of Europe is a gift of the Mediterranean" (p. 38).

This formulation embodies simple geographic determinism and ignores straightforward historical evidence. The three ethnic groups or nations of classical antiquity that most profoundly affected the evolution of Europe were the Jews, the Greeks, and the Romans. The Jews and the Romans formed no mercantile city-states, and some of the major Greek city-states were not mercantile city-states, in Hicks's sense of communities with much external trade and ruled by a trading class.[3] Moreover, the geographic configuration of the Mediterranean played little part in the emergence of some major city-states, such as early Rome. Hicks also explicitly recognizes that the coastal areas and islands of Southeast Asia are similar to those of the Mediterranean but explains that in Asia "opportunities . . . were less and difficulties greater" (p. 39).[4]

Nor is it appropriate to assign a key causal role to the city-state, especially to the commercial city-state, in the evolution of Europe. That this emphasis is misplaced is suggested, for instance, by the comparatively small influence of the Phoenician trading cities, including Carthage (certainly a city-state), on the course of history. They were not centers of intellectual or artistic life, but places where an authoritarian tradition was maintained or even reinforced. The character and influence of the Greek city-states and the different evolutions of Europe and Asia are probably better seen as reflections of a greater intellectual enterprise and restlessness, and a less pronounced authoritarian tradition in Europe than in most of Asia. These differences were already notable by the sixth century B.C. and may have originated in various climatic, political, and religious influences.

Although Hicks emphasizes the role of the city-states in the evolution of Europe, he does not mention what was probably their most important single contribution in this context, namely their role in promoting and protecting personal freedom and intellectual activity. Of course, the cities could play such a role only in the absence of a strongly authoritarian tradition: compare Athens with Sparta (Lacedaimon) or Carthage.

Important as were some commercial city-states in certain periods and in some areas, Hicks greatly overstates their general significance. Many cities, including those that subsequently developed into city-states, originated in activities other than trade. They began as political, military, administrative, or religious centers, including pilgrimage centers or staging-posts for pilgrimages; or as places where life, property, and civic and religious activity could best be protected. Thereafter they often grew into trading centers, an outcome that was facilitated by the relative concentration of population. City-states then developed from trading centers when political and military conditions were favorable. Venice is one example. But many large cities, including those preeminent over long periods, such as Alexandria and Paris, did not become city-states. And not only was Paris never a city-state, but its rise to eminence owed little to trade. Several of the major city-states of the classical world were not mercantile city-states, as interpreted by Hicks. Sparta and Thebes were not primarily mercantile communities. Nor was Rome, which, as Hicks rightly recognizes, was a nonmercantile city-state until it suddenly expanded into an empire after the Second Punic War. The artistic and literary flowering of Western Europe in the twelfth century, most pronounced in France, owed nothing to city-states. Moreover, commercial city-states emerged in only a handful of instances, primarily classical Greece, medieval Italy, the Low Countries, and the Hansa. They played no part in any other major economies, including those of Britain, France, and, of course, the United States.

According to Hicks, city-states and their legal institutions were broadly similar. This generalization covers Carthage and Florence, and the presence or absence of such practices as slavery and infanticide. Such a historical generalization has little to commend it. Hicks considers also that the establishment of external settlements and colonies from the time of the Phoenicians right up to the seventeenth century was "the same story, in some essential respects, in each case" (p. 50). Thus he regards as substantially identical the establishment of Greek colonies in Asia Minor in antiquity; of Venetian quarters in the Levant; the conquests by the Dutch in Southeast Asia in the seventeenth century; the British settlements in North America in the same period; and presumably the Spanish conquests in the Americas. These countries, colonies, and communities differed greatly in their economic and political arrangements, in their degree of political subordination to the country or city of origin, in their relations to other communities, and in their right and ability to trade independently. Little is gained by regarding either their origin or their activities as similar in unspecified essentials.

Hicks links the Venetian-led sack of Constantinople in 1204

and the exploitation of Bengal in the eighteenth century as "evils that belong to the [trading] situation" (p. 52). The supposed connection is, however, extremely tenuous. The sack of Constantinople occurred within a few years or decades of such calamities as the devastation of large parts of the Arab world and Europe by the Mongols, and the first French (Angevin) invasion of Italy, which culminated in the Sicilian Vespers. These episodes had nothing to do with "trading situations." The sack of Constantinople cannot be understood apart from its complex political and religious background, especially the enmity between the Greek and Latin churches, a matter not mentioned by Hicks. And Warren Hastings would not have been impeached if his exactions had been inherent in the situation. Moreover, in Bengal such exactions (or worse ones) by the rulers had long antedated the arrival of the British and were regarded locally as being in the nature of things.[5]

In his discussion of the decline of the trading role of the city-states, Hicks writes that "when the point comes that it [expansion of trade] no longer absorbs the same energy, art can be pursued for art's sake, and learning for the sake of learning. It was at the end of her period of commercial expansion that Athens became the 'mother of arts,' it was after their commercial expansion was completed that Florence and Venice became the homes of the High Renaissance" (pp. 58–59). Three comments are in order on this treatment of the interplay between trade and art. First, the explanation neglects the long history of major developments in the arts in Italy during the period of trade expansion. Second, the efflorescence of the arts in Holland coincided with a rapid expansion of trade, as it also did in Shakespeare's England. (Hicks claims, incidentally, that the nation-state of Holland "had much in common with the city-states"; p. 143.) Third, according to Hicks it was the decline in trading opportunities in the eighteenth century that provided the stimulus to the development of manufacturing industry in England (pp. 143–144). But it is by no means clear that there was such a decline in trading opportunities, nor is it clear why the supposed decline did not lead to a flourishing of the arts.

In Hicks's schema, the modern phase is "the [economic] state the world is in at the present day" (p. 160). All economies now in existence are to be regarded, it seems, as being in the modern phase, because the only distinguishing feature of this category is that the member-economies all exist now. Hicks here completely abandons the scheme that underpins his treatment of history and is the core of his theory. He now regards all economies existing in the world today as being in the modern phase, although many of these have not been through the Industrial Revolution or the Rise of Modern Industry. Thus in Hicks's treatment of the modern phase, recourse to the calendar has replaced even the semblance of an attempt at analysis or theory. The radical shift in treatment is particularly startling when it is remembered that Hicks's city-state phase of society ranges in time from the Greek city-states through the Italian city-states and the Dutch Republic to contemporary Singapore—the latter belongs simultaneously, it seems, to two different economic states of society, namely the city-state and the modern phase, which are elsewhere widely separated in Hicks's scheme of things.

The sketchiness of treatment and the blurring of relevant differences characteristic of the book as a whole are especially pronounced here. Thus it is the entire world that is in the modern phase, a phase that embraces aborigines and tribal societies as well as the highly industrialized societies of North America, Western Europe, and Japan. This is abstraction to a point where it is no longer a useful simplification but an unhelpful travesty of reality. It is the outcome of Hicks's bold attempt at historical generalization across the world and across the ages.

Hicks seems to regard the billions of people of the less developed countries as if they were both uniform among themselves, that is, a homogeneous aggregate, and also similar in culture and conduct to the peoples of the developed world, from whom they differ only in being poorer. They are the proletariat of the modern phase, ready to be absorbed into the industrial working class. Malaysian peasants, Chinese millionaires, Indian laborers, Arabs of the Middle East, tribal Africans, Latin American industrialists, aborigines, and pygmies—all are much of a muchness and are seen as being at the same stage as were the people of Western Europe in the eighteenth and nineteenth centuries. Hicks does not even so much as hint at possible differences in faculties, attitudes, mores, and institutions anywhere in the world, either past or present, or in the less developed world, or between developed and underdeveloped countries. Humanity in total is and was an undifferentiated mass.

Hicks does not, in fact, discuss the so-called modern phase as an economic state of society, but limits his concluding chapter largely to a consideration as to whether the growing "pre-industrial proletariat" of the present less developed world can be absorbed into the ranks of modern industry. His first answer is that the industrial expansion required for this absorption "is indeed enormous; but the expansive power of Modern Industry—the fully science-based industry of the twentieth cen-tury—is also enormous" (p. 158). He sees only two substantial obstacles to a worldwide expansion of modern industry, namely the restrictive autarkic policies of governments of less devel-oped countries and their proneness to spend lavishly on politi-cally popular purposes.[6]

Hicks thinks that governments of less developed countries pursue restrictive policies because they fear certain economic consequences of more liberal policies, primarily displacement of local labor as a result of competition from imports.[7] Reality is considerably more complex than this. The economic policies of these governments reflect the play of political forces, especially the views of the rulers about the most effective way of staying in power, controlling their subjects, pleasing their followers, and dispensing patronage. The policies sometimes also reflect the operation of intellectual fashions from abroad. According to Hicks, the second obstacle to the expansion of modern industry is the readiness of governments of LDCs to devote resources to social expenditure, to prestige expenditure, "or to any expendi-ture for which support can be whipped up" (p. 166). Govern-ment policies do indeed obstruct economic progress in most less developed countries. But it is naive to believe that more favor-able policies would bring an early, worldwide industrial revolu-tion. Such a belief overlooks the limits to rapid modernization set by parameters usually regarded as noneconomic.

A major argument of the chapter titled "The Industrial Revolu-tion" is that widespread hardship (termed "pain and grief" by Hicks) is a concomitant of the capital accumulation involved in this process. Much of the chapter deals with the question of the "lag of [real] wages behind industrialization" and with the reasons why the rise in wages was delayed during the industrialization of England between, say, 1780 and 1840.

It is not clear why a delay in the rise of real wages should bring about "pain and grief." A decline in real wages can cause hardship, but a delay in their rise cannot do so. Hicks offers no evidence whatever for the nature, presence, and extent of the supposed pain and grief. Nor does he in this context mention the experience of any other country in Western Europe or North America. In these areas industrialization was not accompanied even by the semblance of widespread hardship that is supposed to accompany an industrial revolution.

Hicks suggests two reasons for the alleged pain and grief in England during the Industrial Revolution. The first is the rapid increase in population. But why did population increase rapidly if there was large-scale hardship? An increase in population reflects a decline in mortality, that is, a rise in life expectation. This is an improvement in conditions, and is generally the result of improved health, nutrition, housing, and clothing. As a second reason Hicks suggests that a switch from circulating capital to fixed capital can bring about a fall in the rate of growth of circulating capital, and thus slowed growth in the demand for labor. Hicks writes that it "is not at all unreasonable to suppose that something of this kind did indeed happen in England, during the first quarter, or even the first third, of the nineteenth century" (pp. 152–153). He offers no evidence of any significant switch to fixed capital over this period any more than he does of pain and grief. Nor does he mention findings such as those of Professor Sydney Pollard that suggest that any such switch was relatively unimportant.[8] Hicks attaches particular importance to investment in machinery. This category of fixed investment is a relatively small part of total investment in any country over any period for which reasonably reliable statistics are available. Because this form of investment does not require substantial drafts on real resources, it does not entail a significant sacrifice in living standards. It is a misconception that investment spending on machinery involves heavy sacrifices in the early stages of industrialization. Hicks presents this much-canvassed idea without any examination of its substance. He also ignores the technical advances during the Industrial Revolution, which were often capital-saving. Thus improvements in transport reduced requirements of circulating capital, as, for instance, in the holding of stocks.

The unifying theme of Professor Hicks's book is the rise and transformation of the market. He promises (p. 8) that as one continues with the implications of this transformation, "many things . . . will fit into place." One such example is the experience of the Soviet Union.

It is one of Hicks's arguments that developments in the mercantile economy have immensely facilitated government control of the economy itself, primarily by making possible what Hicks terms the "Administrative Revolution in Government," which can be dated almost precisely to the First World War. The opportunity for control was seized "with avidity" by the revolutionary governments of Russia and, later, of China. Hicks observes that these were countries "where the Mercantile Economy had not penetrated deeply" (pp. 162–163). He does not attempt to resolve the apparent contradiction that a development that is supposed to depend on the attainment of a high level of market economy occurs in countries "not deeply" affected by it. Nor does he specify what component of the administrative revolution is crucial to the power of the Soviet government over its people. No administrative revolution worthy of the name was necessary for the development of a highly disciplined party whose leaders were ready to deal ruthlessly with opposition and dissent, nor was it necessary for the construction of minefields and barbed-wire barriers to stop people from leaving the country, or of prisons for the opposition. In short, what can be explained readily in simple terms has been made to "fit into" Hicks's theory of economic history. The characteristically allusive treatment of specific historical incidents and sequences provides superficial plausibility to the fitting-in process.

Hicks regards protectionism and autarkic policies as one of the major obstacles to the economic growth of the present less developed countries, and he claims that the "case of Russia is not fundamentally dissimilar . . . The Russians have made a much better hand at autarkic development than the majority of less developed countries have done, or are likely to do, chiefly because of the greater variety of natural resources that are at their disposal" (p. 164). However, he does not mention the long period of industrial development before 1917. There is here a parallel with his earlier discussion of the Industrial Revolution in England, in which he refers neither to the preceding agricultural revolution nor to the many centuries of development that went before both revolutions. Neither does he instance the well-attested central role of Western science and technology in Soviet technical progress, or the manifold Western contributions to the maintenance of the Soviet economy, which have extended even to the supply of wheat. These facts cast serious doubt on the appropriateness of the term *autarky* when applied to the Soviet Union. Nor does he consider the pertinent differences between prerevolutionary Russia and much of the present less developed world in such matters as people's abilities, mores, and social institutions. The Russia of 1914 or 1917 was not like, say, Zaire in 1980.

Despite its greater endowment of natural resources, Hicks explains that the Soviet Union has "not been able to avoid going through the pain and grief which is characteristic of the early stage of an Industrial Revolution, when adequate capital cannot be drawn from abroad" (p. 64). Here again Hicks does not specify the nature and extent of the pain and grief. He would presumably agree that much of the loss of life and other forms of suffering in the Soviet Union, especially during the forced collectivization during the purges of the 1930s, cannot reasonably be regarded as necessary or inescapable corollaries of industrialization.

The remaining reference to Russia occurs in the context of the mercantilization of agriculture. Hicks writes (pp. 108–110) that from the late Middle Ages until recently the landowners of East Central and Eastern Europe oppressed the peasants more severely than did those in Western Europe.

The decline in population, which was the occasion for this parting of the ways, was itself a transitory phenomenon; in a couple of generations, or a little longer, it had probably been made up. But the habits and the social institutions which had grown up as a reaction to it were not easily eradicated. Prussia and Poland and Russia remained for centuries in the grip of a nobility of landlords, extracting what revenue they could from poor peasants whom they kept dependent upon them, defending as their lifeline an oppressive system which they were unwilling to reform for fear that the house of cards they had built would fall on their heads. (P. 113)

This suggestion of long and severe subjection invites the question why the peasants in the seventeenth and eighteenth centuries failed to escape in order to improve their lot, when much of this region was repeatedly fought over from end to end. However, another aspect of this discussion is of greater interest. In a tantalizing footnote Hicks appears to relate the earlier divisions of Europe into two different agricultural systems to a contemporary division. He writes: "It is no more than a coincidence that the frontier which so long separated these agricultural systems has so striking a resemblance to the Curtain which is dividing Europe at the present day. It can be no more than a coincidence; yet the long experience that has moulded men's minds in one way on one side, and in another on the other, has an effect that is recognizable today, even when the division is expressed in very different terms" (p. 114).

It is hard to take seriously the suggestion that people's habits and mentalities differ significantly on the two sides of the Iron Curtain, and that these differences somehow explain its emergence and acceptance. The very existence of the Curtain and the barriers to exit from one side are clear evidence that mentalities do not differ greatly. If people's mentalities did differ greatly, it would not be necessary to use force to prevent people from leaving the eastern bloc countries. Thus the Curtain by itself is an immediate and direct refutation of Hicks's fanciful speculation. Moreover, the region east of the Curtain includes Bohemia and central Germany, which were highly commercialized and industrialized for centuries, and not simply societies ruled by landowners. In fact, explanation of the existence and location of the Curtain does not call for a theory of economic history or recourse to historical continuities. The Curtain represents a division agreed upon by the Allies in the latter stages of the Second World War. Had the

Soviet forces occupied France, Italy, or Austria, the Curtain would have been drawn that much further west. Indeed, insofar as mentalities and preferences are relevant, it is notable that in France and Italy in open elections now the Communist parties enjoy much greater popular support than they ever did east of the Curtain (or seem to do now, for that matter). It is not only unnecessary but also misleading to look beyond political forces for the establishment of the Curtain, and beyond coercion for the maintenance of a political system on one side of it.[9]

Altogether, Hicks's treatment of the Soviet experience and the industrial revolution shows all too clearly the outcome of attempting to write history without examining the evidence, and of neglecting the time dimension in an apparently historical inquiry. Such an approach invites uncritical acceptance of fanciful and fashionable notions that may be totally without substance. Hicks's treatment of these topics also makes it clear that even foremost economic theorists may be prone to such practices, and thereby vulnerable to the seductive influence of even trivial intellectual fashion and political prejudice.

In his first chapter Hicks not only promises to present a discernible or definable theory of world economic history; he even specifies two distinct though related methods by which he proposes to pursue his quest. The first method is that of inference from statistical uniformities of some aspects of historical events. The second is examination of the implications of particular phenomena in order to deduce how one situation leads predictably to another. But as we have seen, he does not in fact present a general theory of economic history. Hicks rightly abandons his announced quest, since its objective is unattainable by either of his two methods, or indeed by any other.

There are various reasons why the search for statistical uniformities is of little use for the explanation and prediction of the general course of history. It is generally difficult or even impossible to specify the class or category of events from which examples should be selected, or for that matter have been selected. And even if certain statistical uniformities have been discerned between clearly defined phenomena, we often cannot tell whether these uniformities reflect functional relationships between the variables examined. Nor is it possible to predict with confidence whether the uniformities or relationships will persist, because the parameters or their interaction with the phenomena and relationships under observation shift and vary.[10] Finally, the influence of chance, including the operation of factors external to the society or activity under observation, is so frequent and potent that it often swamps the operation of the variables in which one is interested, and which may often have been decisive in the past.[11]

The disproportionate impact of some people on the course of events, and also significant characteristics of people's motivations and conduct, much restrict, or indeed negate, the usefulness of statistical uniformities for explaining and predicting the course of history. To begin with, some individuals affect the course of history, including economic history, far more than the rest of mankind. Obvious instances include Julius Caesar, Christ, Muhammad, Charlemagne, Luther, Marx, Lenin, Stalin, Mao Tse-tung, and Hitler. Their emergence, motivations, and actions or people's responses to them cannot be explained in terms of statistical uniformities or generally in terms of economic factors. Statistical uniformities or economic factors would not have helped in forecasting Caesar's decision to cross the Rubicon, or Ludendorff's action in sending Lenin to Russia, or that of the majority of the British government to declare war in 1914, or for that matter the policies of the Federal Reserve Board in the 1930s. And the same individual's response to apparently similar situations varies greatly at different times: witness Chamberlain's reaction to the international political situation in 1938 and 1939, respectively; and Roosevelt's support of the different responses on the two occasions. Much the same applies to the conduct of groups and collectivities. For instance, German university students reacted very differently to prosperity in the late nineteenth century and in the midtwentieth century.

Retrospective explanations and interpretations can be offered about the sequence of events and the conduct of persons and groups. But even in conditions that are as nearly identical as we can make them, we cannot foretell either the sequence of events or the conduct of people in contexts of historical importance. There are many valid generalizations that can be made about the physical, psychological, material, and spiritual conditions of humankind throughout the ages.

But these generalizations are not about variables that predictably affect the course of history, or whose operation is sufficiently powerful to resist the impact of mere chance or of external factors. In the field of human conduct statistical uniformities are useful for prediction only at levels that are trivial in the context of the historical development of societies, such as that most people will continue to get married. Outside such trivialities, few forecasts and predictions of historical processes based on statistical uniformities have succeeded. Even demographic forecasts have often failed, from the time of Malthus to the present day. Yet demographic forecasters enjoy exceptional advantages. In their field statistical analysis is highly advanced; it also relates to large numbers of instances, and what is perhaps most distinctive and significant in demography, statistical techniques can take advantage of firmly based biological categories such as the limits of the childbearing age. In social studies, this latter advantage is most unusual because the distinctions and categories on which they rely are rarely so clearly defined and stable.

Like many social scientists and some historians, especially Marxist historians, Hicks often personifies collectivities such as city-states or underdeveloped countries, and endows them with powers to make decisions, express sentiments, and pursue courses of action. This familiar practice obscures the fact that these decisions are taken by people either individually or in groups, who face choices, and who *ex ante* have to weigh costs, risks, and results. They normally do not know what the outcome will be, and observers cannot normally predict their decisions.

Hicks's other suggested method, the examination of the implications of situations to predict the sequence of events, is primarily deductive. Unfortunately, this method does not provide a worthwhile theory of economic history either.

Most historical events and sequences do not issue in unique and unambiguous results. Widely different results can emerge from given initial conditions. Close investigation of the *ex post* situation is necessary to reveal which of several and often numerous possible results have actually issued from a particular antecedent situation. And even the definition or interpretation of the initial conditions, as well as the assessment of large and apparently obvious facts, requires more than a casual glance over one's shoulder. To speculate about situations and processes without looking at actual experience is to risk losing touch with reality.

Anyone presenting a theory of history is confronted by countless events and sequences from which it is necessary to choose. Supporters of a particular theory can always find events and interpretations in support of that theory. They can do so whether they think their generalizations (the uniformities they claim to have discerned), that is, the so-called laws of history, reflect the unfolding of God's will or the influence of economic determinism. That way lies arbitrariness, both in the choice of events and in their interpretation. These considerations apply generally to theories of history, and also to attempts to divide its course into specific stages. Successful division of a sequence into distinct stages requires that the stages themselves, the turning points and the processes by which one stage leads to another, be distinct and definable. The life cycles of living organisms satisfy these criteria. So-called stages of history generally do not.

Neither statistical inference nor examination of the implications of situations can serve as the basis for a worthwhile theory of history. This is the reason for the inadequacy of economic determinism as the explanation of world economic history. The explanation and predictions of the course of history derived from economic determinism have been spectacularly unsuccessful, without affecting its appeal. Nor has this appeal been diminished by frequent exposure of its short-comings, such as its evident irrelevance to major decisions that have shaped historical events, or the many obvious instances in which people have taken decisions contrary to their material interests. Indeed, economic determinism has often led its exponents to inferences diametrically opposed to what they thought passed as analysis of a particular situation. In the 1930s some adherents of economic determinism argued that capitalism must necessarily lead to war, on the ground that only large-scale production of arms or even outright war could prevent the collapse of the capitalist system. Other economic determinists insisted that capitalism must lead to appeasement or even to total surrender by the West, because the capitalists could not tolerate the disruption of the profit system.

Although Hicks does not pursue systematically his quest for a general theory of history, the familiar characteristics of such attempts are conspicuous in his book. Heroic abstraction and aggregation and the treatment of collectivities as if they were single decisionmaking units are instances.

Like other architects of general theories of history, Hicks envisages that the relationships between specifically economic activities and such factors as people's attitudes and social institutions are largely one-way. He regards the causal relationship as running almost entirely from the former to the latter, even when the reverse relationship would seem to be far more significant.

Construction of a general theory of history to cover all ages and all mankind is a will-o'-the-wisp. The attempt is both sterile and damaging. It generally diverts attention and effort from more modest but much more informative and intellectually rewarding endeavors. Worthwhile study of history requires the patient and systematic collection of material and correspondingly methodical examination at some depth of evidence drawn from the actual record of history. It requires also the drawing of inferences from the various sources of evidence, and subsequent comparison of results with the findings of other such exercises, including those in cognate fields of study. The same considerations apply to the study of economic development, which is an integral aspect of history. Attempts to construct overarching theories of development and to use them as bases for prediction have been uniformly unsuccessful from Marx onward, however seductive their appeal.

Economic reasoning can be helpful to the study of history, even when it is no more than the use of "bits of theory to serve as hypotheses for the elucidation of some particular historical processes," in Hicks's rather dismissive formulation. Such endeavors may well appear pedestrian beside attempts to construct a general theory of history, but they are likely to tell us far more about reality, either past or present. The quest for a general theory of history can also have more widely damaging results. Many of those who have claimed to have discerned the laws of history have simultaneously claimed it as their right, or even as their duty, to interpret and to enforce these laws. They have claimed it as their mission to bring about and hasten an outcome that was in any case inevitable. And in the pursuit of this march the proponents of these ambitious claims have been ready to tolerate or to perpetrate large-scale and lasting brutality. The pretense of having successfully discovered such laws has served as spurious moral or intellectual justification for such conduct. For instance, it has served to underpin the Marxist-Leninist position at popular, academic, and political levels.

Outstanding scholars, among them Pieter Geyl, Sir Karl Popper, and Professor G. R. Elton, have exposed the futility of attempts to construct general theories of history. But the intellectual and political appeal of these endeavors is such that it is safe to predict that there will always be those who are willing to attempt them.

17
Development Economics: A Retrospective View

This essay summarizes the principal components of the burgeoning development literature of the early postwar years.[1]

The advance of less developed countries depends on ample supplies of capital to provide for infrastructure, for the rapid growth of manufacturing industry, and for the modernization of their economies and societies. The capital required cannot be generated in the LDCs themselves because of the inflexible and inexorable constraint of low incomes (popularized as the vicious circle of poverty and stagnation), reinforced by the international demonstration effect and by the lack of privately profitable investment opportunities in poor countries with their inherently limited local markets. General backwardness, economic unresponsiveness, and lack of enterprise are well-nigh universal in the less developed world. Therefore, if significant economic advance is to be achieved, governments have an indispensable as well as a comprehensive role in carrying through the critical and large-scale changes necessary to break down the formidable obstacles to growth and to initiate and sustain the growth process. External trade is at best ineffective for the economic advance of LDCs, and more often it is damaging.

These ideas became the core of mainstream academic development literature, which in turn has served as the basis for national and international policies ever since. Even when some elements of the core have disappeared from academic writings, they have continued to dominate political and public discourse, an instance of the lingering effects of discarded ideas.

My earliest investigations of economic issues in LDCs were unconnected with these topics.[2] I was drawn into this general area of inquiry through two studies, one of the rubber industry of Southeast Asia, and the other of the organization of trade in the former British West Africa. I spent more than ten years on these studies during the 1940s and 1950s, when I was for substantial periods in each of the two regions. What I saw was starkly at variance with the components of the emerging consensus of mainstream development economics. My inquiries into and observation of economic, social, and political life in these two major regions provoked a lasting interest in general development economics. Although my ideas have developed much since the completion of these studies, they have not moved closer either to the tenets of the development orthodoxy of the 1950s or to their subsequent modification.

Even before setting foot in Southeast Asia and West Africa I knew that many of their economies had advanced rapidly. After all, it required no instruction in development economics to know that before 1885 there was not a single rubber tree in Malaya or a single cocoa tree in British West Africa. By the 1930s there were millions of acres under these and other export crops, the bulk of them owned and operated by non-Europeans. But although I knew this and a good deal else about local conditions, I was nevertheless surprised by much of what I saw, including the extensive economic transformation occurring in large areas and the vigor of economic life of much of the local populations. In Malaya (now Malaysia), for example, the economic activity of the many towns and large villages, the excellent communications, and the evident prosperity of large sections of the non-European population reflected a world totally different from the largely empty and economically backward Malaya of the nineteenth century. The results of somewhat similar, though less extensive, changes were evident also in West Africa, most notably in southern Nigeria and the Gold Coast (now Ghana). How was all this possible if there was any real substance in the central ideas of contemporary development economics?

In the earliest stages local supplies of capital were minimal. In Southeast Asia, however, the export market for rubber (and to a less extent other products such as tin) attracted investment by European enterprises, particularly for the development of rubber estates in hitherto empty jungle. Where local labor supplies were inadequate, as in Malaya and Sumatra, the Western enterprises organized and financed large-scale recruitment and migration of unlettered workers, mainly from China and India. The activities of the Western enterprises induced unintended and unexpected sequences. For instance, Chinese traders were drawn into the rubber trade. Some started their own plantations, while others brought seeds and consumer goods to the indigenous people of Malaya and the Netherlands Indies (now Indonesia). They thereby encouraged the local population to plant rubber trees and to produce for the market. By the late 1930s, more than half of the rubber acreage of Southeast Asia was owned by Asians. This acreage represented the results of direct investment despite initially low incomes.[3]

The history was somewhat different in West Africa. In this region there were (and are) no European-owned plantations. The large area planted to cocoa, groundnuts, cotton, and kola nuts has been entirely occupied by farms established, owned, and operated by Africans. The extensive capital involved was made available partly by European trading firms that financed local traders, and partly by direct investment by Africans, the latter in important instances carried out by migrant farmers in regions far from their homes.

In all of this, the role of traders was crucial: the distinguished historian Sir Keith Hancock has rightly called West Africa "the traders' frontier." The traders made available consumer goods and production inputs and provided the outlets for the cash crops. Their activities stimulated investment and production. The part played by what used to be called inducement goods—a term once a household expression but now rarely encountered in modern development literature—was notable. The sequence showed the inappropriateness of the notion of the international demonstration effect, the idea that access to cheap consumer goods, especially imported goods, retards development in LDCs by increasing the local population's propensity to consume.

The generally rapid economic progress in these areas, of which the large-scale capital formation in agriculture by the local people was a major component, cannot be squared with the idea of the vicious circle of poverty and stagnation. It would have been a freak of chance if I had happened on the only two regions in the less developed world where people had managed to escape the imperatives of a law of economics. In fact, of course, the notion that poverty is self-perpetuating is belied by evidence throughout the developed and less developed world, and indeed by the very existence of developed countries.

The notion is not rescued by the suggestion, much canvassed since the 1950s, that the production of commodities for export resulted merely in enclaves operated by Westerners without benefit to the local people. In the regions I visited, a large part of production, and sometimes the entire output, was (and remains) in the hands of the local population. The same applies to the associated activities of trade and transport. Had this been otherwise, the development of export crops could not have transformed the lives of the local people as it has done. In these regions, as in many others, the pervasive economic advance has made it possible for much larger populations to live longer and at much higher standards.

A developed infrastructure was not a precondition for the emergence of the major cash crops of Southeast Asia and West Africa. As has often also been the case elsewhere, the facilities known as infrastructure were developed as the economy expanded. It is unhistorical to envisage an elaborate and expensive infrastructure as a prerequisite for economic advance. Countless people in trading and transport often performed the services usually associated with capital-intensive infrastructure. For instance, human and animal transport, the contacts between numerous traders, and long chains of intermediaries were partial but effective substitutes for expensive roads and communication systems.

This historical experience (which had counterparts in many other LDCs) was not the result of conscription of people or the forced mobilization of their resources. Nor was it the result of forcible modernization of attitudes and behavior, of large-scale state-sponsored industrialization, or of any other form of big push. And it was not brought about by the achievement of political independence, by the inculcation in the minds of the local people of the notion of national identity, by the stirring-up of mass enthusiasm for the abstract notion of economic development, or by any other form of political or cultural revolution. It was not the result of conscious efforts at nation building (as if people were lifeless bricks, to be moved about by some master builder) or of the adoption by governments of economic development as a formal policy goal or commitment. What happened was in very large measure the result of the individual voluntary responses of millions of people to emerging or expanding opportunities created largely by external contacts and brought to their notice in a variety of ways, primarily through the operation of the market. These developments were made possible by firm but limited government, without large expenditures of public funds and without the receipt of large external subventions.

The nature of these responses in turn exposed for me the hollowness of various standard stereotypes. It was evident that the ordinary people of the LDCs were not necessarily torpid, rigidly constrained by custom and habit, economically timid, inherently myopic, and generally deficient in enterprise. In a decade or two, the illiterate peasantry of Southeast Asia and West Africa planted millions of acres of rubber and cocoa, hitherto unknown cash crops that take five or more years to become productive. The large volumes of direct investment to achieve this were made possible by voluntary changes in the conduct, attitudes, and motivations of numerous individuals, in many cases involving the sacrifice of leisure and the modification of personal relationships. Yet Malays, Indonesians, and Africans were among those who were depicted (as they still sometimes are) as incapable of taking a long view or of creating capital, and as being hobbled by custom and habit.

The establishment and operation of properties producing cash crops are entrepreneurial activities. So also are the ubiquitous trading and transport activities of local people. The contention is thus invalid that entrepreneurial skills and attitudes are lacking in LDCs. Indeed, they are often present but take forms that accord with people's attributes and inclinations and with local conditions and opportunities. In many parts of the less developed world there is evidence of much enterprise and risk taking, often on a small scale individually but by no means confined to agriculture and trading.

The contribution to economic development of the numerous

small and large-scale entrepreneurs (farmers, traders, industrialists, and so on) highlights the generally melancholy record of the entrepreneurial efforts of LDC governments—all too often financed by heavy taxation of cash crop producers. It is often claimed in the development literature, in support of the alleged need for extensive state control and direction in the economies of many LDCs, that their populations lack entrepreneurs. Should the people of a particular country in fact be without entrepreneurial talents or inclinations, it is difficult to see how the politicians and civil servants from this population could make up for the deficiency.

In the less developed world, willingness to bestir oneself and to take risks in the process is not confined to entrepreneurs in the accepted sense of the term. Hundreds of thousands of extremely poor landless rural people have migrated thousands of miles to improve their lot. The large-scale migration from southeastern China and southern India to Fiji, Malaya, and the Netherlands Indies is well known. In my studies I was able to show that very poor illiterate people were well informed about economic conditions in distant and alien countries, and that they responded intelligently to the opportunities they perceived.

When I began my work, the emerging ideas on economic development assigned decisive importance to the ratio between number of people and available resources—land and other natural resources as well as capital. Natural resources and capital were all that mattered. Apart from age and sex differences, people were envisaged as homogeneous. All of these assumptions can be seen in the construction of growth models in contemporary economic literature and in the discussion these models inspired. The only partial qualification was provided by the growing emphasis on differences between people, reflecting investment in them (human capital formation).

My existing skepticism about this approach was soon and amply reinforced by what I saw in Southeast Asia. The differences in economic performance and hence in achievement among groups were immediately evident, indeed startling. The region offered a clear demonstration that people, even with the same level of education, cannot be treated as being uniform in the economic context.

Many rubber estates kept records of the daily output of each tapper and distinguished between the output of Chinese and Indian workers. The output of the Chinese was usually more than double that of the Indians, although all used the same simple equipment: tapping knife, latex cup, and bucket. There were similar or even wider differences among Chinese, Indian, and Malay smallholders on several hundred smallholdings in Malaya that I visited in 1946. The pronounced differences between Chinese and Indians could not be attributed to the special characteristics often possessed by migrants, since both groups were recent immigrants. The great majority of both Indians and Chinese were uneducated coolies, so the differences in their performance could not be explained in terms of differences in human capital formation. The Chinese performance in Malaya was especially notable. Not only had practically all the Chinese been very poor immigrants, but also they were subject to extensive adverse discrimination imposed by the British administration and by the local Malay rulers.

Of course, differences among groups were not limited to expertise in rubber tapping or in other aspects of rubber production. They were pervasive throughout the local economies in the establishment and operation of plantations, mines, and industrial and commercial undertakings. These differences in no way reflected initial capital endowments. These differences in productivity and in personal preferences, motivations, and social arrangements did result in vastly different contributions to capital formation by the various groups. I was to encounter similar phenomena in West Africa, the Levant, India, and elsewhere.

I should not have been so greatly surprised by what I found. After all, I was aware of the pronounced differences in economic performance among different cultural groups as a feature of much of economic history, and of the fact that groups discriminated against were often especially productive and successful. My temporary oversight was probably a result of having succumbed to the then prevailing view that the less developed world newly discovered by Western economists was somehow different. I had also fallen victim to the notion of the primary and overwhelming importance of physical resources (including capital) as determinants of real incomes—a short period of aberration in which I ignored what I knew of economic history.

And I, like others, may have been bemused by figures of average incomes calculated for entire populations without regard to ethnic composition.

Many millions of very poor people in the Third World today, as in the past, have ready access to cultivable land. Such groups as aborigines, pygmies, and various African tribes are extreme cases of poverty amid abundant land. Even in India, much land is officially classified as uncultivated but usable. These considerations undermine conventional labor-to-land ratios. The small size and low productivity of many farms in the Third World reflect primarily want of ambition, energy, and skill, not want of land and capital. Cultivability depends heavily upon the economic qualities of the people as well as on official policies affecting the use of land. Examples of the last include the price policies of governments, control of immigration and inflow of capital, and the terms on which state lands are made available.[5]

Although the discussion of them has been largely taboo in the postwar development literature, the reality and importance of group differences in economic performance cannot be disputed. The subject is virtually proscribed in the profession. These differences are not discussed even when they serve as major planks in official policy, as they do in Malaysia and elsewhere.

Discussion of the reasons for group differences in performance and of their likely persistence would be speculative, and economic reasoning is not informative on these questions. But this provides no excuse for the systematic neglect of group differences by economists. Such differences are plainly relevant for assessment of the economic situation and prospects in Third World countries (and elsewhere too) and for the concept and implications of population pressure. It follows also that the relation between economic development and population growth cannot be examined sensibly on the basis simply of numbers and resources.

Considerations such as those set out so far have reinforced my reluctance to attempt to formulate a theory of economic development, and also my rejection of theories based either on sequential stages of history or on the conventional type of growth model. The inadequacy of these theories is in any case revealed by their inability to account for the well-attested phenomenon of economic decline (whether absolute or relative). Moreover, economic development is but one facet of the history of a society, and attempts to formulate general theories of history have so far been conspicuously unsuccessful, even though many distinguished minds have addressed the question. Not surprisingly, some of these attempts have yielded informative insights, but none of sufficient generality to serve as a basis for a theory of development.

In the more narrowly economic context, I found the approach embodied in the conventional growth models to be unhelpful and even misleading. The approach focuses on independent variables that I came to know were unimportant. It also ignores the interplay between the chosen variables and parameters. Thus, the models take as given such decisive factors as the political situation, people's customs, beliefs, and attitudes, and their state of knowledge.[6] Attempts to increase the stock of capital—for instance, by special taxation or restriction of imports—greatly affect these and other factors treated as parameters, and have repercussions typically far outweighing the effects on development of any increase in capital that might ensue. These shortcomings exist apart from basic problems of the concept and measurement of capital, and of the distinction between investment and consumption. This distinction is especially nebulous in the conditions of LDCs, where the use of inducement goods often results in improved economic performance, and consumption is thus complementary to, rather than competitive with, saving and investment.

Since the Second World War an aggregative and quantitative approach has predominated in development economics. Such an approach may have been inspired by the growth models that confine themselves to aggregates such as capital, labor, and consumption. Acceptance of this general approach has had the comforting corollaries that the economy of an LDC could be studied on the basis of readily accessible statistics, and that it was legitimate to dispense with both direct observation and nonquantitative information generally. This neglect in turn has led to an uncritical acceptance of the available statistics. The very large biases in international income statistics, as well as changes in their incidence over time, have been ignored in much of development economics. Again, in the statistics used in development economics, direct capital formation in agriculture has been undervalued or, more often, neglected altogether. Yet this form of capital formation is quantitatively and qualitatively significant in the advance from the largely subsistence activities characteristic of many LDCs. Perhaps more serious in its repercussions has been the failure to recognize this form of capital formation in analyses of economic growth and hence in proposals for promoting growth. Thus fiscal policies for accelerating capital formation have often been advanced without recognition of their necessary effects on direct capital formation in agriculture. In practice, the untoward results of this oversight have been compounded by the habit, itself encouraged by the aggregative approach, of neglecting prices as determinants of the choice of economic activities.[7]

The use of occupational statistics presents some instructive examples of inappropriate reliance on accessible data and of the neglect, even atrophy, of direct observation. Occupational statistics suggested that in LDCs almost the entire population was engaged in agriculture. For instance, this was a theme of the official reports on West Africa and the literature based on them that I consulted before my first visit. Trade and transport barely figured in the official census or in Lord Hailey's *An African Survey of 1938.* I was therefore much surprised by the volume of trading activity and the large number of traders that I observed. It became clear that the official statistics were misleading because they did not and could not reflect the prevailing incomplete occupational specialization. In households classified as agricultural it was unusual for some of the members to trade regularly or intermittently, regardless of sex and also largely regardless of age.[8]

West African experience, which was clearly not unique, except perhaps in the extent of participation in trading, led me to examine and overturn the prevailing Clark-Fisher hypothesis that economic advancement entails a movement of labor progressively from primary to secondary and then to tertiary economic activity.[9] I showed that the theory rested on misleading statistics; that tertiary activities were a miscellany of activities united only by their output's being nonmaterial; that they do not have the common feature of high income elasticities of demand, and that many tertiary activities were indeed necessary for emergence from subsistence production in poor countries; that in small-scale trade and transport in LDCs labor can easily be substituted for capital; and that the belief was unfounded that technical progress was necessarily more pronounced in the production of goods than in that of services. Furthermore, the common aggregation of economic activities into three distinctive groups was shown to be of no value for analysis or for sensible policy prescriptions. Yet the notion is still alive that the tripartite classification of economic activities not only is valid and firm but can serve as a basis for policy.

In the general context of development economics, the various preceding examples of misleading aggregation are overshadowed by yet another practice. This is the treatment of the world as being two distinct aggregates, the rich and progressing countries and the poor and stagnating countries. The second and much larger aggregate consists of most of Asia and Africa and all of Latin America. This collectivity is envisaged as broadly uniform, wretchedly poor, separated from the rich countries by a wide and widening gap in incomes, and afflicted moreover by generally deteriorating terms of trade in its exchanges with the other aggregate.

In fact, this picture bears no resemblance to reality. It does not do justice to the rich variety of humanity and experience in the less developed world, and to the rapid growth of many formerly poor countries and the prosperity of large groups there. The inappropriate lumping together of all so-called LDCs has made it more difficult for economists and others to reject the prevailing notions to which I have drawn attention above, and therefore to recognize the inappropriateness of the policy prescriptions derived from them. I now see far more clearly than I did when my studies began how inappropriate was the division of the world into the two supposedly distinct aggregates.

In the early postwar development literature trading activity was very largely ignored. It was ignored in the statistics, in the discussion of development prospects, and in the planning literature, as well as in the plans themselves. When considered at all, the discussion of trade was couched typically in pejorative terms. For instance, it was viewed as a hotbed of imperfections and as a source or manifestation of waste. Hence there followed policy proposals to replace private trading arrangements by the establishment of state trading and state-sponsored cooperative societies.

In contrast, the indispensable role of traders, especially in the development of cash crops, was evident in my inquiries both in Southeast Asia and West Africa and in other LDCs I came to know.

I noted what had often been observed by economic historians, administrators, and other observers, that traders provided and extended markets and thereby widened the opportunities open to people as producers and consumers.[10] Traders bought new and cheaper goods to the notice and within the reach of people, a process that induced better economic performance. Sometimes small-scale traders penetrated areas before explorers and administrators had reached them. Without trading activities there could be no agricultural surplus. Traders linked producers and consumers, created new wants, and encouraged or even made possible the production necessary for their satisfaction. More generally, they acquainted people with the workings of an exchange economy and the attitudes appropriate to it. By extending people's economic horizons and by establishing new contacts, the activities of traders encouraged people to question existing habits and mores and promoted the uncoerced erosion of attitudes and customs incompatible with material progress. Moreover, trading widely proved to be a seedbed of entrepreneurial activities extending beyond trading itself. Thus enterprising and successful traders at times initiated or expanded their farming interests (many in any case were part-time farmers). Trading brought to the fore entrepreneurs who perceived economic opportunities and were ready to pursue them. It was not surprising that successful transport and manufacturing enterprises were often established by traders, both local and expatriate.

These dynamic effects of the activities of traders were largely ignored in the postwar development literature. The role of traders in bringing about a more effective interregional and intertemporal allocation of output may have been more widely recognized. But even where this was recognized, the activities of traders and the organization of the trading system were subjected to much misconceived analysis and criticism. For example, the multiplicity of traders and the vertical subdivision of trading activity into many successive stages were often criticized. I showed that these features could be explained by the relative scarcity of capital and administrative skills, the possibilities in trade of substituting labor for capital, and the availability of large numbers of people for part-time or fulltime trading activity. My observations and analysis of trading activities and arrangements gave rise to much subsequent work by economists and anthropologists. Professor Walter Elkan has gone as far as to suggest that this early work pioneered recognition of the presence and significance of what has come to be termed the informal sector in LDCs, and initiated the study of its economics.[11]

In addition, my work enabled me to expose the underlying flaws in familiar proposals and policies for restructuring the trading sector in LDCs. These measures ranged from restriction of the number of traders, and the enforced elimination of particular stages in the chain of distribution, to large-scale state support for cooperative trading and to the suppression of private traders and their replacement by state trading organizations. The adoption of such measures in various LDCs has had the unsurprising consequences of restricting the opportunities for producers and consumers, of entrenching inefficiency in the trading sector,[12] and of obstructing economic progress and the widening of horizons. Most of these so-called reforms have caused widespread hardship and have locked many people into subsistence production (see Essay 6).

Since at least the 1930s both popular and academic literature have decried the fluctuations in the prices of primary products, especially those produced in LDCs. Commodity stabilization schemes have now been major items on the agenda for several decades.

Commodity schemes have usually been proposed as instru-

ments for the reduction of price fluctuations. In practice, however, the objective has usually been the monopolistic raising of
prices. This is transparent today, when commodity schemes are
envisaged as a form of resource transfer from the West to the
Third World. But the monopolistic intention was already clear
in the interwar regulation schemes, such as International
Rubber Regulation. I studied this subject in detail and was able
to document that rubber regulation did not stabilize prices but
did widen fluctuations in output and probably also in producer
incomes.[13] Among other untoward effects, it imposed hardship
on excluded potential producers, who were generally much
poorer than were the beneficiaries.

Subsequently, I examined in depth the operations of the official West African marketing boards.[14] These state organizations
were given the sole right to buy for export and to export the
controlled products. The proclaimed purpose of these arrangements was to stabilize the prices received by producers, and
even to improve them. In fact, they promptly developed into a
system of paying producers far less than the market value of
their produce—they were, in effect, an instrument of heavy, persistent, and discriminatory taxation. Over extended periods
they destabilized producer prices and incomes. I drew attention
to major effects of this heavy taxation, notably that it reduced
the development of cash crops and private savings, obstructed
the emergence of a prosperous African peasantry and middle
class, and served as a dominant source of money and patronage
for those with political power. Thus, paradoxically, although
stabilization is typically invoked as cover for the monopolistic
raising of producer prices, in this instance it was invoked as
cover for persistent underpayment of producers made possible
by the monopsony powers of the boards.[15]

My work on rubber regulation and on the marketing boards
had various spinoffs. First, it showed that the smoothing of fluctuations needs to be clearly distinguished from other objectives
of official schemes, such as monopolistic raising of prices or taxation of producers by underpaying them. Second, it also showed
that even if the reduction of fluctuations was the genuine objective of a scheme, its implementation would encounter formidable conceptual and practical problems. These included the

problems of determining the long-term trend of prices; of choosing between the setting of producer prices at the discretion of the authorities or in accordance with an announced formula; of choosing between stabilization of prices and stabilization of producer incomes; and of choosing the frequency and amplitude of the adjustments in producer prices. Third, my work and the response it elicited from Professor Milton Friedman led me to question whether the exercise of government power was desirable or necessary for producers to achieve price or income stabilization if they felt the need for it.[16] If stabilization of disposable incomes is desired, producers on their own account can set aside reserves on which to draw in times of adversity. If necessary, they can form voluntary associations to help them achieve this purpose.

The truth of the French saying *Rien ne vit que par le détail* impressed itself upon me in the course of my work in Southeast Asia and West Africa. The work also underlined the pertinence of Bacon's maxim "It cometh often to pass that mean and small things discover great better than great can discover small." Much of this work uncovered phenomena and relationships that had not been acknowledged adequately either in previous studies of these regions or in the more general economic texts. I list briefly a number of these matters not already discussed here; fuller treatments are to be found elsewhere in my publications. However, several of the issues raised or illustrated are of some general significance and interest.

The supply of smallholders' rubber had commonly been instanced as a classic case of a backward-sloping supply function. In fact, it was possible to establish not only that the supply curve was forward-rising but also that this response was fully recognized in the implementation of official policy (for instance, in the imposition of special export taxes to curtail smallholders' exports under rubber regulation). The much higher density of planting on rubber smallholdings than on the estates used to be attributed to the crude methods used by smallholders. In fact, it could be shown to reflect differences in the availability of factors of production to the two broad groups of producers. Further, even the short-period supply price of rubber could not be estimated simply by reference to current outlays, but had also to include the expected reduction of future revenues through the current consumption of the latex-containing bark. Again, cost of production was found to vary greatly with the current product price (much more so than with the scale of operations). Thus cost of production, and therefore the supply price, depended significantly on expected future prices as well as on current prices.[17] Once it is recognized that current and prospective product prices affect costs, it is not legitimate to treat supply as independent of demand (as is the standard practice in microeconomic theory).

I found that the standard expositions of monopoly and of its measurement were incomplete, even misleading. Rubber regulation covered many thousands of producers, none of whom controlled even 2 percent of total supplies of a highly standardized product or had any influence on prices. The controlling authority, on the other hand, faced a much less than perfectly elastic demand. This combination was very different from the situation typically analyzed in monopoly theory. In the study of West African trade, statistics accessible to me showed that the degree of concentration was systematically higher for standardized products than for differentiated products. This relationship was contrary to what I expected to find from contemporary discussions of product differentiation. Again, in Southeast Asia and West Africa the number of trading points diminished steadily from the urban center to the outlying rural areas. Yet I found this phenomenon to have no systematic relation to the intensity of competition: the effective degree of monopoly could not be predicted at all reliably from the number of traders present. The small trader in a remote village was exposed to competition from many sources, including itinerant peddlers and farmers acting as part-time traders. The number of traders, however, became important in determining the strength of competition whenever entry was officially restricted. Even then, diversity among the traders (such as ethnic diversity or differences in length of establishment) could modify the effect of numbers on competition.

That detailed statistics can be revealing was shown by statistics of the prices of official rights to export rubber from Malaya.

These could be made to reveal both the de facto extent of restriction and the very low supply price of large quantities of smallholders' rubber. Closer examination of the statistics of total estate production and those of locally registered companies disclosed that rubber regulations treated companies registered in the United Kingdom more favorably than locally registered companies, and estates more favorably than smallholdings. The statistics could be used also to measure the effect of the 100 percent excess profits tax on the level of production.

Direct observation in conjunction with certain statistical series, especially transport statistics, helped to uncover the large volume and importance of kola nut production and trade in Nigeria, activities entirely in the hands of Africans and virtually unremarked in official and other publications. Again, detailed examination of the working of import and price controls in wartime and postwar West Africa made clear that quite momentous political and social consequences could follow from apparently innocuous official measures.

During the latter part of the 1950s I first wrote on two major issues in development economics: comprehensive planning and foreign aid. I was subsequently to develop my analysis and conclusions when these two subjects came to loom more largely both in the academic development literature and even more in public discussion. I noted then that comprehensive central planning was certainly not necessary for economic advance; it was much more likely to retard it. It did not augment resources, but only diverted them from other public and private uses. It reinforced the authoritarian tradition prevailing in many LDCs. And it also divorced output from consumer demand and restricted people's range of choice.

On foreign aid I wrote little, beyond saying that it was not indispensable for the progress of poor countries and that it often served to underwrite and prolong extremely damaging policies commonly pursued in the name of comprehensive planning.

I see no reason to retract these findings and assessments. But I must acknowledge a serious misjudgment. I failed then to appreciate the pervasive significance of the politicization of economic life in LDCs. Except in my treatment of the West African mar-

keting boards, I was apt to analyze the more specifically economic implications and effects of individual policy measures
without appreciating adequately how they contributed to the
general politicization of life in many LDCs. By the late 1950s
the principal measures included state monopoly of major
branches of industry and trade, including agricultural exports;
official restrictive licensing of industrial and other activities;
controls over imports, exports, and foreign exchange; and the
establishment of many state-owned and state-operated enterprises, including state-supported and state-operated so-called
cooperatives. Several of these individual measures gave governments close control over the livelihood of their subjects. When
applied simultaneously, these measures conferred even greater
power on the rulers.

In these conditions the acquisition and exercise of political
power became all-important. The stakes, both gains and losses,
in the struggle for political power increased. These developments enhanced uncertainty, anxiety, and political tension,
especially in the many LDCs that comprised distinct ethnic,
religious, or linguistic groups. They thereby diverted people's
energies and resources from economic activity to the political
arena.

These developments and their repercussions have become
much more pronounced and widespread since the 1950s. Not
only the economic but even the physical survival of large numbers of people have come to depend on political and administrative decisions. Productive ethnic minorities have been conspicuous among the victims. What I saw only dimly in the 1950s has
therefore become a major theme in my more recent writings.

Notes

Index

Notes

1. Traders and the Development Frontier

1. Hoh-cheung and Lorna H. Mui, *Shops and Shopkeeping in Eighteenth Century England* (London, 1989), pp. 291–292.
2. Jacob M. Price, "What Did Merchants Do? Reflections on British Overseas Trade, 1660–1790," *Journal of Economic History,* 49 (June 1989), 267–284.
3. Richard Grassby, "English Merchant Capitalism in the Late Seventeenth Century," *Past & Present,* no. 46 (February 1970), 106.
4. Adam Smith, *The Wealth of Nations* (London, 1776), bk. III, chap. 4.
5. The sequences described here are the exact opposite of those envisaged by the international demonstration effect, a major theme of the development literature of the 1950s and 1960s. The protagonists of the international demonstration effect argued that awareness of new consumption possibilities obstructed development by raising consumption at the expense of saving and investment. Among other relative considerations, this reasoning disregarded that the acquisition of consumer goods required improved economic performance, such as additional work or replacement of subsistence production by production for sale and direct investment in agriculture.
6. Two early examples are *The Indian Second Five Year Plan* (Delhi, 1956) and the World Bank report *The Economic Development of Nigeria* (Baltimore, 1955). These influential documents served as models for other countries.

2. Economic Progress and Occupational Distribution

1. "For convenience in international comparisons production may be defined as primary, secondary, and tertiary. Under the former

we include agricultural and pastoral production, fishing, forestry and hunting. Mining is more properly included with secondary production, covering manufacture, building construction and public works, gas and electricity supply. Tertiary production is defined by difference as consisting of all other economic activities, the principal of which are distribution, transport, public administration, domestic service and all other activities producing a nonmaterial output"; Colin Clark, *The Conditions of Economic Progress* (London, 1940), p. 182. See also A. G. B. Fisher, *Economic Progress and Social Security* (London, 1946), pp. 5 and 6.

2. A more extensive discussion, including detailed examples, of trading and related activities in West Africa is in P. T. Bauer, *West African Trade* (Cambridge, 1954). Other studies of trading operations in Third World countries include Sidney W. Mintz, "The Jamaican Internal Marketing Pattern," *Social and Economic Studies,* 4 (March 1958), 95–103; idem, "The Role of the Middleman in the Internal Distribution System of a Caribbean Peasant Economy," *Human Organization,* 15 (Summer 1957), 18–23; idem, "The Employment of Capital by Market Women in Haiti," in *Capital, Saving, and Credit in Peasant Societies,* ed. Raymond Firth and B. S. Yamey (Chicago, 1964); Alice G. Dewey, *Peasant Marketing in Java* (New York, 1962); idem, "Capital, Credit, and Saving in Javanese Marketing," in Firth and Yamey, *Capital, Saving, and Credit*; Leon V. Hirsch, *Marketing in an Underdeveloped Economy: The North Indian Sugar Industry* (Englewood Cliffs, NJ, 1961). See also W. Arthur Lewis, *Development Planning* (London, 1966), chap. 2.

3. Lord Hailey, *An African Survey,* 2d ed. (London, 1945), pp. 1425–26.

4. The relative increase in the numbers engaged in retail distribution in Great Britain and elsewhere during the depression of the early 1930s is a more familiar example that can be largely explained in terms of reduced supply price arising from the contraction of opportunities.

5. This point is emphasized by Professor Simon Rottenberg in a Note, *Review of Economics and Statistics,* 35 (May 1953), 168–170.

6. Clark, *The Conditions of Economic Progress,* pp. 6–7.

7. Fisher, *Economic Progress and Social Security,* pp. 6–7.

8. Perhaps more fancifully, purchases of fur coats, oysters, caviar, lobsters, pheasants, and orchids sustain hunting, fishing, and farming, which are primary activities.

9. Of course, in West Africa the time may come when eight hours of a person's time may be worth more than the profit margin on the sale of three beer bottles.

10. A. G. B. Fisher, "A Note on Tertiary Production," *Economic Journal,* 62 (December 1952), 820–834.

11. The adjective is Professor Fisher's in a related context.

12. Fisher, "Note on Tertiary Production," p. 829. He refers there to two criteria or approaches: income elasticity of demand for products and rates of technical progress. Elsewhere in the article he refers to the customary definition of tertiary products as services.

13. Ibid., p. 826.

14. Ibid., p. 827.

3. Population, Welfare, and Development

1. Robert S. McNamara, *One Hundred Countries, Two Billion People: The Dimensions of Development* (London, 1973), pp. 31, 35–36, 45–46.

2. *The Times,* 30 March 1990.

3. *Report of the Commission on International Development* (New York, 1969), p. 55.

4. Queen Elizabeth I contrasted her lot unfavorably with that of her prisoner, Mary Queen of Scots, because the latter had been delivered of a bonny baby while she, Elizabeth, was of barren stock.

5. John C. Caldwell, "Towards a Restatement of Demographic Transition Theory," *Population and Development Review,* 2 (September 1976), 321–366.

6. A. MacFarlane, "Modes of Reproduction," in *Population and Development,* ed. G. Hawthorn (London, 1978), p. 108.

7. "The weariest and most loathed worldly life / That age, ache, penury, and imprisonment / Can lay on nature, is a paradise / To what we fear of death"; *Measure for Measure,* act 3, scene 1.

8. Any increased use of condoms in LDCs as a result of the AIDS scare is irrelevant here.

9. Having children in the expectation of an eventual return in the form of either their economic contribution as youngsters or support in old age should not be construed as a form of exploitation. The children will in turn enjoy similar benefits when they become parents.

10. For simplicity, the argument assumes that the costs are borne by taxpayers of the country in question. To the extent that they are borne by foreign donors, the conclusion in the text has to be altered to include outside donors.

11. For intertemporal comparisons of per capita income to be informative about living standards, adjustment should be made for changes in the age distribution of the population. This is necessary to reflect the fact, for example, that children have both lower incomes and lower requirements than adults. However, the need for age standardization in national income statistics is rarely recognized, especially in nontechnical discussion. Unadjusted national income statistics overstate the short-run reduction in income per head when population is growing rapidly.

12. In Britain, farmland rent represented about 40 percent of the value of agricultural output in the 1880s, and under 10 percent in the 1960s; P. T. Bauer, *Equality, the Third World and Economic Delusion* (London and Cambridge, Mass., 1981), p. 50.

13. One wonders what would have happened if the widely canvassed proposals for increasing fertility worldwide had been adopted in the 1930s and 1940s and had increased the numbers in the reproductive age groups. However, before these proposals could be implemented, the predictions on which they were based were already discomfited.

14. Caldwell, "Restatement of Demographic Transition Theory."

4. Foreign Aid

1. The familiar terms *bilateral* and *multilateral aid* are also misleading in implying reciprocity between donors and recipients. There is no such reciprocity since donors give and recipients receive. Under bilateral programs the resources go direct from donor to recipient governments, and under multilateral programs they go through international organizations for subsequent reallocation.

2. In some instances, subsidies go through governments rather than to them. In our context the distinction is immaterial because the direction and use of the funds require government approval in the recipient countries.

3. This disregard accords with much modern macroeconomic theory, including unrefined Keynesian methodology. Here is a key passage from *The General Theory of Employment, Interest and Money* (London, 1936), p. 245: "We take as given the existing skill and quantity of available labor, the existing quality and quantity of available equipment, the existing technique, the degree of competition, the tastes and habits of the consumer, the disutility of different intensities of labor and of the activities of supervision and

organization, as well as the social structure." It is debatable whether such assumptions are helpful for the analysis of fluctuations in output and employment in advanced industrial economies. They are plainly inappropriate for the examination of the factors behind the economic performance and advance of entire societies. For this purpose, acceptance of these assumptions deprives the analysis of all predictive power.

4. In the 1980s, multi-million-dollar official relief funds were set up to help refugees who had fled as a result of persecution by aid-recipient governments.

5. Further and detailed examples will be found in P. T. Bauer, *Reality and Rhetoric: Studies in the Economics of Development* (London and Cambridge, Mass., 1984), chap. 3.

6. *New York Times,* 1 March 1981.

7. In accordance with standard practice, foreign aid in this essay refers to official economic aid, that is, gifts from donor governments to recipient governments, both directly and also indirectly through international organizations. It includes the grant element in subsidized loans. It excludes military aid, private investment, and the activities of charities; the West includes Japan, Australia, and New Zealand—that is, it refers to the OECD countries.

8. Paul A. Samuelson, *Economics: An Introductory Analysis,* 2d ed. (New York, 1951), p. 49.

9. The world is a closed system which has not received resources from outside. All developed countries began as underdeveloped. Academic readers will recognize the model underlying the vicious circle of poverty and stagnation. The crucial variables and relationships of this model are the following: the growth of income is a function of the rate of capital accumulation, that is, of investment; investment depends on saving; and saving is a function of income. Hence the growth of income depends on the growth of capital, and the growth of capital depends on the growth of income. The model behind the thesis of the vicious circle of poverty pivots on the notion that the low level of income itself prevents the capital formation required to raise income.

10. References to the work by Kuznets and others are in P. T. Bauer, *Equality, The Third World and Economic Delusion* (London and Cambridge, Mass., 1981), pp. 242 and 280.

11. Examples include British aid and the large amounts of aid distributed by the International Development Association, an affiliate of the World Bank. These are allocated explicitly on the basis of recorded per capita income.

12. For instance, P. T. Bauer and Cranley Onslow, "Making Sure Overseas Aid Goes Where It Is Needed," *The Times,* 15 November 1977; P. T. Bauer, *Reality and Rhetoric: Studies in the Economics of Development* (London and Cambridge, Mass., 1984).

13. This is most obvious in Africa and the South Pacific but also to a lesser extent in Asia and Latin America.

14. Examples range from Nkrumah in the 1960s to Nyerere and Mengistu in the 1980s.

15. This was a major theme of the Brandt Report. *North-South: A Program for Survival* (Cambridge, Mass., 1980).

16. Of course special groups in the donor countries often benefit from aid. For instance, in the 1970s the supply of ships financed by British aid to India, Poland, and Vietnam benefited labor, management, and shareholders in British shipyards. But the government funds involved could have been used for other forms of so-called employment creation. The ships could also have been sold to the highest bidder or given away to British owners.

17. Besides the three most persistent and widely canvassed arguments for aid, discussed in the text, numerous secondary and ad hoc arguments and rationalizations emerge from time to time, such as restitution for past wrongs, global redistribution, and compensation for adverse external change. These arguments hinge on the assumption that aid promotes development or relieves poverty. They therefore fall away when these assumptions are shown to be untenable, as they are in this essay. Moreover, they are, so to speak, insubstantial in their own right. I have reviewed them at length in "Foreign Aid and Its Hydra-Headed Rationalization," in *Equality, The Third World and Economic Delusion.* A fairly new but now very influential argument is that aid is necessary to alleviate the burden of Third World debt. This argument is dealt with in the next essay. Even more recently, aid is being advocated also to enable Third World governments to fight the drug traffic, protect the environment, and preserve endangered species. Even the African elephant has been pressed into the service of foreign aid.

   One persistent and recurrent theme of the literature of foreign aid and cognate subjects is that there is a long-term tendency for the terms of trade of LDCs to deteriorate, and that therefore aid from the West is required as a form of redress.

   Insofar as aid does not promote development or help the poor, the argument is irrelevant. It also begs the question why governments have not set aside resources to provide against adversity at times when terms of trade have been more favorable.

Moreover, the allegations of persistent deterioration of the terms of trade of LDCs are altogether unfounded. It is doubtful whether there is any sense in averaging the terms of trade of such a highly diverse aggregate as the Third World, that is, most of mankind. The terms of trade of its components move in different and often opposite directions. Because of the extensive diversity of the Third World it can always be suggested by choosing particular years, commodities, and countries that the terms of trade of Third World countries have deteriorated. Insofar as averaging or aggregating Third World terms of trade is at all sensible, it is worth noting that by historical standards the commodity terms of trade of this collectivity have been distinctly favorable since the Second World War. Changes in the more relevant indicators—indicators that allow for changes in the real cost of exports, improvement in the range and quality of imports, and the huge expansion in the volume of trade—have been even more favorable. The aggregate real purchasing power of the Third World over imports has expanded greatly in recent decades.

5. The Third World Debt Crisis

1. *International Herald Tribune,* 2 January 1989.
2. The seventeen countries are Argentina, Bolivia, Brazil, Chile, Colombia, Costa Rica, Ecuador, Ivory Coast, Jamaica, Mexico, Morocco, Nigeria, Peru, Philippines, Uruguay, Venezuela, and Yugoslavia; World Bank, *World Debt Tables 1987–88* (Washington, D.C., 198X).
3. Deepak Lal, *Wall Street Journal,* 22 April 1983, and *The Times,* 6 May 1983.
4. Bank of International Settlements, *Annual Report, 1988–89* (Basle, 198X), p. 135.
5. Relevant statistics in yearbooks published by the Food and Agriculture Organization.
6. Relevant statistics are in reviews published by the Commonwealth Secretariat. See also an article in the *Financial Times* (London), 28 July 1989.
7. Fluctuations in export earnings resulting from changes in external market conditions are outside the control of the government. It is often argued that such fluctuations have been responsible for the difficulties of debt service. This view disregards the possibility of setting aside prudential reserves in favorable periods. Third World governments nowadays have less reason than in the past to follow

such a course because, as explained in the preceding essay, balance-of-payments difficulties often serve as ground for securing more Western aid.

6. Marketing Reform

1. These views are expressed very clearly in the official *Report of the Nigerian Livestock Mission* (London, 1950). Thus "the handling of almost the entire trade by a host of redundant dealers and middlemen, the frequent handlings of stock" are among the factors that "represent for Nigeria economic wastage on a prodigious scale and in large measure accounts for the unjustifiably wide gap between the prices received by the producer and those paid by the consumer" (p. 95).

2. The same tendency to spend time and effort in the search for the most satisfactory terms is observable in the behavior of many African consumers. The desire to make money go further is strong. For example, in northern Nigeria the salt marketed by a particular merchant firm commands a premium over the same salt marketed by other firms. The salt comes from the same British factory; but the firms supply their own sacks, and those of this particular firm are slightly heavier and therefore ultimately make better shirts.

   The ready response of many East African cotton growers to price differences was recognized in the *Report of the Uganda Cotton Industry Commission* (Entebbe, 1948). The commission recommended (pp. 8–9) that a higher price be paid to the grower if he brought his cotton to a recognized market than if he and his cotton were transported at the expense of a ginner to his ginnery. The commission considered that the suggested price difference might work to the disadvantage of ginners. It was conceivable that, while growers and their cotton were being transported by ginners, "growers passing a cotton market might wish to dismount and sell their cotton at the higher price prevailing at the market as compared with their ginnery destination." But the commission did not think this would be a serious difficulty, "as the high rails of the . . . lorry would prevent them getting out and the driver who is responsible for getting them to the ginnery would certainly not slow down when passing a store market." The physical obstacles and hazards were thus thought to be sufficient to thwart the recognized desire for profit maximization.

3. In West Africa, the advantages of specialization of marketing functions between the foreign-owned trading firms and African mid-

dlemen are graphically illustrated in some towns. In eastern Nigeria, it is quite usual to see African traders sitting just outside the produce-buying stations of the European firms (or even inside their compounds). They buy produce from smaller traders, who bring in palm oil and palm kernels in small quantities and, after cleaning and blending, resell the produce to the firms. It pays the firms not to buy directly from the small traders but to allow African dealers to carry out the bulking and blending of small parcels, because their margins of profit are less than would be the cost of supervising and maintaining a staff of salaried employees engaged in the same work.

The same principle applies in the sale of imported merchandise. The intermediaries break bulk and save resources at all stages between the first seller and the final buyer. The organization of retail selling in Ibadan (and elsewhere) exemplifies the services rendered by petty traders both to suppliers and to consumers. Here there is no convenient central market, and it is usual to see petty traders sitting with their wares at the entrances to the stores of the European merchant firms. The petty traders sell largely the same commodities as the stores, but in much smaller quantities. It does not pay the European-owned stores to deal in these smaller quantities on the terms on which the petty traders are prepared to handle this business. On the other hand, consumers find it preferable to deal with the petty traders rather than to buy in less convenient quantities from the adjacent stores.

4. For example, in some West African towns market women and their associations are said to have stopped fishermen from retailing their own catches.

5. It is often held that much of the borrowing by farmers in LDCs is used to finance occasional extravagant consumption and that it would be in the interests of the population to restrict the possibility of borrowing for such purposes. This, however, is an entirely different issue from the one discussed in the text.

6. The discussion here is not concerned with the regulation of produce routes introduced solely for purposes of veterinary control.

7. One example of proposals for compulsory routing of produce may be mentioned: the Nigerian Livestock Mission, in its report in 1950, recommended that a large abattoir be awarded the sole right to buy cattle in Kano and an undefined area around. The purpose was to prevent cattle from being taken on the hoof to the consuming markets in the south; *Report of the Nigerian Livestock Mission*, p. 141.

8. A proposal along these lines was put forward by J. Mars in his contribution to *Mining, Commerce, and Finance in Nigeria,* ed. Margery Perham (London, 1948). One of his suggestions was that the outlying trading stations of the European firms be compulsorily closed. He argued that compulsory centralization would increase the extent of competition. "It has been pointed out that the tendency towards oligopsony and eventual monopsony is absolutely inevitable in the produce business of Nigeria if up-country stations of exporting firms remain open. If all such up-country stations were compulsorily closed down, the tendency towards monopsony would be much weakened if not eradicated" (p. 132).

9. To be consistent, Mars should have advocated compulsory cessation of export produce buying in West Africa so that producers would be forced to take their produce to overseas markets, where the largest numbers of buyers are concentrated. On the same reasoning, housewives throughout the country should be forced to buy eggs and butter from central markets in large cities.

10. It is often said that excessive competition forces dealers or processors to cheat producers more scandalously and persistently; this argument is examined later in this essay.

11. Compulsory restriction of the number of intermediaries is a prominent feature in the marketing of cotton in Uganda. Some of these measures are discussed in the *Report of the Uganda Cotton Commission* (Entebbe, 1939).

12. Unless producers are the creditors of bankrupt intermediaries. But strong competition among buyers means that there will be many buyers willing to pay cash in the struggle for supplies.

13. Two kinds of supervision would be involved. The zonal monopolist would have to be regulated by the authorities, in an attempt to prevent the abuse of monopoly power; and the local clerks and employees of the monopolist would have to be supervised much more closely by responsible officers to prevent their clerks from exploiting producers who, *ex hypothesi,* cannot remove their custom if dissatisfied with their treatment.

14. The 1948 *Report of the Uganda Cotton Industry Commission* recognized that East African cotton growers did not feel satisfied if they had no choice of buyers: "Although there is a fixed price for their cotton, they feel that they are more likely to get a square deal if they have the opportunity of going elsewhere if dissatisfied" (p. 9).

15. A West African example of the two contrasting situations is described in Essay 15.

16. An uncompromising and influential discussion of abuses in marketing and of their effects is in the *Report of the Commission on the Marketing of West African Cocoa,* Command Paper 5845 (London, 1938). The relevant portion of this report was reproduced in the British government White Paper *The Future Marketing of West African Cocoa,* Command Paper 6950 (London, 1946), which confirmed the establishment of statutory export monopolies in the West African cocoa trade.

17. A trader inventing a new type of abuse may secure temporary abnormal gains until his competitors and/or customers become familiar with the new practice. Such a phenomenon is unlikely to be significant in an activity such as produce buying.

18. The protection afforded by experience over time is not available if the buyer or seller enters the market only at long intervals. This situation does not apply in the marketing of farm produce.

    The heterogeneity of units of measure in a marketplace in Haiti is described and discussed in Sidney W. Mintz, "Standards of Value and Units of Measure in the Fondes-Nègres Market Place, Haiti," *Journal of the Royal Anthropological Institute,* 91 (January–June 1961), 23–38.

19. Experience in the operation of compulsory inspection and grading of Nigerian export produce is discussed in a later section.

    According to the 1948 *Report of the Uganda Cotton Industry Commission,* "The buying of seed cotton takes place either at ginneries or at stores situated at the various buying centres away from the ginneries. We are satisfied by the evidence that cheating takes place both at ginneries and at stores, but that it is more prevalent at ginneries since there is little or no competition between buyers and also there is more rush and crowding. In fact wherever we have been we have heard bitter complaints by growers of the manner in which buyers deliberately keep them waiting until late in the day, when a huge crowd assembles and in the rush and scramble to get their cotton sold in time to go home before dark the growers are easily swindled" (p. 15). Clearly, if there are several competing buyers, dissatisfied growers need not put up with delaying tactics by individual buyers. This incident supports the analysis in the text. The commission went on to note that officers appointed to stop cheating "are frequently bribed to look the other way," a finding that again bears out the argument in the text.

20. As used here, the term *price differences* does not refer to differences in returns of producers who are in different locations. The presence of these differences, which persist even if equilibrium is

reached, has also given rise to demands for specific marketing reforms, discussed in the next section.

21. It is unlikely that prohibiting the export of poorer quality products will enable the exporting country to influence the world price appreciably. For instance, exports of West African palm oil or East African cotton are a small part of total world supplies; *a fortiori,* the quantities of so-called substandard produce are far smaller still. Even for cocoa, West African supplies of the substandard qualities are a negligible part of world cocoa supplies. However, when market prices can be affected, the gains of monopoly have to be set against the adverse effects considered in the text.

   Prohibition of the *sale* of poorer qualities of a product in the home market can be used as a device to restrict supplies and to raise price. The Nigerian Livestock Mission in 1950 disapproved of the sale of certain kinds of offal, such as guts, hides, and lungs, which in some Western countries are not usually regarded as edible. The sale of these goods in West Africa is deplored as being "a very unsatisfactory position from the consumer point of view"; *Report of Nigerian Livestock Mission,* p. 109. These remarks ignore the obvious fact that consumers willingly buy these products; their withdrawal from sale would merely force consumers to eat less meat.

22. If this were not so, producers would voluntarily incur the additional expenditure, even if the export of lower grades were permitted.

23. For example, the satisfaction expressed in the annual reports and other official statements of the Nigeria Cocoa Marketing Board in the 1950s was misplaced when the board emphasized that it no longer bought and exported certain lower but commercially exportable grades, or when it opposed the establishment of local processing enterprises on the grounds that they would use inferior grades, the production of which the board wished to discourage.

24. Essay 14 provides a detailed discussion of this practice in West Africa.

25. This effect is analogous to the second type of effect produced by the imposition of a minimum exportable standard, discussed in the preceding section.

26. Compare the analysis in the preceding section of the third type of effect produced by the imposition of minimum exportable standards.

27. A producer or buyer can never compel an examiner to inspect his produce; the examiner can always state that he is engaged elsewhere.

28. Inspection at this stage is necessary because timber does not cross a wharf but is either rafted alongside the ship or shipped from lighters. Inspection must thus take place in a form that prevents substitution between the time of inspection and the time of shipment.

29. Abner Cohen, "The Social Organization of Credit in a West African Cattle Market," *Africa,* 35 (January 1965), 8–20.

8. Commodity Stabilization

1. OPEC is also a government-supported commodity cartel. However, it has not pretended to be a price or income stabilization scheme. Its undisguised objective has been to raise oil prices monopolistically.

2. Under these arrangements, monopoly is superimposed on conditions approaching perfect competition. The individual producer of the controlled commodity faces a demand curve that is horizontal up to the amount he is permitted to produce or to export, and vertical beyond that point. The central organization is faced by a downward-sloping demand curve reflecting world demand.

3. The incidence of this taxation was on the producers, not on overseas users. This was wholly so in the case of groundnuts, palm oil, palm kernels, and cotton. And it was largely true also of cocoa. West African supplies of the products other than cocoa were a small part of total world supplies. West African cocoa was a larger proportion, but the short-period inelasticity of the supply of this crop and the substantial long-term elasticity of supply from other sources brought it about that the incidence of the taxation ultimately was very largely on the West African producers of cocoa.

4. The West also transfers resources specifically to LDCs that export primary products by various arrangements other than cartels. Such aid operates whenever the prices of the commodities in question fall below certain specified levels. The scheme known as STABEX is one example.

9. Wage Regulation in Less Developed Countries

1. The term *regulated wages* is used here to refer to wages determined by government, statutory authorities, and trade unions, in contrast to those emerging from the play of market forces. Even without such organized prescription of wages, the institutions of society affect wages, as they do all other prices. But such general influences

act by affecting the conditions of supply and demand, and not by setting rates with given conditions of supply and demand, or by monopolistic measures restricting the supply reaching the market.

2. Unavoidable scarcity, sometimes termed natural scarcity, reflects the limitations of the total available supply, while a contrived scarcity results from the withholding from the market of part of the total supply. A contrived scarcity is superimposed on a natural scarcity because economic resources are in limited supply. But the two concepts are logically distinct and have very different implications for policy. The distinction corresponds to the traditional distinction between rents on the one hand and monopoly earnings or prices on the other. The convenient terms *natural scarcity* and *contrived scarcity* were introduced by Professor W. H. Hutt.

3. For instance, according to a report by the International Labour Organization (hereafter ILO), *Minimum Wages in Latin America* (Geneva, 1954), p. 22, "Brazil, Chile, Costa Rica, Cuba, Haiti, Mexico, Paraguay and Uruguay have had considerable experience in the fixing and enforcement of minimum wage rates. In each of these countries it may be said that, taken together, the rates fixed have had a substantial influence on wages as a whole."

4. The discussion here refers to industrywide bargaining and wage determination. It does not bear on collective negotiation by workers of a single enterprise, which raises issues quite different from those considered here.

5. According to the ILO report *Labour Policies in the West Indies* (Geneva, 1952), p. 173, "The regulation of hours of work, whether by collective agreement, by administrative order or by general legislation, has developed during the period 1939–49 as part of the general process of the introduction and strengthening of modern labour legislation in the area, and of the development of collective bargaining."

6. Mr. Joshi was addressing the Preparatory Asiatic Regional Conference of the ILO, New Delhi, 1947.

7. ILO, *The International Labour Organization: The First Decade* (Geneva, 1931), p. 314.

8. Subbiah Kannappan, "The Impact of the ILO on Labor Legislation and Policy in India," in Aronson and Windmuller, *Labor, Management, and Economic Growth,* p. 188.

9. ILO, *Problems of Wage Policy in Asian Countries* (Geneva, 1956), p. 64.

10. The first issue, published in London in 1906, of *Rubber Producing Companies,* an annual reference book of the rubber industry,

designed in part to attract capital into the industry, contained the following passage (p. V): "It may therefore be well for intending investors to consider what advantages the cultivated rubber of the East may have over the wild and uncultivated rubber of the West.

"The first consideration is that of labour. This is in favour of the Malay Peninsula and Ceylon, both countries being conveniently situated for the supplies of cheap coolie labour to be drawn from Southern India."

11. The *Report of the Indian Factory Labour Commission of 1908* (London, 1908), pp. 32–33, refers explicitly to the adverse effects on industrialization of restrictive measures. The commission was especially concerned with working hours, but its remarks apply equally to other restrictive measures: "we are strongly opposed to the imposition of any unnecessary restriction on the employment of labour in factories, especially at a time when the further industrial development of the country is of such vital importance . . . the strongest practical objections exist to the general enforcement in India of any law rigidly restricting the working hours of adult males . . . the imposition of a direct restriction on the hours of adult labour would be repugnant to the great majority of capitalists, both in India and abroad, who have invested, or are considering the question of investing money in India . . . the opinion is widely and strongly held that, if interference with adult labour be permitted, pressure will be brought to bear in order to utilise that power of interference in a manner calculated to promote the interests of Lancashire and Dundee, rather than of India . . . [and this] would undoubtedly adversely affect India's industrial development . . . we are strongly opposed to any direct limitation of adult working hours, because we consider there is no necessity for the adoption of this drastic course, because we are convinced that it would cause the gravest inconvenience to existing industries."

12. If the monopsonist is a group of employers acting in concert, the labor has to be rationed among them formally or informally.

13. According to a mimeographed memorandum by the Information Department of the British Colonial Office, "Notes on the Development of Trade Unionism and Labour Relations in the Colonies" (London, 1953), p. 5: "The degree of employer organization varies considerably between territories, but in general it can be said that the greatest degree of organization is to be found where either the formation of workers' associations has demonstrated the need for combination on the part of the employers, or the common problems of an industry . . . have brought about co-operation."

14. The processes and results up to 1939 are examined in detail in Sheila T. van der Horst, *Native Labour in South Africa* (London, 1942), chap. 13.

15. W. Galenson and H. Leibenstein have ingeniously suggested in an important article, "Investment Criteria, Productivity, and Economic Development," *Quarterly Journal of Economics,* 69 (August 1955), 343–370, that higher capital intensity in certain activities brought about by higher wage costs may promote development even when there is surplus labor. The suggestion is that although the current national income may be reduced, the difference between production and consumption—that is, the volume of investible resources—may be increased. The formal validity of this argument depends in part on an assumed equivalence of future and present output, on specific assumptions on factor productivities and consumption habits in different sectors, and on the irrelevance of consumer preferences. However, even if these assumptions and premises are accepted, the policy appropriate to the promotion of development would be a tax proportionate to the wage bill rather than the indiscriminate imposition of minimum wages and conditions, since such taxation would conduce to the most efficient deployment of different types of labor, and possibly of other resources, within individual enterprises.

10. Price Control in Less Developed Countries

1. The discussion here is concerned mostly with price control over imports, as this throws into clearest relief certain issues of practical interest. Most of the discussion would, however, apply also to price control over locally produced commodities, including manufactured goods.

   This essay is not concerned with, and therefore disregards, the possibility that effective price control over monopolist producers or distributors can serve to increase their output. The usual type of price control over commodities in underdeveloped countries is introduced not for this reason, but to deal with situations, often colloquially called short-supply situations, in which the relevant supply (usually total supply, but at times supply from certain sources) is fixed.

2. The following passage from a thesis by B. G. Kavalsky at London University illustrates the ineffectiveness of price control in northern Rhodesia in the 1940s, as well as other aspects of economic life there.

"The case of Mulfulira in 1944 provides an interesting example of the operation of price control. The control price was set for grain and meal and immediately evaded through a change in the measure given to customers. The management then introduced special cups and dishes, which when filled with grain or meal gave the correct weight, and enforced their use. The marketeers' next step was to cut round pieces of cardboard of the same colour as the meal and fit them as a shelf some inches up from the bottom of the mug. When the authorities cottoned on to this, the marketeers switched to beating up the bottoms of the mugs, and when this was stopped, they cut down the tops gradually over a long period, so as not to be immediately noticeable. The effect of all this was that in 1945 none of the measuring cups bore any relation to the original size, and the price had been restored to its earlier level.

"Other managements tried similarly to control the price by the introduction of scales. The figures on the scale were quickly scratched out and the old prices charged till eventually the matter was settled by the breaking of the scales. When the controlled price of fish was made eight pence a pound as against the actual selling price of two shillings a pound, and the riverside price of six pence a pound, the fish sellers simply left the market and refused to operate at that price. The customers were most unhappy about the situation and asked the management to stop the controls as they would rather have higher prices than no fish at all." The passage is reprinted in Kavalsky's summary of a longer discussion of this subject in W. V. Brelsford, *Copper Belt Markets* (Lusaka, 1947), pp. 22–23.

3. The distinction between an increase in demand and a contraction in supply, though often important both for analysis and for policy, is not directly relevant here. For simplicity of exposition, the discussion is confined to a contraction of supply with an unchanged demand.

4. Scattered information on the level of controlled and open market prices in India will be found in R. G. Agrawal, *Price Controls in India* (New Delhi, 1956), and in B. R. Shenoy, *Indian Planning and Economic Development* (Bombay, 1963).

Some information on controlled and actual prices of consumer goods in West Africa in the late 1940s is presented in P. T. Bauer, *West African Trade* (Cambridge, 1954), app. 5.

5. This type of situation is vividly described in certain official reports, especially locally published reports. Examples include the

Report of the Commission on Enquiry into the Distribution and Prices of Essential Imported Goods (Accra, 1943); *Report of the Commission of Enquiry into Conditional Sales* (Lagos, 1948); and *Report of the Commission of Enquiry into Disturbances in the Gold Coast* (London, 1948).

6. The applicants may include regular traders in the particular commodities, traders in other commodities, and people not usually trading at all. In the 1940s and 1950s in West Africa, children often applied to merchants for supplies of controlled goods. This phenomenon also occurred in Pakistan and some other LDCs.

11. Industrialization and Development

1. Immigration policy in West Africa provides an instance of the pursuit of two incompatible objectives; see P. T. Bauer and B. S. Yamey, "Immigration Policy in British West Africa," *South African Journal of Economics,* 22 (December 1954), 211–232.

2. The improvement in the physical quality of palm oil exports does not necessarily reflect an economic improvement. The identification of the two concepts rests on a confusion between technical and economic efficiency, a confusion that in turn reflects a disregard of the relevance of costs and prices. This issue is discussed in Essay 6.

3. The term *industrialization* as used in much of the development literature is ambiguous in that it denotes different situations or processes in which three components are present in different proportions: the growth of manufacturing, which often but not invariably accompanies certain stages of material advance; modernization of attitudes, institutions, and economic processes; and state support of manufacturing. The components or elements are frequently present simultaneously, but they are distinct. Most often the term is used to denote state-sponsored or -subsidized manufacturing. Kilby employs industrialization in this sense, with occasional instances of the first use of the term.

4. Income elasticity of demand denotes the responsiveness of demand to changes in income; it is expressed as the ratio of the proportionate change in income associated with it. A low income elasticity of demand, i.e., one of a numerical value of less than unity, is often confused in the literature with a negative income elasticity of demand, i.e., one with a value of less than zero.

5. A succinct yet comprehensive critical review of the argument for subsidized industrialization in less developed countries is found in Harry G. Johnson, "Commercial Policy and Industrialization," a lecture delivered at the University of Panama, 12 August 1971, and published in *Economica,* 39 (September–December 1972), 264–275.

12. Policy and Progress

1. *Study Submitted by the Center for International Studies of the Massachusetts Institute of Technology to the Senate Committee Investigating the Operation of Foreign Trade* (Washington, D.C., 1957), p. 37.
2. Alexis de Tocqueville, *Journeys to England and Ireland (1833),* ed. J. P. Mayer (London, 1958).

13. Import Capacity and Economic Development

1. S. J. Patel, "Export Prospects and Economic Growth: India," *Economic Journal,* 69 (September 1959), 490–506.
2. Anne E. Krueger, "Export Prospects and Economic Growth: India: A Comment," *Economic Journal,* 71 (September 1960), 436–442.
3. Patel, "Export Prospects," p. 496.
4. There is a class of exports from some LDCs for which the demand may at a certain point become perfectly inelastic, namely manufactures on which quotas are imposed. Although in certain conditions this may well be practically important and relevant to the framing of trade policy, it does not apply to the major exports of most LDCs.
5. The export prospects of underdeveloped countries are often said to be compromised by a low income elasticity of world demand for their exports. These discussions generally confuse the effects of a low income elasticity of demand with those of a negative income elasticity of demand. The income elasticity of demand for the major exports of the underdeveloped world is unlikely to be low, let alone negative.
6. If the income elasticity of foreign demand is negative, and the long-term decline in demand is not offset by an increase in domestic demand, excess capacity may develop in the industries in question. This effect may raise problems when the resources are specific. But they are no different from those created by changes in domestic demand.

14. Price Response

1. The merits of these policies are considered in Essay 6.
2. Nigeria Cocoa Marketing Board, *Second Annual Report, Season 1948–9* (Lagos, 1950), p. 22.
3. Idem, *Fifth Annual Report, Season 1951* (Lagos, 1952), p. 10.
4. Nigeria Oil Palm Produce Marketing Board, *Sixth Annual Report* (Lagos, 1954), p. 14.

15. Competition and Prices

1. The Nigerian railway charged a flat rate for the movement of groundnuts throughout the Kano area.
2. The penalties approximated the difference between gross receipts and the short-run avoidable (or escapable or prime) costs of purchase; that is, they were designed to eliminate all profit from buying more than the quota.
3. In one period during the war, members of an obscure African tribe, the Kakanda, who engaged in canoe trading on the Benue River, outbid the licensed buyers at certain upriver stations. They bought groundnuts at these stations above the gazetted minimum prices, took them down the river, and sold them to licensed buyers at the higher gazetted prices prevailing on the lower reaches of the river. These activities were stopped by administrative regulation although they helped both African producers and the enterprising Kakanda.
4. Generally, the margin available to be competed away was larger at the outlying stations, especially at the subsidy stations, where in some cases the transport differential and the subsidy together exceeded £9 per ton. On the other hand, at road stations near the railway line the differential was only a few shillings. Thus, even though there might have been a large number of buyers operating under keenly competitive conditions at road stations near the railway line, the overpayments would perforce have been less than at the more remote stations with fewer buyers but larger transport differentials.
5. This information was kindly collected by the Produce Department of the United Africa Company in Kano.
6. The number of clerks and middlemen operating in different localities tended to be proportionate to the number of buying agents. The degree of competition among clerks and middlemen was largely influenced by the number of buying agents and the market positions of the latter. See also the final section of the essay.

16. Economic History as Theory

1. It is interesting to note Alfred Marshall's statement: "the two great forming agencies of the world's history have been the religious and the economic"; *The Principles of Economics,* 7th ed. (London, 1916), p. 1.

2. Hicks uses the term *mercantile economy* to cover the market (exchange) economy generally, and also economies or polities with much external trade. This ambiguity blurs the argument in some contexts, but not in this particular instance.

3. In his observations on the early history of the Greek city-states Hicks concedes that the ruling classes were landowners and not merchants. He argues, however, that once trade was active "even a landowning class is likely to have been engaged in trade to an extent which is sufficient for the trade orientation" (p. 40). But this attempt at reconciliation contradicts Hicks' emphasis on the key role of the specialized merchant in the earlier development of the mercantile economy (pp. 27-29).

4. Hicks writes that "until the rise of Singapore in very recent times," Southeast Asia "has not been a place for city-states" (p. 39). This formulation suggests that by declaring itself independent of Malaysia, Singapore overnight became a city-state. It is rather baffling that a city could suddenly become a city-state and thus enter one of Hicks's "economic states of society." It is not clear how Hong Kong, Penang, and some other contemporary trading centers would fit into this scheme of things.

5. In 1527, about the midpoint between the sack of Constantinople and the trial of Warren Hastings, Rome was sacked by the imperial forces of Charles V in the course of a triangular struggle with Francis I of France and Pope Clement VII. This sack, the worst ever experienced by Rome, had nothing to do with what Hicks would call the trading situation. The sack of Rome bore a much closer resemblance to the sack of Constantinople than did the latter to the activities of British merchants and civil servants in eighteenth-century Bengal.

6. The modern phase is the only period in which Hicks ascribes a central influence or role to government policies as such. Thus in his discussion of the Industrial Revolution in eighteenth-century England, Hicks does not mention the propitious circumstances of limited government, moderate taxation dependent on the approval of a Parliament made up largely of property owners, and a legal system and judiciary favorable to the rights of property

owners. Nor does he refer to other aspects of the social and political background that encouraged the taking of long views and the experimental outlook, and promoted long-term investment in agriculture and industry.

7. In Hicks's rationalization of these restrictive policies, there is a curious reference to the displacement of Indian handloom weavers as a result of the import of textiles. Hicks notes that from this development "there would be a favourable effect, somewhere; but it might be anywhere; there would be no particular reason why it should be in India" (p. 165). This formulation ignores the fact that the consumers of the cheaper textiles obviously were Indians, who must have benefited from lower prices or improved quality. Moreover, even if they did not spend the increase in their real incomes on other Indian products, somebody else must have spent more on them, because otherwise the country could not have paid for the imports—payment certainly was not in bullion.

8. Sydney Pollard, "Fixed Capital in the Industrial Revolution in Britain," *Journal of Economic History,* 24 (September 1964), 299–314.

9. In 1948 the minister of propaganda in one of the Eastern European countries was asked privately for his opinion about the percentage his government would poll in a free election. He put it at between 5 and 10 percent. He predicted, however, that twenty years of consistent political education would obliterate the past sufficiently to enable the Communist party to secure a majority in a free election. The minister's views and the reason for his long-term optimism, namely that the past would have been forgotten in twenty years, furnish an interesting comment on Hicks's opinion on the persistent differences in mentality on the two sides of the Iron Curtain.

10. The central issue in this range of problems has been summarized by Sir Karl Popper in his phrase "But trends are not laws"; *The Poverty of Historicism* (London, 1957).

11. The influence of mere accident on the course of history is large, although many people, especially those with a religious or Marxist turn of mind, are reluctant to admit this.

17. Development Economics

1. Detailed references to the early development literature are given in P. T. Bauer, *Dissent on Development* (London, 1971; and Cambridge, Mass., 1972), especially chaps. 1 and 2.

2. See P. T. Bauer, *The Rubber Industry* (London and Cambridge,

Mass., 1948); *Report on a Visit to the Rubber-Growing Smallhold-ings of Malaya, July–September 1946* (London, 1948); *West African Trade* (Cambridge, 1954); *Economic Analysis and Policy in Underdeveloped Countries* (Durham, N.C., 1957; and Cambridge, 1958); with B. S. Yamey, *The Economics of Underdeveloped Countries* (Chicago, 1957); and with B. S. Yamey, *Markets, Market Control and Marketing Reform* (London, 1968).

3. The plantation rubber industry comprises both smallholdings—that is, properties of less than a hundred acres each—and estate properties of more than a hundred acres each. Smallholdings, which account for well over half the total area, have always been in Asian ownership. By now virtually all the estates are also owned by Asians, mainly Chinese.

4. See Bauer, *The Rubber Industry,* chap. 15 and app. D; idem, *Economic Analysis and Policy,* chap. 1.

5. The distinction between cultivable and uncultivable land is arbitrary. Adam Smith noted that grapes could be grown in Scotland. The arbitrary nature of the distinction is highlighted by the experience of areas such as the Netherlands, Venice, and Israel.

6. As previously noted, these growth models have been inspired by Keynes. See Essay 4, note 3.

7. See Bauer, *Economic Analysis and Policy,* chap. 2; idem, *The Economics of Underdeveloped Countries,* chap. 10.

8. See Bauer, *West African Trade,* chap. 2.

9. See Colin Clark, *The Conditions of Economic Progress* (London, 1940), and A. G. B. Fisher, *Economic Progress and Social Security* (London, 1946).

10. Since I refer to my observations in the early postwar period I use the past tense. However, the role of traders still applies generally wherever they are allowed to operate. See Bauer, *West African Trade,* chap. 2; idem, *Markets, Market Control and Marketing Reform,* chaps. 1–3.

11. Walter Elkan et al., "The Economics of Shoe-Shining in Nairobi," *African Affairs,* 81 (1982).

12. It is difficult to explain in retrospect why it was almost universally accepted as axiomatic in the early development economics that cooperative enterprises had such particular economic virtues that they should enjoy extensive state support and protection. A cooperative society is simply a form of economic organization. As such, it does not inherently have access to efficiency superior to that of other types of organization, private or public. If cooperative societies had such attributes, they would not have needed official

favors. The economics of cooperative societies is discussed more fully in Essay 7.

13. See Bauer, *The Rubber Industry,* especially pt. 3 and statistical app. 2.

14. See Bauer, *West African Trade,* pt. 5; idem, *Markets, Market Control and Marketing Reform,* chaps. 8 and 9.

15. When I first published my findings, they were received with indignation by official spokesmen and by fellow economists. As late as the mid-1950s the supporters of the marketing boards argued that the boards were engaged only in price stabilization. By the 1960s it was widely accepted that they were, and had been all along, instruments of taxation. It is also now generally agreed that the proceeds of this taxation were in large measure wasted.

16. See Milton Friedman, "The Reduction of Fluctuations in the Incomes of Primary Producers: A Critical Comment," *Economic Journal,* 64 (December 1954), 698–703.

17. On the supply of rubber, see Bauer, *The Rubber Industry,* chap. 4 and app. E.

Index

Abuja, 53
Africa (general discussion), 5, 146, 191; population growth, 26–27, 34, 36; land, 29; foreign aid to, 40, 47, 48, 49, 50, 53, 212n13; infrastructure spending, 51; British colonization of, 64; 80–85; cooperative organizations, 89; wage regulation, 100; price controls, 112; economy, 197. *See also* Central Africa; East Africa; West Africa; *specific countries*
African Survey, An (Hailey), 6, 196
Aggregation of economic activities, 18, 195, 197; in tertiary production, 12, 15; Third World debt payments and, 59; monetary demand and, 120
Agriculture, 191; in LDCs, 3, 4, 6, 33, 66, 74, 78; markets, 3, 64–65, 66, 68, 70, 77, 78, 83, 84; direct investment in, 4, 43, 189, 207n5; Third World debt and, 60, 61; exports, 64–65, 80–83, 133, 138; government control of, 64, 65; loans and credit to producers, 67–68, 87, 88, 89, 90, 214n5; competition in, 68–69; cooperative organizations, 74–75; export quality and standards, 80–85; use of intermediaries, 89; subsistence, 108–109, 139; capital formation in, 189, 196; surplus, 198. *See also* Production; *specific commodities*
AIDS, 209n8
Allocation: of resources, 8, 11, 12–13, 107, 110; of supplies, 115–117
Annual Report on Nigeria, 7

Arbitrage, 10
Argentina, 39, 59, 109, 213n2
Asia: South, 24, 147; population growth, 36; foreign aid to, 40, 47, 48, 49, 50, 212n13; infrastructure spending, 51; collective bargaining, 100; price controls, 112; wages, 146; economy, 197. *See also* Southeast Asia; *specific countries*
Australasia, 36
Australia, 210n7
Autarkic policies, 176, 178, 179

Balance of payments, 48, 128, 129, 151, 213n7. *See also* Debt, Third World
Bank of International Settlements, 60
Barriers: import, 49, 142; entry, 71, 74, 76, 113; emigration, 104; industrialization, 104; to movement, 108
Barter system, 8
Birth control, 21, 24, 35, 36. *See also* Population growth
Black market. *See* Price(s): market-clearing
Bolivia, 213n2
Borrowing. *See* Debt, Third World
Brandt Report, 212n15
Brasilia, 52–53
Brazil, 26, 29, 40, 60, 220n3; debt, 59, 213n2
British Colonial Office, 100, 107
British Commonwealth, 100. *See also* England
Burma, 46, 96, 102, 107
Burundi, 53

Caldwell, John, 22, 35
Capacity restrictions, 93, 98. *See also* Production
Capital, 192; formation, 3, 4, 30–31, 44, 187, 191, 192, 196; equipment, 14; economic development and, 44; inflow, 46, 48–49, 61, 194; export of, 61; accumulation, 176–177; circulating vs. fixed, 177–178. *See also* Labor/capital substitution
Capitalism, 184
Caribbean, 30, 100
Cartels, 63, 219n4; commodity, 93–94, 95; price stabilization and, 93–95, 98, 219n1; producer, 97
Cattle markets, 85–86, 215n7
Central Africa, 29, 30
Ceylon. *See* Sri Lanka
Chenery, Hollis B., 39–40
Chile, 213n2, 220n3
China: primary production, 11; population growth, 34, 37; migration of laborers, 142, 144, 189, 192, 193
City-state systems, 171–174, 183, 227nn3,4
Clark, Colin, 11
Clark-Fisher hypothesis of labor movement, 196
Clove exports, 61
Cocoa, 61, 96, 188, 189, 191, 217n16, 219n3; cartels, 95; exports, 97, 136; prices, 153, 154–157, 218n21
Cocoa Marketing Board (Nigeria), 152–153, 154, 218n23
Coffee, 93, 95, 97
Collective bargaining, 41, 100, 131, 220n4. *See also* Trade unions
Collectivization, forced, 46, 52
Colombia, 29, 40, 213n2
Commodities: price stabilization, 92, 93, 95, 199–200; cartels, 93–94; primary, 97; rationing of, 113, 117, 118; volume control, 115; conditional sales of, 117, 118
Communist party, 228n9

Competition: market, 65, 68–69, 77, 79; defined, 69; price, 69, 70–72, 75–76, 77–78, 158–165; excessive, 71–72, 75, 216n10; intermediary, 71, 75, 77, 159, 161, 226n6; control and restrictions on, 72, 87, 88, 93; purchasing monopolies and, 72–74; quality of exports and, 83; protective tariffs and, 124
Comprehensive planning, 203
Conditional sales, 117, 118
Conflict, armed, 41, 45–46, 52, 184
Consumer goods, 2–3, 12, 15, 24, 113, 123; incentive, 139, 195. *See also* Commodities
Consumption, 33, 105, 141, 189; input/output ratios, 21–22; investment and, 195
Contrived scarcity, 99, 220n2
Cooperative organizations: monopolistic, 74–75; government-subsidized, 87–89, 90–91, 198, 229n12; provision of services, 87–88; unsubsidized, 89, 90; cartels, 93–94; employer's associations, 107, 221n13. *See also* Trade unions
Copper industry, 97
Costa Rica, 213n2, 220n3
Cotton industry, 103, 104, 189, 218n21, 219n3; price differentials in, 214n2, 216n14. *See also* Textile industry
Cuba, 39, 54, 220n3
Cyprus, 30, 112

Debt, Third World: default on, 56, 57–58, 62, 63; as form of foreign aid, 56, 57, 62, 63, 212n7; and living standards, 56, 59, 60; economic impact, 56–57, 62; relief/service, 57–58, 59, 60, 61, 63; social impact, 57; defined, 59–60; /GNP ratio, 59; political impact, 62. *See also* Balance of payments
Deficit finance, 147, 149
Demand: income elasticity of, 12,

14, 15, 19, 136, 150, 197, 209n12, 224n4; for tertiary products, 15; competition and, 69; prices, 92, 148; elasticity of, 104, 105, 136, 148, 225n4; labor, 109; for imports, 114; curve, 118, 219n2; inflation of, 118, 119; price elasticity of, 148

Depression of 1930s, 208n4

Development aid. *See* Foreign aid

Development boards, 127, 130–131

Direct investment. *See* Investment: direct

Distribution: occupational, 6, 15, 17; resource allocation and, 8, 11, 12–13; of income, 12; age, 22; reform, 65; price controls and, 112; costs, 113; internal, 113; chain, 199; retail, 208n4

Dodoma, 53

Drug traffic, 212n17

East Africa, 30, 96, 113, 214n2

Eastern bloc countries, 54

Economics (general discussion): welfare, 21, 23–24, 25, 123; history of, 166–186; development, 187–204

Ecuador, 213n2

Edinburgh, Duke of, 20

Education, 25, 35, 131

Egypt, 171

Elkan, Walter, 199

Elton, G. R., 186

Emigration and immigration, 104, 106, 108, 111; quotas and control, 126, 194. *See also* China: migration of laborers; India: migration of laborers

Employment: distribution, 6, 15, 17; occupational specialization, 7–8, 15–16, 99, 105; in tertiary production, 12, 13; foreign aid and, 55; Third World debt and, 57; wage regulation, 99, 100–101, 102, 104, 105, 106, 107, 108–109, 110; 219n1; wages and, 132, 137.

See also Labor; Unemployment

Energy supply, 32

England: trading activity, 1–2, 5, 90, 214n2; Falklands War, 39; foreign aid programs, 55, 60, 212n16; colonization of Africa, 64, 90, 95, 96, 130, 158, 188; agriculture, 93, 210n12; taxation of African colonies, 96; and British Commonwealth, 100; colonization of Hong Kong, 143, 144; industrialization of, 177, 227n6; colonization of Malaya, 193

Environmental issues, 56, 212n17

Ethiopia, 5, 31; foreign aid to, 39, 47, 53; governmental policy on foreign aid, 46, 52, 53; armed conflict in, 52

Exchange and exchange rates, 48; Third World debt and, 61; control policies, 114; shortages, 141; fixed, 149; output and, 150

Exchange economy, 2, 3, 5, 8, 68, 198. *See also* Trading activity

Exports: Third World, 42, 55, 97, 98; foreign aid and, 55; Third World debt and, 59, 60; restricted, 60, 81, 83, 95, 138; agricultural, 64–65, 80–83, 133, 138, 190; quality and standards of, 80–85, 218nn25,26; prices of, 84, 94, 95, 148; quotas on, 94; monopolies, 95, 140, 152, 204, 217n16; duties and taxes, 96, 130, 201; income elasticity of, 136; reserves of, 136–137, 213n7; stagnation of, 147; elasticity of demand, 148, 150; world, 148, 149; real cost of, 212n17. *See also specific commodities and countries*

Extended family system, 25–26

Falklands War, 39

Famine and malnutrition, 31, 56

Far East, 40, 61

Farm production. *See* Agriculture; *specific countries*

Favored consumers, 119, 120, 121
Federal Reserve Board, 182
Fiji, 192
Financial system, international, 57
Fisher, A. G. B., 11–12, 18, 19
Foreign aid, 203; grants, 38, 56, 59,
  87; soft loans, 38, 56, 63;
  subsidies, 38, 45, 47–49, 57, 58,
  87, 88, 130, 211n7; wealth
  transfers, 38, 45, 48–49, 53, 55;
  economic development and, 39,
  43, 46, 48, 49–50, 51, 52, 63;
  politics of, 40, 45–46, 53, 54; to
  Third World, 40, 41, 42, 51–52,
  54, 56, 97; rationalizations for, 42,
  43, 212n17; /GNP ratio, 45, 50,
  51; project, 46, 51, 53; recipient
  government policies, 46–48, 49,
  52–54; per capita income as
  determinant of, 47, 50, 63; balance
  of payments and, 48; and foreign
  trade, 49; reform of policies, 51;
  poverty relief and, 52, 53, 55; and
  employment, to LDCs, 55, 212n17;
  defined, 56, 210n1, 211n7; as
  element of Third World debt, 56,
  57, 62, 63, 212n17; direct loans,
  58; stabilization schemes as, 97;
  technical assistance as, 102. See
  also specific countries
Foreign exchange: earnings, 49;
  auctioning of, 121
Foreign trade, 48. See also Trading
  activity
Fossil fuel, 31, 32
Friedman, Milton, 201

Germany, Federal Republic of, 29,
  51–52
Geyl, Pieter, 186
Ghana (Gold Coast), 6, 7, 23, 61,
  96, 188
Ginneries. See Cotton industry;
  Textile industry
GNP: /foreign aid ratio, 45, 50, 51;
  /Third World debt ratio, 59
Gold Coast. See Ghana

Grassby, Richard, 2
Gross reproduction rate, 33
Groundnut Marketing Board
  (Nigeria), 158–160
Groundnuts, 148, 189, 219n3

Hailey, Lord, 6, 196
Haiti, 217n18, 220n3
Hancock, Sir Keith, 189
Hastings, Warren, 174, 227n5
Health services, 25
Hicks, J. R., 105, 166–172, 173,
  174–175, 176, 177, 178, 179, 180,
  181, 183, 184-185
Hirschmann, Albert, 133
Holland, 29. See also Indonesia
Hong Kong: population, 29, 31, 32,
  141, 144; exports, 61, 103, 143;
  manufacturing industry, 103;
  development policies, 142–146;
  economic development, 142;
  market economy, 142, 143, 144–
  145; tax policy, 142, 143; British
  rule in, 143, 144; government
  subsidies, 143–144; education,
  144, 145; government, 146,
  227n4; wages, 146
Hong Kong: A Study in Economic
  Freedom (Rabushka), 142
Hutt, W. H., 220n2

Ibadan, 214n3
Immigration. See Emigration and
  immigration
Import(s): substitution, 46, 48, 126,
  127, 132, 137, 138; barriers, 49,
  142; foreign aid and, 53; demand,
  114; controls and restrictions, 115,
  140, 195, 222n1; cost of, 115, 134;
  licenses, 118, 139; prices, 119;
  inelasticity of supply, 119; and
  economic development, 147
Incentive goods, 139, 152, 153, 195.
  See also Commodities
Income: distribution, 12, 17, 27;
  elasticity of demand, 12, 14, 15,
  19, 136, 150, 197, 209n12, 224n4;

national, 14, 15, 21, 22, 45, 50, 107, 110, 194, 210n11; as measure of welfare, 21, 22; population growth and, 26, 31, 35; real, 26, 28, 193; disposable, 31; price stabilization and, 96, 201, 219n1; wage regulation and, 109, 110. *See also* Per capita income

India: population growth, 22, 23, 36–37; land, 30, 194; war with Pakistan, 41; foreign aid to, 45, 50, 212n16; collective bargaining, 100; wage regulation, 100, 103, 107, 109; labor legislation, 102, 104, 221n11; textile industry, 103, 104, 228n7; migration of laborers, 111, 189, 192, 193, 220n10; price controls, 112; exports, 147–150; foreign exchange crisis, 147, 149

Indian Head Mills, 126

Indonesia, 39, 94, 109, 189, 191, 192

Industrialization, 2, 122, 133–137; state-sponsored, 190; defined, 224n3. *See also* Manufacturing

Industrial relations, Anglo-Saxon model of, 131, 132. *See also* Collective bargaining; Trade unions

Industrial research, 131

Industrial Revolution, 2, 175–176, 177, 178, 179, 181, 227n6

Inflation, 114; Third World debt and, 48, 59; of industrial costs, 104; of demand, 118, 119; price controls and, 120

Infrastructure: spending, 45, 51; capital-intensive, 190

Intermediaries: in trading activities, 10, 11, 17, 64, 65, 70, 71, 74, 190, 214n3; in markets, 65–66, 67, 68, 69, 70, 72, 214n3; competition among, 71, 75, 77, 159, 161; control of, 71; and prices, 71; defined, 113; price controls and, 113, 114, 118; merchant sales to, 116, 117, 119; licensed, 118;

commission, 159, 160; restrictions on number, 216n11

International demonstration effect, 205n5

International Development Association (IDA), 59, 211n11. *See also* World Bank

International Labour Conference, 101–102

International Labour Organization (ILO), 100, 101–102, 107, 109, 220n3

International Monetary Fund, 58

International Rubber Regulation Scheme (IRRS), 94–95, 200

Investment, 211n9; direct, 4, 5, 43, 44, 56, 189, 191, 207n5; restrictions, 46–47; portfolio, 56; Third World debt and, 61; competition and, 126; by merchants, 126; foreign, 135; barriers, 142; fixed, 177; consumption and, 195

Iran, 41

Iraq, 41

Iron Curtain countries, 180–181, 228n9

Ivory Coast, 29, 40, 213n2

Jamaica, 213n2

Japan, 94, 211n7; land, 29; population, 36; industrialization, 103, 175; wages, 146

Joshi, N. M., 101

Kavalsky, B. G., 222n2

Kenya, 29

Keynes, J. M., 210n3, 229n6

Kilby, Peter, 122–123, 124–125, 126, 127, 128, 129, 130, 131, 132, 133, 134, 135–136, 137, 138–140

Kola nuts, 189, 203

Korea, South, 40, 59, 147

Krueger, Anne O., 147

Kuznets, Simon, 44

Labor: occupational specialization,

Labor (*cont.*)
  7–8, 15–16, 99, 105; supply, 11,
  33, 99, 102, 103, 106, 108; in
  tertiary production, 15; unpaid vs.
  paid, 15, 16–17; shifts, 18, 196;
  division of, 26, 27, 28, 171;
  population growth and, 32;
  markets, 33, 101, 106, 107;
  elasticity of substitution in, 33;
  /land ratios and substitution, 33,
  194; price of, 99, 105, 108;
  legislation, 100, 102, 104;
  restrictions, 101; costs, 102–103,
  104, 105, 106, 110; elasticity of
  supply, 103; demand, 109; *See
  also* Employment; Monopsonies;
  Trade unions; Unemployment;
  Wages
Labor/capital substitution and
  ratios, 9, 10, 11, 17, 33, 102; in
  tertiary production, 12, 13–14,
  197; in trading activities, 199
Lal, Deepak, 59
Land: per capita, 21, 28; economic
  growth and, 29, 194; prices, 29–
  30; tenure, 31; /labor substitution
  and ratios, 33, 194
Laos, 53
Latin America: consumer goods, 24;
  population growth, 26–27, 36;
  land, 29; mineral resources, 30;
  economy, 40, 197; foreign aid to,
  40, 212n13; economic growth, 43;
  infrastructure spending, 51; debt,
  60; collective bargaining, 100;
  wage regulation, 100, 107, 109;
  price controls, 112. *See also*
  specific countries
Lenin, V. I., 182, 186
Less developed countries (LDCs):
  trading activities and traders, 1, 3,
  4, 5, 11, 76, 78, 112–113, 115,
  120, 187, 196, 199; trade policies,
  2; agriculture (general discussion),
  3, 4, 6, 33, 66, 74, 78, 196; capital
  formation, 3, 4, 31, 187, 196;
  living standards, 3, 28;
  manufacturing, 4, 103; labor

supply, 11, 33, 102, 106;
  population growth, 20, 21, 22–23,
  24–25, 27, 28–29, 32, 34–36, 37;
  consumer goods, 24; education,
  25, 132; urban growth, 26;
  employment, 32; external
  commercial contracts and, 37;
  imports, 49, 114–115; politics, 50,
  54, 176, 203–204; foreign aid to,
  54–55, 211n7; government control
  of agriculture, 64, 83–84; exports,
  81, 83–84, 97, 128, 136, 225n4.
  See also Third World; *specific
  countries*
Letters of credit, 84, 85
Licensing of traders and agents,
  115–116, 117–118, 121, 140, 161,
  204
Living standards, 2, 3; labor supply
  and, 11; population growth and,
  28, 177, 210n11; Third World
  debt and, 56, 59, 60; labor
  demand and, 109; commodity
  prices and, 115
Loans. *See* Debt, Third World
Lusinchi, Jaime, 56–57

Malaya, 191, 193, 220n10;
  population growth, 28; rubber
  exports, 188, 189, 202–203. *See
  also* Malaysia
Malaysia, 29, 30, 31, 188, 194; land,
  32; immigration to, 39; economic
  growth, 40; exports, 61, 94. *See
  also* Malaya
Manufacturing: in LDCs, 4, 103;
  government supported/subsidized,
  122, 130, 136–137, 138, 139, 140,
  224n3; protective tariffs and, 123–
  126, 139, 140; private investment
  in, 124; machinery sales, 126–127;
  technology transfer in, 133–134,
  136, 138; capital-intensive, 134
Markets and marketing, 191;
  agricultural, 3, 64–65, 66, 68, 70,
  77, 79, 217n18; export, 3, 57, 80;
  regional, 3; growth and
  stabilization of, 13, 93; labor, 33,

101, 106, 107; Third World, 42; foreign aid and, 54; control of, 64, 65, 70, 78, 79, 80–85; competition in, 65, 68–69, 77, 79; reform, 65–66, 70, 74–75, 199, 217n20; use of intermediaries in, 65–66, 67, 68, 69, 70, 72, 214n3; centralization of transactions, 68–69, 70, 214n3, 216nn8,9; inflexible, 73–74; differentials, 81–82; world, 82, 83, 84, 95–96, 148; cooperative organizations and agreements, 87, 113; legislation, 93; boards, 95–97, 128, 129, 130–131, 140, 152–153, 154, 200, 203–204, 230n15; protective tariffs and, 124, 125; number of traders in, 158, 163, 226n4, syndicates, 160–161; transformation of, 166–167, 170, 178; defined, 171. *See also* Trading activity
Mars, J., 216nn8,9
Marshall, Alfred, 105, 227n1
Marshall Plan, 42, 51–52
Marx, Karl/Marxism, 169–170, 182, 183, 185, 186, 228n11
Massachusetts Institute of Technology, 141
McNamara, Robert S., 20
Mengistu Haile Mariam, 212n14
Mercantile economy, 170, 227nn2, 3. *See also* Trading activity
Mexico, 29, 40, 220n3; debt, 59, 60, 213n2
Middle East, 24, 30, 40, 112. *See also specific countries*
Middlemen. *See* Intermediaries
Mineral oil, 97
Mineral resources, 28, 29, 30, 31–32, 193. *See also* Resource(s)
Mining industry, 106
Monopolies, 70, 202; control of, 73; profits of, 73, 89, 112–113, 116; statutory, 73, 74, 75, 78, 158–159, 217n16; competitive markets and, 76, 125; price stabilization and, 93, 95, 200; export, 95, 140, 152, 204, 217n16; product market, 106;

trading, 112–113; defined, 113; zonal, 216n13. *See also* Monopsonies
Monopsonies (labor purchasing monopolies), 68, 72–74; price stabilization and, 93; defined, 105–106; absence of, in LDCs, 106–107; labor policies in, 106, 109, 221n12; wage regulation and, 109
Morocco, 213n2
Myrdal, Gunnar, 141

Natural resources. *See* Resource(s)
Natural scarcity, 220n2
Netherlands East Indies. *See* Indonesia
Net reproduction rate, 33
New Zealand, 210n7
Nigeria: agriculture, 6, 7, 83, 84, 139, 140; trading activity, 6, 7, 66, 203, 214n1; population growth and statistics, 22–23, 34, 132; land, 30; petroleum industry, 60, 129, 136; exports, 83, 84, 85, 123, 127–128, 136, 139, 140, 152, 216n8; cocoa industry, 96, 136, 152–153; industrialization and manufacturing, 122, 124, 125, 130, 133, 134, 135–136, 137, 138; protective tariff system, 123–124, 125–126; machinery sales, 126–127; palm oil industry, 127–128, 152–153; marketing boards, 128, 129, 152–153, 154, 158, 159; education, 131; trade unions, 131; statistical data errors, 132; political conflict, 140; groundnut industry, 158, 159–165; economic growth, 188; debt, 213n2
Nigerian Livestock Mission, 215n7, 218n21
Nkrumah, Kwame, 212n14
Nurkse, Ragnar, 133
Nyerere, Julius Kambarage, 212n14

Occupational distribution, 6, 15, 17. *See also* Employment; Labor

Occupational specialization. *See*
Employment: occupational
specialization
OECD countries, 210n7
Oil Palm Produce Marketing Board
(Nigeria), 128, 129, 152–153, 154
Oils and oilseeds, 148
Oligopolies, 125
Oligopsonies, 68, 70, 216n8
OPEC, 145, 219n1
Organizations and associations. *See*
Cooperative organizations

Pakistan, 41, 103, 112, 224n6
Palm oil industry, 97, 127–129,
152–154, 214n3, 218n21, 219n3
Paraguay, 220n3
Para-statal organizations, 60
Patel, S. J., 147, 148, 149
Pearson Commission, 21
PEMEX, 60
Penang, 227n4
Per capita income: and economic
progress, 11, 21; population
growth and, 27, 28; Third World,
40–41; and foreign aid, 47, 50, 63
Peru, 60, 213n2
Petroleum industry, 60, 129, 136
Philippines, 39, 213n2
Pioneer oil mills, 128
Point Four Program, 41
Poland, 212n16
Politics and economy (general
discussion), 170–171, 190–191
Pollard, Sydney, 177
Popper, Sir Karl, 186, 228n10
Population growth: LDC, 20, 21,
22–23, 24–25, 27, 28–29, 32, 34–
36, 37; forecasts, 21, 33, 34, 35;
per capita income and, 21, 22,
27–28, 30; policies, 21, 25, 27, 34,
36–37; external effects of, 25–27;
environmental effects of, 26;
urban, 26; economic progress and,
28–29, 36, 141; and living
standard, 28, 177, 210n11; capital
formation and, 30–31; famine
and, 31; unemployment and, 31,

32–33; energy supply and, 32; and
labor force, 32
Population transfers, 52
Poverty, 40, 52, 55, 141–142, 190,
194
Price, Jacob, 2
Price(s), 196; product, 10, 12, 14,
17, 26, 199, 202; differentials, 64,
82, 83, 153, 217n20; stabilization/
equilibrium, 64, 77–79, 92–97,
115, 200–201, 217n20, 219n1;
market reform and, 65–66;
competition and, 69, 70–72, 75–
76, 77–78, 158–165; agreements,
70; agricultural, 70, 71, 72, 75;
intermediaries and, 71; uniform,
79–80; exports and, 84, 94, 95,
148; movements and changes, 92–
93, 95, 96, 152; depression of, 95,
96; wage regulation and, 104, 105;
controls, 112, 113–114, 115, 116,
117, 118–119, 120, 194, 222nn1,
2; market-clearing, 113, 114, 115,
116, 117, 118, 119, 120; import,
114–115, 117, 132; supply/
demand ratios and, 114–115, 116,
119, 120; elasticity of demand,
148, 150; incentives, 152, 153,
154; and production, 153;
gazetted, 159, 162, 163, 226n3;
supply, 201–202
*Problems of Wage Policy in Asian
Countries* (ILO), 109
Produce Control Board (West
Africa), 154
Production: subsistence, 1, 2, 3, 5, 8,
31, 52, 98, 108–109, 139, 197,
199, 207n5; for sale, 2, 4, 207n5;
tertiary, 6, 11, 12, 13–15, 16, 17–
18, 19, 196–197, 207n1; primary,
11–12, 13, 16, 17, 18, 97, 136,
199, 207n1; secondary, 12, 13, 14,
16, 17, 207n1; input/output ratios,
21–22, 153; elasticity of
substitution in, 33, 104, 105;
capital investment in, 47; Third
World debt and, 57, 61;
agricultural, 64, 65, 67–68, 79;

market incentives for, 66, 79, 82, 152, 153; cooperative organizations, 74–75; extension of, 93, 98; restrictions, 93, 98; taxation of producers/farmers, 95–97, 139, 192, 200, 219n3; costs, 103, 134, 202; prices and, 153

Productivity: influences on, 28, 133–134; land, 29; wage regulation and, 110; capacity, 150; of resources, 150–151

Product(s): markets, 2, 64; prices, 10, 12, 14, 17, 26, 199, 202; quality, 64, 80–83, 84; standardized vs. differentiated, 202. *See also* Commodities; Consumer goods

Profit sharing, compulsory, 103

Propaganda, 38

Property rights, 26

Protectionism, 178. *See also* Tariffs, protective

Purchasing power, 110

Quotas, 94, 161, 226n2

Rabushka, Alvin, 142, 144

Rationing of commodities, 113, 117, 118

Redistribution, 53

Religion, 169, 227n1

Research, industrial, 131

Resource(s): allocation, 8, 11, 12–13, 107, 110; mineral, 28, 29, 30, 31–32, 193; Third World debt and, 60; transfers, 97, 98, 136, 200, 219n4; capital/labor ratios and, 102, 192; investible, 107, 222n15; output and, 150; productivity of, 150–151

Rhodesia, 222n2

Robinson, Joan, 105

Royal Dutch Shell, 5

Rubber industry, 98, 187, 191, 193, 229n3; cartels, 93, 94–95; prices, 94–95, 201–202; exports, 97–98, 201, 202–203; labor supply in,

102–103, 220n10; wages, 108; foreign investment in, 188–189; regulation of, 200, 201

Rubber Producing Companies, 220n10

Sahel, 5, 31

Salt market, 214n2

Samuelson, Paul, 43, 141

Service sector. *See* Production: tertiary

Singapore, 29, 31, 32; economic growth, 40, 175, 227n4

Smith, Adam, 2, 4, 171, 229n5

South Africa, 106, 109

South America, 102

South Asia, 24, 147

Southeast Asia, 5, 172, 173; consumer goods, 24; population growth, 26–27; land, 29, 30; immigration to, 39; economy, 40, 43, 188, 190, 192; rubber industry, 102–103, 187, 188–189, 191; trading activity, 113, 202

South Pacific, 212n13

Soviet Union, 54, 171, 178–181

Sowell, Thomas, 38

Spain, 30

Specialization. *See* Employment: occupational specialization

Spengler, Oswald, 169–170

Sir Lanka, 52, 94, 220n10

STABEX, 219n4

Stabilization strategies. *See* Price(s): stabilization/equilibrium

Statutory monopolies, 73, 74, 75, 78, 158–159, 217n16

Stevenson Rubber Restriction Scheme, 94–95

Subsidies: as foreign aid, 38, 45, 47–49, 57, 58, 87, 88, 130, 211n7; agricultural, 64; wage regulation and, 105; manufacturing, 130, 136–137, 138, 139. *See also* Foreign aid

Substitution: labor/capital, 9, 10, 11, 12, 13–14, 17, 33, 102, 197, 199; elasticity of, 33, 104, 105; import,

Substitution (*cont.*)
46, 48, 126, 127, 132, 137, 138;
men/equipment, 135
Sudan, 47, 52, 53
Sugar industry, 93, 97
Sumatra, 189
Supply: restrictions, 64, 93, 98;
competition and, 69; price
stabilization and, 92, 94, 95;
scarcities, 99, 220n2; elasticity of,
104, 219n3; rationing, 113, 117,
157; for imports, 114, 115;
allocation, 115–117; licensing,
115–116, 117; short, 115, 120,
121, 221n1; inelasticity of, 219n3
Switzerland, 29
Syndicates, 160–161

Taiwan, 29, 30, 40, 61
Tanzania, 5, 31, 46, 47, 50
Tariffs, protective, 123–126, 139
Taxation: of producers/farmers, 95–
97, 139, 192, 200, 219n3;
marketing boards and, 96,
230n15; of merchants, 116, 120;
of profits, 121, 203; income, 125;
of exports, 130, 201; labor
deployment and, 222n15;
subsidized manufacturing and,
138; and trading, 139; of imports,
195
Tea industry, 93, 97
Technical change, 12, 14, 209n12;
productivity and, 28; wage
regulation and, 110; production
and, 197
Technology transfers, 133–134, 136,
138
Terms of trade, 212n17
Textile industry, 4–5, 12, 126. *See
also* Cotton industry
Thailand, 40, 61
Theory of Economic History, A
(Hicks), 166, 170
Third World: trading activities, 2,
11, 212n17; population growth,
21, 24, 28, 34, 35–36, 37, 40;
economy, 28, 34, 40; land, 29,

194; foreign aid to, 40, 41, 42, 51–
52, 54, 56, 97; per capita income,
40; poverty, 40, 42, 194; defined,
41; hostilities in, 41, 45–46, 52;
exports, 42, 55, 97, 98; markets,
42; foreign direct investment in,
43; loans to, 43; politicization of,
45–46, 50. *See also* Debt, Third
World; Less developed countries
Tigre, 51
Timber, industry, 85
Tin industry, 93, 95, 97, 188
Tobacco industry, 97, 102, 107
Tocqueville, Alexis de, 145
Toynbee, Arnold, 169–170
Trader-lenders, 67
Trade unions, 74; wage regulation
and, 99, 219n1; collective
bargaining, 100, 131, 220n4;
Nigerian, 131
Trading activity, 191, 197–199;
economic repercussions, 1–2, 5,
198; mercantile, 1–2, 113, 114–
116, 117; resource allocation and,
1, 5, 13; consumption goods, 2–3;
agricultural, 3–4, 64–65; new
markets and, 3; capital formation
and, 4; suppression of, 5, 52, 61;
numbers engaged in, 7, 199, 226n4;
pricing policies and, 10, 112, 113–
114, 115, 116; use of
intermediaries in, 10, 11, 17, 64,
65, 70, 71, 74, 190, 214n3;
restrictions on, 49, 67, 199; illegal,
75–76; external, 112, 113, 187,
227n2; monopolies, 112–113;
wholesale, 112, 114; licensed, 115–
116, 117–118, 121; conditional
sales, 117; state-controlled and
-operated, 120, 198, 199; taxation
and, 139; in city-state systems,
171–174. *See also* Competition;
Markets and marketing
Transfers: wealth, 38, 45, 54;
population, 52; resource, 97, 98,
136, 200, 219n4; technology, 133–
134, 136, 138. *See also* Foreign
aid

Transport, 191, 203; resources, 8, 9, 10, 13; costs, 12–13, 163, 165, 226n4; agricultural, 75, 78, 79, 190; and prices, 79; Third World, 80; facilities, 108; and capital, 178; substitution, 190, 197
Truman, Harry, 41–42
Turnkey projects, 126–127

Uganda, 5, 31, 46, 216n11, 217n19
Unemployment, 55, 108; population growth and, 31, 32–33; Third World debt and, 56, 57
Unilever, 5
Unions. See Trade unions
United Africa Company, 226n5
United Nations, 54, 141; Development Program, 39
Uruguay, 109, 213n2, 220n3

Venezuela, 40, 59, 60, 213n2
Vertical integration, 1, 67
Vietnam, 39, 46, 54, 212n16

Wages: arbitration, 99; minimum, 99, 100, 102, 104, 107; regulation of, 99, 100–101, 102, 104, 105, 106, 107, 108–109, 110, 219n1; supply price of labor and, 99; in monopsonies, 106; differences in, 108; technical change and, 110;

employment levels and, 132; manufacturing, 137, 177; industrialization and, 177
War. See Conflict, armed
Wealth transfers. See Transfers: wealth
Welfare economics: population growth and, 21, 23–24, 25; manufacturing tariffs and, 123
West Africa, 5; agriculture, 7, 9–10, 31, 189; occupational specialization in, 7–8; trading activity, 7, 8, 9, 12–13, 66–67, 85–86, 158, 187–188, 189, 196, 202, 208n2, 216n9; labor/capital substitution, 9, 10, 11; container trade, 9, 14; commodity distribution, 10–11; consumer goods, 24; economic growth, 43, 188; cocoa industry, 95, 219n3; marketing boards, 95–97, 200, 203–204; price controls, 112, 203, 224n6; imigration policy, 224n1
Windfall profits, 116, 117, 118, 119–120, 121
World Bank, 40, 46, 56, 59, 211n11

Yugoslavia, 213n2

Zaire, 5, 26, 31, 179
Zanzibar, 61